# The Roots of Sorrow

## A Pastoral Theology of Suffering

Phil C. Zylla

D1523024

BAYLOR UNIVERSITY PRESS

*Cover Design* by *the*Book Designers

Library of Congress Cataloging-in-Publication Data

Zylla, Phillip Charles.
  The roots of sorrow : a pastoral theology of suffering / Phil C. Zylla.
  223 p. cm.
  Includes bibliographical references and index.
  ISBN 978-1-60258-632-1 (pbk. : alk. paper)
1.  Suffering—Religious aspects—Christianity. 2.  Pastoral theology.
I. Title.
  BT732.7.Z95 2012
  231'.8—dc23
                    2012007887

Printed in the United States of America on acid-free paper with a minimum of 30% pcw recycled content.

This book is dedicated to the memory of Stanley J. Grenz.

*In the fall of 2004 Stan and I had discussed the idea of writing a book together on the theology of suffering. I was very excited about working with a mentor and friend on a topic that had become so important to me. We spoke often about how a new approach was needed that would integrate a pastoral theology of suffering with the motifs of systematic theology. Our vision of a shared project was compelling and exciting as we anticipated the blending of our voices into a single volume. Sadly, Stan Grenz died suddenly on March 11, 2005. Those who know his work will recognize the imprint of his influence in this book. With gratitude for his scholarship and friendship, I dedicate this book.*

# Contents

# The Roots of Sorrow

*I'm a rollin'*
*I'm a rollin' through an unfriendly worl'*
*I'm a rollin'*
*I'm a rollin' through an unfriendly worl'*

We live with a tension that may be best explored from the point of view of the poets and the spirituals—*"we're a rollin' through an unfriendly worl'."*[1] In the spirituals there is a strange mixture of acceptance and resistance. Our experiences of suffering defy explanations, and yet, there is a need to understand how we might live hopefully in a broken world. This book is written with a similar tone: an accepting resistance or a compassionate protest. We cannot deny the reality of suffering, but we also dare not acquiesce to suffering. We resist suffering even as we try to understand where God is in the sorrows of our lives.

The roots of sorrow require a spiritual vision for the suffering and oppression of the most broken persons and communities of the world. A theology that takes seriously the experiences of the most afflicted will call for a deep searching into the fabric of suffering itself. One may sense the experience of godforsakenness and abandonment of the most afflicted in the roots of sorrow. It is here, in the experiences of the most afflicted, that a theology of suffering will be required to probe the questions of God's own presence or absence. This requires entering the abyss and moving into the mystery of the very experience of affliction itself. Anyone who has suffered will tell you that the encounter with affliction was almost always by surprise, it almost always went deeper than words could express, and at its very core, there was an experience of abandonment and hopelessness at the root of life itself.

It is to these complex situations of suffering that this book is addressed. There are two key audiences in mind for this book. This book is written for those who are called to bring hope-words to the afflicted. It is hoped that this book will bring clarity to our understandings of God in the context of the most serious situations of suffering. In this sense, this volume is directed toward the practitioners of compassion: pastors, pastoral counselors, chaplains, psychologists, social workers, nurses, and others who are called to bring comfort to the most afflicted. One of the most exacting challenges of these practitioners is to offer an articulation of the presence of God in the places of God's seeming absence. It is a very daunting task to bring words of hope and meaning to the meaningless encounters with tragedy and horror in life. Often our attempts fall short of a helpful reorientation, and we wonder if there might be a better approach to the situations of suffering in our ministry of care.

A second audience is in mind for this volume. It is also written for all those who have come to the end of their world and have had their faith in God eclipsed by sorrows too deep for words. It is written for persons who have had theological explanations of suffering given to them but have found that these "answers" do not sustain hope or provide enduring comfort. At the root of sorrow is a profound loneliness, an experience of not-being-understood. This vast chasm is a reality for many whose perspective is obscured by calamity and the anguish of suffering in its many forms. This book takes seriously the experience of suffering and our search for God in the midst of painful life situations. A core aim of this volume is to instill hope and courage into those who are being tested by relentless life trials. It is a reorientation to hope for those who sing, "*I'm a rollin' through an unfriendly worl'.*"

Throughout this volume I will try to maintain a tenacious commitment to the concrete experiences of the afflicted. Too often we are willing to ignore dimensions of suffering that fit our explanations rather than opening ourselves to the complexity and multivalent reality of suffering as it is experienced by the afflicted. A rigorous exposition of the various dimensions and kinds of human suffering that are experienced actually matches the kind of language that the Bible uses in regards to suffering. However, we have often become detached from the harsh conditions of life, and, at times, our theologizing does not fit the facts of the situation.

To write a book on God and suffering is a dangerous quest for several reasons.

## One Realizes the Impotence of Words in the Face of Unspeakable Anguish

Words melt away in the presence of affliction. This is why it is so important to ground our theological reflection on the theme of suffering in the real, concrete, and complex experiences of the afflicted. In so doing, the quality of theological reflection is measured against the highest order of concern: the suffering of the most afflicted. This is a very high standard for, as we will see, the serious situations of the most afflicted should not be lightly dismissed. Such experiences seldom fit into neat and tidy theological schemas. Suffering is immense and difficult. The scope of suffering is unexplainable and can, at best, be felt with an intuitive imagination that exponentially deepens one's own solidarity with those who suffer. Most human suffering goes unattended and unknown. There are thousands who suffer in silence and who do not have theological explanations for the darkest moments. A mature theology of suffering must find language that "at least says what the situation is."[2] This admonition may seem innocuous to us, but it is actually an important concern that assists us to pay close attention to the reality of suffering as it is experienced. In order to say what the situation is, we must construct an accurate depiction of the experience of suffering. This will require skillful attention to the perplexing aspects of suffering in its multivalent expression. We are often inaccurate or incomplete in our understanding of the complexity of the situation itself. To describe the situation, or "at least say what the situation is," is a very important theological exercise.

Edward Farley identifies four key aims in the hermeneutical task of interpreting situations. The first aim is "simply identifying the situation and describing its distinctive and constituent features."[3] The second aim is recovering elements that have been repressed or forgotten. This is in response to the tendency of filtering out what is really going on in order to "simplify the situation." Very often our simplified version of what is going on in a situation has been modified by our worldview or our own perspective or knowledge of the facts. To remedy this, we need to probe what has not "gotten through." The third aim involves correcting the abstraction "committed by the focus on a single situation."[4] We must keep in mind that "all situations occur within broader situations," and this demands that we reflect on what Farley calls the "intersituational."[5] If we fail to locate the situation in this "larger and longer" context of the intersituational, we are prone to distort what is really going on. This scheme prepares us for the fourth aim, "discerning the situation's demand," which again calls us to reconsider our settled theology or our "idolatries." Farley concludes this schema by noting that this final phase is the theological task and "one of the most complex elements of interpreting situations."[6]

It is only when we have finally taken into account the full context of the intersituational and have discerned the situation's demand that we are able to give expression to what we see. Therefore, the wording activity of pastoral theology in the situation of the afflicted will call for skills of attention, discernment, recollection, and honest speaking. All of these together make for the complex task of wording the void and giving expression to the complexities of any given situation of suffering. We turn now to a second reason that this volume is a risky adventure.

## Trust in a Loving God Is the Final Resort for Those Who Are Clenched in the Tight Grip of Acute Suffering

This book is written with the sensitive recognition that for many who are suffering the stakes are very high. For them this is their last line of defense before the despair sets in. While it is my hope that this book will build the courage of the forsaken, it is never far from my thinking that tremendous pain, anguish, and torment chip away the defenses and leave the brokenhearted "holding on by a thread." For some, questions of faith and trust in a good and caring God are questions of the intellect—a matter of convictional belief and doctrinal assent. For others, that is for those who suffer in extremis, such questions are truly life and death. There is no partial faith in such circumstances. It is "all or nothing." This touches on the mystery of faith itself. A deeper perspective is required to hold out for a particular understanding of God's presence in the situation of the most afflicted. Trust in God's caring intervention is hard to hold on to in the depths of the abyss of suffering. Faith itself is tested at the root by the ongoing situation that seems to indicate God's absence. The problem of sustained trust in God in the seriousness of suffering must not be dismissed lightly by carefully worded dogma or sentimentalized religious reflection. The real situations of anguish and suffering require nothing short of the "leap of faith"—a total abandonment toward one's source of hope.

I turn now to a personal note about the writing of this book. Rabbi Kushner stated in the introduction to his famous book *When Bad Things Happen to Good People* that he always knew one day he would write his book about suffering as he responded to the premature death of his son Aaron to progeria.[7] I am compelled to say much the same thing. When our daughter, Chelsey, was born with a congenital birth defect, spina bifida, I was a young pastor. It was difficult to articulate what we were going through as a family. My wife and I felt like we were entering an abyss. At the time, I was beginning my doctoral dissertation. There was a profound gap between the meaning of words of theology that I was studying and the experience of our daughter's suffering. I began to journal, to reflect, and to jot down my thoughts and experiences. I wanted to pay attention to the contours of our own hoping and the deeper realities of suffering that our family was going through.

Those were painful years. We watched our child go through surgery after surgery. The relentless days and weeks at the hospital took their toll on us. We tried to maintain the rhythms of our life in ministry, but the staggering demands of our daughter's suffering wore us down. Many times we could only blindly pursue the horizon of hope as though we were caught in a sandstorm of life. We "wept and wondered."[8] Through the years I began to find some words for the experiences of suffering that our family was going through. This book is an attempt to weave those reflections into something helpful for those who suffer and for those who courageously journey alongside them as caregivers.

It is only now, after nineteen years of sharing in Chelsey's suffering, pain, and hardship, that I feel equipped to express what we have been learning as a family on this anguishing pilgrimage. Our family has experienced much agony and Chelsey herself has endured more suffering than any child should ever have to experience. She has been confined to a wheelchair all of her life. We have watched her struggle with major health concerns and severe limitations on her life. Chelsey has endured sixteen surgeries in nineteen years. At times, in the darkest periods of our journey, Chelsey has gone through life-threatening and harrowing experiences. We have tasted the bitter cup of disappointment and loss. Even to this day her future is quite uncertain, and the day-to-day struggles that she endures are numerous. We have come to live with ambiguities and losses that we cannot even name. They have attached themselves to our souls. We continue to learn together how to navigate this difficult terrain. We still weep and wonder. This is the life situation that has formed the canvas for the picture of suffering found in this volume.

However, we are also deeply aware that suffering, in its most excruciating forms, goes far beyond the encounters we have had as a family. We have become profoundly aware that the suffering of our daughter (with all of the supports of health care and medical technology) may seem negligible to so many others in their hurt. The explorations of this volume seek to empathize with the unimaginable grief of others. It is a work of solidarity with all who suffer. This book is an attempt to pay attention to the grief of the family whose young mother is murdered or the pain of parents who are sentenced to watch their child die slowly of cancer. We know little of the gut-wrenching anguish of the Somalian mother who cannot provide daily food for her dying baby. One could rehearse countless situations of extreme affliction—all of which seem unbearable, anguishing, and for which there are few words. A third reason, therefore, arises to make the writing of this book so dangerous.

## The Immense Scope of Suffering Itself

*"Your wound is as deep as the sea; who can heal you?" (Lam 2:13)*[9]

The tendency to compare our grief, hurt, and anguish comes naturally to us. This matter of comparisons often leaves the suffering person bewildered. They wonder if their suffering is greater or lesser than another's. There are no measurements for affliction. The intensity, the relentless progress, the insistent presence of suffering are all extremely difficult to weigh. It is so hard to determine whether the degree of suffering one is experiencing can adequately be compared to the suffering of others. This often leads to an impasse within the suffering person who does not know how to calibrate the anguish they are experiencing.

Furthermore, there are several dimensions to all suffering. A thoughtful reflection on the theme of suffering must take into account all of the variations in suffering. The explorations in this volume will take into account four key dimensions of suffering: physical pain, psychological anguish, social degradation,[10] and spiritual desolation (see chap. 3, "What is Suffering?"). But even these descriptions fail to take on board the full weight of suffering. Suffering is immense. It is a difficult river.

Learning to talk about God in our suffering is a key dimension of this volume. Gustavo Gutiérrez invites our consideration of some key questions: "How are human beings to speak of God in the midst of poverty and suffering?"[11] And, "How are human beings to find a language applicable to God in the midst of innocent suffering?"[12] The core questions of this book are grounded in the reality of suffering itself, not in the esoteric arguments that sometimes make up the world of philosophical theology and common approaches to theodicy.

It is hoped that this volume will significantly assist those whose callings and vocational commitments require them to journey deep into the afflictions of others with compassion. The intention of this volume is not simply to defend God in the face of unspeakable suffering but to articulate the dimensions of hope for those who suffer in extremis. In order to give clarity to the direction of this volume, I wish, at the outset, to express several key features of the approach to the theology of suffering taken up in this book.

### Giving Voice to the Serious Situations of the Most Afflicted

*"What did you want to say," the interpreter asks the poet. And the poet replies: "I wanted to say precisely what I said." . . . "What I said is precisely what I wanted to say because this is what I saw," says the poet.*[13]

We all must grow in appreciating the voice that we bring to the crucial dialogue in theology *and* the voice that others bring to us. Theology, correctly conceived, is dialogical. The mystery cannot be fully expressed, but there is a return to the founding Word for an expression of understanding of the foundations of things. It is true that "mystery is an embarrassment to the modern mind,"[14] and yet we are called to sensitively articulate[15] our faith seeking understanding. Theologians who have dared their suspicions on this profound theme of suffering caution us to refrain from arrogant conclusions as we search for ways to give voice to affliction.[16]

No one has all there is to say on a topic as profound and numinous as suffering and God. This book is an attempt to articulate, from the perspective of those who are suffering, the words that make sense about God's presence/absence. I am interested in preserving the mystery while bringing clarity and light to the questions of suffering in the spirit of humility and great respect for those who suffer.[17]

Yet, there is a need to articulate understandings. I am hopeful that the sensitive articulation of the theology of suffering in this book will give voice to those who are suffering in extremis. Further, it is hoped that the words expressed here about God and suffering will facilitate mature reflection for those who are called to work alongside the afflicted. A theology of suffering includes our dared suspicions about hope in the face of extreme anguish. It calls for our best words to articulate the presence of God in the midst of life's darkest corners. This volume seeks to respond with clarity to the deepest questions of those who suffer.

Such understandings are elusive at best. Therefore, this book is written with the sense that, while we cannot know all that there is to know about God in suffering, it is possible to say something about what the situation really is. This once again calls for a grounded perspective on the theme of suffering. We must carefully explore the actual situations of the suffering person and community rather than making large generalizations about evil and suffering.

This leads to an opening premise that I will contend for throughout the book:

> *Suffering is not a problem to be solved or a riddle to be explained, but rather it is a reality to be confronted in cooperation with God's own expressed intentions in the world.*

Some will find this to be disappointing, as it does not approach the "problem of suffering" as a philosophical problem or connect it to the wider mystery of evil in the world. However, the disappointment that matters is the sense of spiritual anguish of the person who truly seeks theological insight into the nature of their affliction only to discover that the "answers" of theology are quite removed from the reality of suffering that they are experiencing. If theology is going to be relevant to the suffering of persons and communities it will mean risking conversation right in the midst of the fires of suffering itself. This is the posture that this book will seek to sustain as we explore the question of God's presence/absence in the experiences of suffering in our lives.

### A Recognition of the Complexity of Faith in the Face of Suffering

While there are many dimensions of a theology of suffering that will be explored in this book, it is important from the outset to take at face value the complexity of faith as the subject of the experience of suffering. We see, for example, in the book of Job the arduous task of explaining the suffering of one life. The reality of suffering is always complex, and, in the task of developing a theological paradigm for a theology of suffering, one must always be cognizant of the complexities that abide within the experiences of the most afflicted.

A theology of suffering will be faithful to the biblical record of God's own self-revelation, while living up to the questions and probing the deeper dimensions of lived reality. Articulating the reality of God's presence and redemptive activity in a broken world requires that we keep in the foreground the profound grief and complex anguish of the distressed. A theological understanding that starts with the experience of the most afflicted offers precisely what Job's friends were not willing or able to offer—an articulate theological expression of faith in the midst of the darkest circumstances of life. While taking seriously each situation of suffering itself, the aim of this book is not simply to develop a phenomenology of suffering but rather to make concrete connections between actual experiences of suffering and the vivid revelation of a God who suffers with us.

This brings us to the question of God's suffering. Does God suffer? The position taken in this volume is that the passibility of God is assumed in the biblical revelation. In due course we will tackle the philosophical question of God's own suffering and how this must be understood. Although I am not keen to engage the philosophical debates about the suffering of God, these cannot be ignored completely. Therefore, I take the position in this volume that such approaches fail to convince us of the necessity of the immutability of God and that such arguments seek to protect a rather modernist theological interpretation of God's own relationship to the created order.[18]

### Prayer as Absolute, Unmixed Attention

I am struck by the simplicity and beauty of Simone Weil's depiction of prayer as "absolutely unmixed attention."[19] A theology of suffering will require a creative response to the deepest realities of human experience in groaning prayer. While there is a great chasm between God and our experiences of suffering, it is also in these experiences that the possibility of divine encounter is most richly described as "attention." This is a call for a particular posture in the world as we come to the mystery of suffering. We cannot pretend to know all that there is to know about God and God's presence/absence in our lives and our experience of the world. However, the biblical call to prayer is the invitation to move, in the deepest hour of need and desperation, toward God. Absolute, unmixed attention allows us to enter into the deeper recesses of our experience for connection to God. The Apostle James offers the invitation, *"Draw near to God and he will draw near to you"* (Jas 4:8).

This call to attentiveness is strategic to the development of a mature theology of suffering. In this volume I share the conviction of Dorothee

Soelle, who states, "It is this attention from which creative ability springs, and at its highest level it is equivalent to prayer."[20] It is in prayer that we overcome the human penchant for acquiescence to suffering and fate and frame the conditions for the resistance of suffering. I share the view that prayer is "an act by which people dare to put their desires into words and thereby handle their suffering differently from the way society recommends to them."[21] Soelle equates the gut-wrenching prayer of Christ in Gethsemane as the core of such prayer and states, "Prayer is an all-encompassing act by which people transcend the mute God of an apathetically endured reality and go over to the speaking God of a reality experienced with feeling in pain and happiness. It was this God with whom Christ spoke in Gethsemane."[22] I would go further than Soelle in understanding *attention* as the way to relate our own experiences of suffering and hope to God and as a way to understand or, perhaps better, to encounter God in the situation of our brokenness. Prayer, in this sense, is more than a subversive move to express our situation but is rather a moving into the realm of God's own mystery, for "in him we live and move and have our being" (Acts 17:28).[23] This approach integrates a spirituality for theology of suffering with a more nuanced biblical theology of creation. Using Romans 8 as a paradigmatic text, I will explore the threefold groaning in that pericope: the groaning of "the whole creation" (Rom 8:22), the groaning of the Spirit with "groans that words cannot express" (Rom 8:26), and the inward groaning of the redeemed community of God (Rom 8:23). This tripartite groaning is expressive of the communion of the saints in the Spirit with the ultimate purposes of God in redemption. A theology of suffering must take up the reality of a broken and groaning creation as the context in which our understandings of God's presence and the future God is making for us are related.

## Paradigm for a Theology of Suffering

I have elsewhere argued for the importance of the paradigmatic in pastoral theology,[24] stating that "paradigms are flexible but settled sets of core convictions that are derived from living with ambiguity, practicing displacement, and managing complex and often competing bodies of information."[25] In this volume I will advocate that a mature theology of suffering requires absolute, unmixed attention to both the contours of suffering and the subtle persistence of hope. This dialectic between hope and suffering is crucial to the development of the proposed theological paradigm. Suffering suffocates hope; hope persists "in spite of" suffering.[26]

The biblical idea of persistence of hope in the face of unspeakable suffering will be presented paradigmatically in three pivotal movements. The movements are meant to create a path from ambiguity and inaction. Suffering often immobilizes the church. We fail to act and we fail to respond to the deepest needs of the most afflicted. This is not simply a matter of not caring but it is a matter of working without a paradigm to enact the practices of ministry. The following three movements will be explored as the basis for a pastoral theological engagement of suffering.

## Movement One
### *The Movement from Mutism to Lament*

Unspeakable suffering leads to "mute suffering."[27] We are unable to express what the situation is because of the enormity of the anguish, the complexity of the reality, and the depth of the pain. Mutism is the incapacity to state any or all of the dimensions of a situation. Often the first response to suffering is that one can say nothing. The biblical idea of mutism as "groaning" will be underscored. Romans 8:26 states, "We do not know what we ought to pray for, but the Spirit himself intercedes for us through wordless groans." The word-forming activity of the spirit of God and our own capacity to express the unspeakable in suffering are explored as the first paradigmatic movement of a theology of suffering.

This will call for a theology of lament and the renewed practice of lamentation, dirge, spiritual songs, and theopoetic articulation of the situation of suffering. The renewal of attention to lament will be taken up in a careful study of the poem of Lamentations 3 (chap. 3) and in the work of renewal of lament in the pastoral practices of the church (chap. 5).

## Movement Two
### *The Movement from Loneliness to Community*

Loneliness is *the suffering in suffering.*[28] To experience oneself as abandoned, forgotten, neglected, and forsaken smothers one's sense of belonging and identity in the wider spiritual community. This volume will explore the experiences of "godforsakenness" to express the depths of experience of those who find themselves to be abandoned by others, by the community as a whole, and, ultimately, by God. The roots of sorrow are embedded in a deep-seated need for belonging and, more than that, for a theology of community that takes seriously the inclusion of the weak, the forgotten, the broken, and the suffering as a core dimension of our calling in the world.

As a result, we turn to a theology of community for an understanding of the way forward for those who experience themselves as forsaken and rejected. This movement will include both an understanding of the church as the community of compassionate protest and the reality of the communion within the Triune God.

Movement Three

*The Movement from Indifference to Compassion*

Compassion means "to suffer with." One etymological depiction of compassion considers its Latin root, "*compassus*, the past participle of *compati*, which means to suffer, bear (*pati*) with (*com*)."[29] This deeper dimension of compassion is often overlooked, yet it reveals the very center of Christian theology and the heart of the paradigmatic approach of this volume to the theology of suffering. Compassion is the capacity to move toward suffering rather away from it. However, compassion is not a natural inclination. When we encounter suffering we are appalled. We move away from suffering. We must come to terms with the important assertion that we are not immediately attracted to those who are suffering, but rather we are repelled by their situation. Our immersion in the conditions of human existence will bring us face to face with many situations of extreme suffering that call for compassion. However, when we realize that compassion will call for our "suffering with" the other, this "often evokes in us a deep resistance and even protest."[30]

This calls up the analysis of indifference and apathy as an important dialectic with compassion. Before we can fully live into our mandate as the compassionate community of God, we must come to terms with the source of our indifference to the suffering of others. Indifference is "the failure either to see, to acknowledge or to act on behalf of others."[31] This volume therefore follows the movement from indifference (the desire to remove oneself from the situation of the most afflicted; the avoidance of suffering) to compassion (the desire to move into the situations of the most afflicted with active help). Our exploration of this movement will involve delving into the source of our avoidance of pain and suffering. Furthermore, I will probe into the cultivation of *compassionate protest* as the appropriate response to suffering. In order to do this we must also look carefully at the theological implications of such a movement for our understanding of God as the source of true compassion.

At the root this volume is a call to exercise compassion and enter into the suffering of others with active help. In order for us to do this, we must have a clear understanding and picture of what that help would look like. We will explore the contours of apathy, indifference, and the theological understandings of suffering that sometimes cause us to "become strangers to pain."[32] The movement from indifference to compassion will allow us to balance the *premature acceptance* of suffering with the *mature acceptance* of suffering. While we cannot fully know the boundaries between the "suffering we can and cannot end,"[33] it is part of the mission of the church in the world to act as the community of compassionate protest of suffering.

Each of these movements, in its turn, reveals a core dimension of hope in the face of unspeakable suffering. In this way the paradigm for a theology of suffering enters into the dialectic with hope itself. As the movements unfold, three dimensions of hope will parallel the movements described above.

### The Hope That Someone Will Listen

Lament is the expression of the deepest cry and anguish of the human soul. Such expression itself is demonstration of the power of hope to persist in the face of unspeakable brokenness. The lament is a hopeful word-form which relies on the capacity of someone to hear, to acknowledge, and to listen to the cries of anguish that come from the darkest places in human experience. Lamentation is the outcry of the anguished and reflects the hope that someone will hear, that someone will pay attention and draw near to the situation of the afflicted in their abandonment and isolation. Lamentation is the biblical permission to express the deepest questions and most profound human emotions in the context of suffering. The hope of being heard is at the root of the lament form and this will be explored in some detail in chapter 3. What is the structure of lament in the Scriptures? What are the dimensions of the movement from the initial mutism (inability to say anything about the suffering) toward the ability to express the deeper need for being acknowledged (lament)?

At the root of this hope is the need to be understood. Most afflicted persons and communities feel that, at the core of their experience, they have been forgotten and their situation has become unbearable for others. This reinforces the suffering in suffering (loneliness) and demonstrates that, at the root of hoping, is the expectation that someone will listen to the plea for help.

## The Hope That Someone Will Come

The movement from loneliness, forsakenness, and isolation to community is the second movement of a theology of suffering. There is a profound difference between solitude and isolation. The movement out of isolation involves an acceptance of suffering, which will lead to an experience of community. The tension here lies between the premature acceptance of suffering, which leads to inauthentic forms of community, and the mature acceptance of suffering, which leads to the hopeful participation in the compassionate community of God. Solidarity, in this deeper sense, allows the afflicted to live fully their place in the human community. The most infinitesimal consolation can give rise to a great hope within the human spirit. The desire for another to enter into the suffering is rooted in a hope of belonging even for those who are living in the bleakest circumstances of life. The hope that someone will come is an expression of the hope of true communion. All human beings, regardless of the anguish of their situation, long for participation in an authentic community. The place of suffering is not only the place of godforsakenness, as it is sometimes felt by the afflicted, but is rather a cry for participation in the compassionate community of God. It is a forward look to the experiences of God's own abiding presence despite every evidence to the contrary.

## The Hope That Someone Will Care

The final movement of the paradigmatic engagement with suffering is the hope that someone will care. The structure of apathy as cowardly withdrawal from the afflicted will be explored in the movement from indifference to compassion. It is here, in the hope that someone will care, that we discover one of the central themes of a biblical theology of suffering. Compassion is moving into the center of suffering itself. For the afflicted the need of help is at the center of the reality of suffering. Help is required, and the last hope of the most afflicted is the hope that someone will care.

The love of God, expressed most fully in God's own reconciling action in the cross, is at the center of a theology of compassion. We will explore fully the implications of this paradigm for the work of ministry and for the reconciling mission of God in the world with which the church, as the compassionate community of God, is aligned.

This analysis of the dialectic between hope and suffering in the experiences of the most afflicted leads us to the completion of the paradigm in the expression of a theology of suffering.

### God Hears Our Cry

The cries and lamentations of the afflicted come to the ears of God, who, in the person of the Holy Spirit, hears our plea for help. The Holy Spirit intercedes for us with groans too deep for words. The Holy Spirit abides with us in our brokenness, pays attention to the hidden reality of our situation, and ultimately understands the most wounded expression of lament. God is not an apathetic God. Rather, the biblical expression is that God leans his ear toward the cry of the oppressed. The community of God, in its turn, participates in paying attention through actions of solidarity. Listening to the cries of the brokenhearted is one of the most crucial themes of a theology of suffering, and it connects the activity of the Holy Spirit as intercessor with our own participation in the community of God as those who live out God's character in a broken world.

### God Enters into Our Brokenness

The biblical picture of the incarnate Christ who leaves the throne of heaven (Phil 2:5-11) and moves into the most afflicted circumstances of the world is the picture of God as the One who comes. The incarnation reveals the action of God's entering into the circumstances of the suffering world. Dietrich Bonhoeffer's declaration that "only a suffering God can help"[34] leads to an exploration of the centrality of the incarnation and crucifixion of Christ as the center of a theology of suffering. That God came into the reality of the world's brokenness in redemptive love is crucial to a theology of suffering. This action of Christ in coming to the world and participating in suffering itself is at the core of a biblical theology of suffering. Furthermore, this action of God in Christ offers perspective on the question of God's own suffering. We see in the vulnerability of the cross of Christ the hint of God's own suffering.[35]

### God Comforts Us in Our Affliction

*"Praise be to the God and Father of our Lord Jesus Christ, the Father of compassion and the God of all comfort, who comforts us in all our troubles, so that we can comfort those in any trouble with the comfort we ourselves have received from God." (2 Cor 1:3-4)*

God is the author of compassion. Compassion involves "suffering with" those who are in anguish and moving into the situations of the most afflicted with active help. This is the center of a Christian theology of suffering. The movement of God into the world's brokenness and every situation of fear and oppression is the core biblical message about who God is. God is love. We will seek, in our final paradigmatic turn, to articulate the very central message of the theology of suffering as the suffering love of God the Father for the brokenness of the world. Compassion, then, is the final movement and completion of the paradigm for a theology of suffering.

### These Hopes

fragile glimpses of a
better future
glances at the wide-angled
vision
struggle for a word that
describes the road
we share
asking the honest question
"why?" untroubled
finding a solidarity, a
kinship in loss
our griefs combine without
explanation
and tell us of a better way—
the way of shared
suffering and
fragile glimpses of a
better future. (PCZ)

## CHAPTER ONE

# Common Explanations of Suffering

Pastors and caregivers are called to come alongside the grieving, to hear their anguished cries for help, and to feel the awful, gut-wrenching pain of the affliction of the soul. Who among us has not trembled inwardly with the weight of our own misgivings that derive from hearing the distressed lament of a suffering person, "Why, God? Why? Why have you forsaken me?" This chapter seeks to explore the rhetoric that occurs in pastoral responses to those who are afflicted. In part these "explanations" or "answers" to suffering are truncated responses to the deeper reality of suffering. Often well-meaning, but terribly unsatisfying, these approaches to the reality of suffering come up short in their capacity to take on board the complexity of suffering and the lived experiences of affliction. While inadequate to fully explain suffering, these responses are often used in order to bring some pastoral consolation or understanding to the life situation of those who are undergoing extreme affliction. I will seek to uncover what some of these common explanations of suffering are and how these are often used in Christian ministry.

To embrace suffering with hope is a courageous act of faith. A theology of suffering requires facing up to our doubts, and with our many unrealized hopes, to ask key questions about God. We are seeking to understand the very roots of sorrow. We are interested in assisting our fellow sojourners in the Christian life with the subtle persistence of hope. Our incapacity to address the core concerns of the afflicted gives rise to pastoral responses that often leave the suffering person feeling more overwhelmed by their situation. It might help us to orient our searching to the kinds of questions that people ask when they are in the throes of affliction. A first might be, "Where is God?"

## Where Is God in Suffering?

Here is the way a father I met in ICU put it to me some time ago while we were both there with our critically ill children: "It makes you wonder where *the Man Upstairs* is when this is happening." He explained, "We were just having a nice day together. We went out for a drive. We came to a blind corner where an accident had not been cleared . . . I had no way out. My son's seatbelt wasn't on quite right. It tore up his insides—the small intestines I think. Maybe some damage to the inner organs . . . I don't know what they're saying exactly but he's been in surgery now for 2½ hours. I don't understand why these things happen."

I did not bring up the subject of God, but there I was, with my daughter, wondering too. One of the things that make us human in the face of adversity is the capacity to weep and wonder.[1] Here, as in most situations of suffering, the core question arises, "Where is God in the calamities, afflictions, and sufferings of our life?" Is he "asleep at the wheel" as my new friend in ICU felt? Or has he wound up the world like a clock, put it on its course, and removed himself from the situation?

We all have some ideas about this but few certainties. This chapter deals with the tendency to explain our suffering with premature answers and incomplete theological conclusions. While the reality of suffering remains a mystery, we have a strong penchant to prematurely resolve the situation of suffering with answers and explanations that are incomplete and partial. In this chapter I hope to identify some of the factors that lead to this tendency and to expose some of the faulty thinking that gives rise to these answers and explanations. The search for God in the realities of suffering is a core pastoral theological issue. When we introduce God into our reflections on the experience of suffering, much turmoil emerges. It is difficult to explain God's part in the experience of tragedy. When terrible, inexplicable pain and anguish enter our experience, it is impossible for us to say how God is providentially overseeing all events. We wonder why God would not prevent tragedy if this were possible. This confusion increases exponentially when we consider that innocent people are being tortured, afflicted, oppressed, and killed. To understand the pronounced presence and/or absence of God in suffering is to inquire into a mysteriously deep realm. It is human to ask where God is in our experiences of suffering. This is the realm of the unseen and the unknown—a realm that one might say is more felt than compre-hended; more a matter of trust than knowledge; something that, much like the encounter with suffering itself, may be described as an "experi-ence of God." It may be experienced as a touch of God's nearness, or the persistence of hope, or the beauty of love repeated in the complex reality of anguish.[2]

The desire and longing for God's nearness in suffering is a dimension of the life of faith. Often, this sense of God's presence or the anticipa-tion of well-being is contradicted by the circumstances. At other times, in the face of overwhelming evidence to the contrary, one perceives the comforting presence of God in suffering.

The tension between God's immanent nearness and the experience of God's absence or silence leads to many complexities in the life of faith. Such a tension may lead to premature answers that are incomplete or that fail to live up to the deeper test of affliction. In our apprehensions of suffering we may relapse to a faulty theological withdrawal from the root questions about why affliction happens and the core causes of suf-fering. A theological explanation, even a weak one, often substitutes for a careful analysis of the source of suffering itself and the complexities of the suffering situation. Truncated answers often satisfy us without exploring carefully enough the root causes and complexities of the situ-ation of suffering itself. A theological critique of this approach is that it insufficiently explores both God's involvement in the situation of suffer-ing and the other causes that have given rise to the suffering.[3]

We will look with greater attention at some of the more common explanations of suffering and the premature answers that are often given as theological explanations to the question of God's presence and action in suffering. For now, I will turn to yet another question that arises in the suffering person, namely, the purpose of suffering.

## What Is the Purpose of Suffering?

We are conditioned to think incrementally about life. We have such and such time and so many resources, and therefore, we can expect a cer-tain, almost mathematical result: $x + 3 = 12$. Our expectation is largely that we can control life. If we put in certain efforts, we should be able to expect certain results. Life is supposed to be fair.

For those who are suffering, an incredible sense of unfairness settles in. When affliction enters into one's experience, there is no choice. It is not a matter of being brave in the face of a serious encounter or standing up to the abyss of forsakenness with a hopeful disposition. Suffering is a sudden, anguished experience that pounces on our lives. Suffering is erratic, unpredictable, and incomprehensible. Suffering has no logic. It weaves and jabs. It moves in and away at the same time. It stabs and hides. Suffering has no predictable pattern that can be easily discerned or pronounced—no beginning and no clear end. The erratic weavings of suffering cannot be comprehended in a plain, expected sequence. Without such bearings one can never really know "where one stands." Is this the beginning or the end? The math does not compute.

We are conditioned to think that everything has a purpose. Our minds work hard to "make sense" of things that seem random or senseless. Suffering and our experiences of affliction often fail to fit into simple categories of purpose. Very often, therefore, we discover ourselves conditioning our understanding of a critical situation toward a meaning construct or purpose that we hold as a steady or certain conviction.

Let us go back to the situation of the father I met in ICU, whose son was horribly injured in the intestines and vital organs while out on a pleasurable afternoon drive. The father, and family together, tried to make sense of it by observing that "it could have been worse." Even though the boy suffered the painful tearing up of his abdominal region requiring extensive surgery, even though his life was vitally threatened, the father finds comfort in knowing that the CT scan ruled out severe head trauma. Our sense-making activity then allows for a degree of trauma, bad luck, and heartache. If things had been worse, they would have been sense-less, but it makes sense that accidents happen and that little boys have to suffer for a while.

When it comes to theology, our understanding about God in suffering, our sense-making activity follows these purpose lines of thinking and extrapolates theological allies for making sense of suffering. The common "purpose texts" are often used to give us an understanding of the reality of suffering and its confusing presence in our experience. Christian understandings of God's purposes and intentions are often summarized in ways that short-circuit a complete explanation of the reality of suffering. Such abbreviated and truncated responses to suffering should not stand up. However, aligned with the human tendency to look for purpose, these explanations take a shortcut to a fuller understanding of the reality of suffering and give the impression of a complete answer.

A brief look at three commonly used "purpose texts" will demonstrate how these verses are used to outline an explanation of suffering.

*"And we know that in all things God works for the good of those who love him,*
*who have been called according to his purpose." (Rom 8:28)*

Purpose, in this text, is tethered to the deeper recognition that our calling as believers is tied to God's "purpose." Whatever may be happening in our circumstances, God is providentially orchestrating it "for the
good of those who love him." We try to understand what that means,
and, without thinking about the wider implications of the theology of
suffering, our penchant for sense-making activity shifts the nuance of
the verse to cause—"God causes all things to work together for good"
(NASB). This shift allows us to come to terms with suffering and to
acquiesce to it as a mystery. Somehow we want to believe that God is
acting in a way that is mysterious to us and that does make sense to God.
Here, we are invited to align ourselves with God's purposes without
understanding of the deeper cause of our suffering. We are invited to
grin and bear it without really knowing the "why" of suffering. This is
beyond our capacity, and we are invited to trust that God has a deeper
purpose. Andrew Lester illustrates this "purposing" activity: "When
two missionaries were killed in an automobile wreck in my country,
the paper quoted members of the supporting church as saying that God
willed the accident in order to bring about some greater good that was
not yet visible. The line between 'God can bring something good out of
suffering' and 'God caused the suffering to bring about good' seemed
blurred."[4] We will see how this response becomes embedded, then, in
particular theories about suffering in the common explanations.

*"'For my thoughts are not your thoughts, neither are your ways my ways,' declares*
*the LORD. 'As the heavens are higher than the earth, so are my ways higher than*
*your ways and my thoughts than your thoughts.'" (Isa 55:8-9)*

The prophet Isaiah declares the sovereign perspective of God. That
God is far above our knowing and his capacity to discern far outweighs
our limited and finite perspective is a given in this text and throughout the Scriptures. However, this view does not mean that we cannot
know aspects of our suffering and investigate the deeper situation that
causes our suffering. The idea that God knows more than we do about
our suffering does not imply that we should not seek understanding of
our situation. It does not justify acquiescence and resignation to situations of suffering that can be avoided or changed. It does not absolve us
of responsibility for participating in the justice of God in situations of

oppression, tragedy, or human suffering caused by the ongoing effects of human cruelty.

In fact, the prophet Isaiah is quick to point out that to live at peace with injustice, to acquiesce to senseless suffering, and to neglect the cause of the afflicted is to deny the actual concerns of God in the world. The reality that God's perspective is higher than ours ought not to keep us from adopting the very perspective of God in the situations of the most afflicted. The concerns of Yahweh are to be our concerns. The mind of God is to be our mind. The fact that we cannot attain to the whole view of God does not absolve us of responsibility for living in fidelity to the vision of God that we do understand.

> Is not this the kind of fasting I have chosen: to loose the chains of injustice and to untie the cords of the yoke, to set the oppressed free and break every yoke? Is it not to share your food with the hungry and to provide the poor wanderer with shelter—when you see the naked, to clothe him, and not to turn away from your own flesh and blood? (Isa 58:6-7)

One more "purpose text" will aid our reflection on how the misuse of scriptural admonitions can lead to a faulty posture of apathy and withdrawal from the causes of suffering.

> *"There is a time for everything and a season for every activity under heaven. . . . He has made everything beautiful in its time. He has also set eternity in the hearts of men; yet they cannot fathom what God has done from beginning to end. . . . I know that everything God does will endure forever; nothing can be added to it and nothing can be taken from it. God does it so that men will revere him." (Ecc 3:1, 11, 14)*

Here is another purpose text that can be read in such a way as to reinforce the mystery of suffering, which can lead to a premature withdrawal from the problems and pains of human misery and suffering. The fact that there is a time for everything, as indicated by Qoheleth in the ancient text, is received as a kind of fatalism. The text can be seen to mean that we have little or no capacity to change the situation of others because it is ordained to happen. God's timing is perfect and therefore we are not to interfere.

This understanding of Qoheleth's message, however, is an improper reading of the text of Ecclesiastes. In fact, the message of Qoheleth is that because of God's infinite concern for the world and because of the reality of his sovereign governance of the affairs of the world, the believer is called to a life of fidelity. "Now all has been heard: here is the conclusion of the matter: Fear God and keep his commandments for this is the whole duty of man. For God will bring every deed into judgment, including every hidden thing, whether it is good or evil" (Ecc 12:13-14). Yet, our inability to "fathom" what God is up to leads to nonaction. We fail to act on our situation because of the biblical injunction that God knows what God is doing. The implication of this thinking is that our part is not to question God but to surrender quietly. Putting all of this in the category of "purpose" can sufficiently disengage us from the task of resisting suffering or protesting its root causes.

Each of these "purpose texts" brings comfort and sense to random and senseless sufferings. When a child dies, when a tragedy occurs, when a calamity strikes that does not fit into our normal range of appropriate grief (how much suffering is "normal" for a boy in a car accident?), then we *need* these deeper theological explanations. We need to have God function in a way that brings purpose to random and inexplicable suffering. Many problems are rooted in this need to bring purpose and meaning to random and senseless suffering. We devise "explanations" that help us to cope, to bring meaning, and to assist with the senselessness of our various encounters with affliction. At times these explanations are inadequate and fail to take into account the many other factors that are required for a mature Christian perspective.

## Three Tendencies with Respect to Questions about Suffering

While not an exhaustive list, we may note at this point three common tendencies with respect to Christian explanations of suffering. These tendencies exist in various degrees of certainty and precision. However, they operate in our unexamined assumptions about what is going on in the situation of the suffering. Before we move into the common explanations of suffering and the theodicies that support them, a brief exploration of these three tendencies will assist our aims.

### The Tendency to Explain Suffering

The tendency to explain suffering often leads us to the temptation to short-circuit our understanding of the deeper realities that give rise to suffering and a careful analysis of the root causes of suffering. Closely tied to our "sense-making" activity is the tendency to articulate premature or incomplete answers that prevent us from looking deeper into the causes of suffering itself. We may in fact begin to ignore aspects of suffering that can be changed or confronted when we acquiesce in this manner.[5] Suffering cannot be fully explained, and, as we have already noted, the situation of the suffering is always multivalent, complex, and multicontextual. However, this does not stop us, in our efforts of pastoral care and ministry, from offering explanations of suffering. In order to expose the inadequacy of the simple answers that we often give to those who suffer, I have developed the following evaluation grid for the explanations that we do offer.

## Five Tests of Our Explanations of Suffering

*Do Our Answers Alienate the Suffering Person?*

As we will see, some of our answers to suffering will leave the suffering person even more alienated and alone in their sorrow. The answers may fit our own theological interests or agenda but fail to respond to the deeper concern of the suffering person. The account is given of a thirty-two-year-old woman whose experiences of loss were severe. Her suffering began early in high school when her mother died. In a few short years, her brother was murdered, her father died of a heart attack, and her fiancé was killed in an accident. Her theology did not allow for a direct expression of anger at God and prevented her from truly expressing her sorrow. She writes in her journal, "I now identify massive amounts of storehouse anger. . . . [For] years I've tried to hide my anger at God. I've felt distant, out of touch, not spiritually connected, of little faith . . . unworthy of God's love. . . . I withdrew from God, sometimes not even able to go to church. . . . Walls were up around my heart. . . . [This] suppressed anger has kept me alienated from God."[6] Some of our answers cause alienation from God. When we deny persons the capacity to lament and to be angry with God, the suffering person may turn in on themselves and find that they have been cut off from fellowship with God.

*Do Our Explanations Adjust and Interpret the Facts to Fit Our Assumptions?*

We will often miss important dimensions of the situation of suffering or ignore these altogether, adjusting and interpreting the facts to fit in with our assumptions. Our theological categories often become hardened, and we prefer to ignore some information that may not align easily with these.

The account is given of a theological student and spouse whose new baby had suddenly died. People projected their theological assumptions on to them to explain this unexpected death. They said, "You know, it's probably a good thing that your son died. He probably would have grown up to be a problem. Maybe he'd have been a drug addict or would have refused to follow Christ. God knows these things in advance, and he was probably just saving you from those problems."[7]

*Do Our Interpretations Fit the Horrific Situations beyond Our Own Experience?*

In the same way, sometimes our interpretations of suffering are truncated by our relative lack of experience. If we cannot relate to the seriousness of the situation or the complexities that lie within a profound affliction, we might inadvertently minimize these realities to conform with our own experience. We must be careful to attend to all of the horror of the situation and not protect ourselves from the harder questions that may emerge when all of the facts are known.

Liberation theologians in other parts of the world remind us that the situation in North America is radically different from the situation in many other parts of the globe. Our lack of understanding of these contextual horrors of suffering in the cities of poverty and violence prevents those of us who live in the relative comfort of the West from truly accepting the full dreadfulness of suffering on a massive scale. For example, in the African context "the question [of suffering] again reverberates in the face of poverty, famine, displacement, refugee situations, and the resultant violence that has become the daily lot for millions of Africans living as they are 'in a continent which tends to become a veritable empire of hunger.'"[8]

When we unknowingly limit our understanding of the situation of suffering to those experiences that we have personally encountered, we truncate the situation of suffering itself and fail to take seriously the harsh conditions of much of the globe. A mature theology of suffering will of necessity move into the situations and complexities of famine, global hunger, injustice at a national scale, and other elements of suffering that are beyond our personal purview. To limit our understanding of suffering to the boundaries of our individual experiences is to fail to come to terms with the reality of suffering as it really exists in the world.

*Do Our Answers Fit the Anguish of the Victims and Reassure Them?*

While our answers sometimes bring consolation and encouragement to the surface of a situation, they do not always provide for the deeper issues of psychological anguish and spiritual desolation that often accompany true suffering. Our construction of pastoral responses must be tested against the deepest emotional trauma possible. If we live and answer on the surface, we will often miss the profound sense of melancholy and human anguish that accompany the situations of those who are victimized by suffering.

Much of the Bible is written in the language of lament and protest. There are whole sections of the New Testament that are written to beleaguered Christians who are being crushed by life. Our spiritual explanations of suffering must match the seriousness of the questions with which people are called to live.

This test of our explanations must include our capacity to withhold our explanations, which is a vital element of authentic pastoral concern. While our tendency is to offer words and answers, many situations of suffering require an articulate silence. The orientation for our active voicing of the situation must always be to the victim. When we enter into the suffering of others with true compassion, our first response will be similar to theirs—we will enter the ineffable space of shared lament. Anguish is a difficult space to endure. Authentic pastoral engagement will move into the uncomfortable place of not-knowing and hold the person who has experienced one of life's harsh blows. This is not a place for easy answers or pat explanations but a liminal space of solidarity with the afflicted.

*Do Our Explanations Attempt to Defend God?*

The final test of our "answers" or "explanations" of suffering is in regards to the defense of God and God's good name. This is a difficult aspect of theological reflection on suffering because we are taught, from early age, not to disrespect God. When theological defense of God becomes the primary aim we are in danger of imposing the balance due of affliction onto our fellow human beings. While the biblical witness allows for lament, protest, and complaint to God, some theological formulations seek to protect God and fail to live up to the seriousness of suffering.

Christian literature is filled with tracts and Bible studies that protect God's name at the expense of the suffering person. This theologizing activity is very dangerous and usually offers a prerogative to God that amounts to God's own terrorizing of human persons. Here is an example of such an explanation of suffering:

> God cannot shape without pain. Where there is no pain, no shaping is achieved. The tools He must use are sharp and abrasive. Quarry stones cannot resist but the "living stones" may. When they do, their sorrow and pain is wasted. If God cannot shape one for his distinctive place in eternity without

the use of affliction, may this not explain why many people continue to suffer physical illness in spite of long continued prayer for healing? If character is God's supreme aim in the universe and if character cannot be developed without pain, does this not illuminate the passage: "Whom the Lord loveth he chasteneth" (Heb 12:6)? Maybe God just cannot get that special stone He needs for a particular place any other way.[9]

### The Tendency to Avoid Suffering

We like to think of ourselves as compassionate people who are basically caring, responsive to pain, and understanding in the situation of the afflicted. We more or less assume that compassion is a natural response to human suffering. We like to think that our natural instinct to the reality of affliction is one of care and concern. In fact, our first response is to move away in dread, to avoid suffering at all costs, and to withdraw from the situation of the afflicted.[10] Dread, not compassion, is the natural response to the suffering of the afflicted. Our acknowledgment of the innate resistance to suffering is an important step in reforming compassionate ministry. If we lull ourselves into the conviction that we are intuitively caring, we will miss much of the opportunity for compassion. In fact, suffering repels us and calls up an inner resistance that is a more natural response to suffering and affliction.

If we compared our likely responses to the situations of suffering of others, we would begin to recognize a deep-seated resistance to compassion—not that we are uncaring, but that at its core, entering into the suffering of others is costly, difficult, and counterintuitive. The following chart compares the responses of dread and compassion to the situations of the afflicted.

| Dread | Compassion |
| --- | --- |
| looks away | pays attention |
| withdraws from suffering | moves toward the suffering |
| excuses ourselves | takes responsibility to relieve suffering |
| does not seek out causes | investigates the root causes of suffering |
| shrinks back from helping | counts the cost of helping |
| moves toward safety | engages the risk of "suffering with" others |

It is important to acknowledge the avoidance of suffering through the response of dread as we orient ourselves to the more challenging task of compassion. While we like to think that we are attentive to suffering, we are often looking away. Incapacitated moral seeing is a function of fear that comes when we are witness to the excruciating demands of suffering. We see as much, or as little, as we want to see. Therefore, compassion is first of all a "way of seeing" or an orienting perspective that notices the situation of suffering with full attention. The risks of inattention distract us from the good and remove from our field of vision the situation of the afflicted.[11]

Dread and fear also hold back our actions of relieving suffering, which is an elemental part of true compassion. There are significant risks in helping others who are suffering. The response of dread shrinks back from responsibility, moves toward safety and self-protection, and fails to search out the root causes of suffering. Compassion, on the other hand, is a full risk-taking enterprise. The compassionate response to suffering takes the responsibility to help, even if the helping action is costly and difficult. The compassionate response looks into the origin of the situation of the afflicted and offers active help in the alleviation of suffering and the causes that brought it about.[12]

In the end, the actions of mercy and compassion move us into the situation of the suffering with active help. We not only posture ourselves toward the sufferer and enter into their situation as our own, but we also actively help to alleviate the situation of suffering and confront its foundational causes. The tendency to withdraw, to fail to acknowledge, or to avoid suffering requires us to reexamine the very nature of our responses to the situations of suffering that we encounter. This tendency to avoid suffering is part of the human condition and signifies an opportunity for the moral formation of God's people as the compassionate community of God.

### The Tendency to Defend God

In *The Problem of Pain* C. S. Lewis describes in philosophical and abstract terms how Christian theology and suffering intersect. Lewis' is a distant theological reflection that God uses pain as an instrument to rouse us, to bring us back to him, and to draw us into relationship with himself. The early C. S. Lewis offers this maxim: "Pain is God's megaphone to rouse a deaf world."[13] Years later, after losing his wife to cancer, Lewis revisits the theme of suffering in his book *A Grief Observed*. The tone changes significantly in the mature Lewis. The experience of cancer taking the life of someone he loved dramatically alters his perspective and softens his language. His own encounter with personal tragedy and suffering had melted his previous articulate discourse, and this in turn required a reframing of his original ideas. Of suffering Lewis says, "But go to Him [God] when your need is desperate, when all other help is vain, and what do you find? A door slammed in your face and a sound of bolting and double bolting on the inside."[14] Like others who suffer the pangs of grief, Lewis is bewildered by the reality of affliction as he watches his beloved Joy die. In his perplexity he writes more softly of suffering. No longer is it a simple tool to make us pay attention to God; now suffering is a reality to be lived with in patience. He comes to the conclusion that there is "nothing we can do with suffering except to suffer it."[15]

Suffering modifies our language. If we try to articulate, as distant observers, the situation of suffering, there will be a leaning toward defending God. "The language we use depends on the situation we are in."[16] The tendency to defend God is a natural instinct. We are often like Job's friends who fail to enter fully into Job's situation. Their theological answers to suffering presume from a safe distance and carry the diminished language of the observer.

We sometimes prefer to keep our answers clear. It is difficult to muddy the waters with problems that may tarnish God's reputation, and sincere believers feel sometimes that it is their responsibility to defend God's honor. Yet, a mature theology of suffering will take into account the concrete situations and the sufferings and hopes of our fellow human beings.[17]

The stakes are high in the task of theology. To open up questions about God and suffering is to bring to the forefront the possibility of blaming God for the reality of suffering as we know it. This is uncomfortable for us, especially if we are part of a faith community of covenant love and loyalty to God. This was Job's real problem. While his friends were content to leave their theology untested and to defend God's honor, Job wanted an explanation for the reasons of his suffering. He wanted to explore the deeper understanding of God's presence and absence in the midst of his losses, anguish, and suffering. It was crucial to Job that he openly express his grief and learn to articulate the depths of his affliction. Job desired the understanding of his friends, and he wanted to experience the enduring care of God for him in the midst of his brokenness, hardship, oppression, and anguish. Job states his plight as clearly as he can: "If only my anguish could be weighed and all my misery be placed on the scales. It would surely outweigh the sand of the seas—no wonder my words have been impetuous. . . . Therefore I will not keep silent; I will speak out in the anguish of my spirit, I will complain in the bitterness of my soul" (Job 6:1-3; 7:11).

When our theological answers are structured more to defend God than to communicate the reality of suffering honestly, we need to modify our approach.[18] Our language in theology must bear the marks of compassionate participation in the suffering of others. We will have some inclination to protect God's image and to ensure that our theology does not diminish God's sovereign power. However, we must take seriously the challenge of theologians who caution that a theology of affliction may result in "bringing us back to a God who only becomes great when he makes us small."[19]

## Five Common Explanations of Suffering

By attempting to give meaning to suffering, we often settle for incomplete "answers." These answers pacify our need for understanding and for the sense-making that we require to cope with life. While we have the intuitive feeling that these answers are incomplete and only partially explain the deeper reality of suffering, we often use these to control the meaninglessness or enigma of suffering. All of these "answers" or "explanations" have elements of being correct (half-truths are always half right) and may, in some part, bring certain meaning to suffering. At the same time, these explanations can become a hindrance to greater and more congruent theological reflection on the meaning of suffering.

Offering pastoral care to persons in affliction requires deep sensitivity to the multivalent reality of suffering. There are explanations of suffering that are offered to suffering persons to give comfort and guidance in their pain. If these explanations of suffering are oversimplified, they can be used in ways that are debilitating to those we seek to help. These explanations are still in widespread usage even though the reduced theological assumptions on which they are based are faulty and deeply inadequate. These common explanations have various iterations that appear in popular literature[20] and in some theological works.[21] We will explore five explanations here and look for parallel examples of how these "answers" appear in other Christian literature.

*Suffering as Punishment*

In this view the assumption is made that we always get what we deserve and that suffering is a consequence for wrongdoing. Misfortunes are seen as punishment for sins. It is a commonly held assumption and is reinforced by biblical teachings. This retributive approach to the meaning of suffering is supported with biblical texts such as Isaiah 3:10-11: "Tell the righteous it will be well with them, for they will enjoy the fruit of their deeds. Woe to the wicked! Disaster is upon them! They will be paid back for what their hands have done." Again, in Proverbs we read, "No harm befalls the righteous, but the wicked have their fill of trouble" (Prov 12:21).

The *doctrine of retribution* simply stated is that the wicked are punished and the righteous are rewarded. In the Old Testament book of Job, this "convenient and soothing doctrine"[22] is based on the idea of fairness. The Lord sees all and acts toward human beings appropriately: the righteous are rewarded and the wicked are punished. The emphatic inclusiveness of the texts that support the doctrine of retribution make it seem like there is no room for other nuances to enter in. Consider, for example, the argument of Eliphaz the Temanite to the suffering Job: "Consider now: Who, being innocent, has ever perished? Where were the upright ever destroyed? As I have observed, those who plow evil and those who sow trouble reap it" (Job 4:7-8).

The theological premise behind the doctrine of retribution is that all suffering is the result of actions we have done—to the righteous, good rewards, and to the wicked, punishment. Suffering is a punishment for our sins, our rebellion, and our "sowing of evil." This may be classified retributive suffering.[23] In the Old Testament, this is the most comprehensive type of distress or suffering mentioned. Tied intimately with the judgment of God, the most basic idea of retributive suffering is that it is the kind of suffering that comes as a result of sin.[24] From this outlook, suffering is the result of sin that must be punished by a just God. In this view, we should expect to suffer at God's hand for our disobedience because "it is our own fault and we often have only ourselves to blame."[25]

Philip Yancey tells of a deacon in Claudia's church who came to see her when she was in the hospital with cancer. The church leader "solemnly advised her to reflect on what God was trying to teach her. 'Surely something in your life must displease God,' he said. 'Somewhere, you must have stepped out of his will. These things don't just happen. God uses circumstances to warn us, and to punish us. What is he telling you?'"[26]

The question never occurs to this church leader that there are times when the doctrine of retribution does not fit the facts. There are situations where innocent people suffer and are caught as victims in the throes of an untoward reality. We may be able to explain much suffering with the balance of rewarded good and punished evil, but there are many situations that simply do not fit. While the doctrine of retribution may seem like a "neat and attractive solution to the problem of evil," it leads people away from a deeper encounter with God whom they now fear, and so often this explanation does not fit the facts of the circumstances of suffering.[27]

Rooted in the idea of human responsibility for suffering, the idea that suffering is caused by God's punishment of our transgressions is still an active explanation that is often placed on the suffering innocent. If the cause is not self-evident, the afflicted is advised to look more deeply within to the secret sins and the hidden rebellion that must in fact be the ultimate cause of the suffering. However, guilt and punishment for sin is tricky. Note Kaiser's qualifying word, "we *often* have only ourselves to blame."[28] How will we discern whether our suffering is a punishment by God, thus a deserved chastisement for our disobedience, or innocent? What are the criteria for knowing that your sin is the cause of a particular situation of affliction?

There are occasions where suffering must not be labeled as retributive justice for sin. Victims of a crime or abuse or a terrorist attack experience "radical (unmerited) suffering."[29] These are innocents, and their situations of profound loss and tragedy are the result of the moral evil inflicted by others. There are many situations where retributive justice simply does not fit. This does not imply that there are not consequences for sin; however, the explanation for all suffering is often unfairly attributed to this cause-and-effect approach. Seen this way, suffering as punishment is only a partial view of the causes for suffering and applicable in only a limited way.

We move to a second category of suffering, the mystery of the resolved life in God's tapestry.

### The Resolved Life in God's Tapestry

In this view, suffering is a mystery that can only be understood from God's perspective. We are not urged to expose the roots of suffering, nor are we to identify the causes of suffering and alleviate them. From this outlook, suffering is a temporal experience that will be resolved in the long term, when we gain God's ultimate perspective on the situation. This perspective contends that human beings are limited and finite and see the situation of suffering only from the underside. Our limited vantage point is like the backside of a tapestry. We can see the knots and the loose strings, but not the beautiful art that God can see on the opposite side of the tapestry. This is the difference between God's perspective and our perspective on suffering.[30]

Suffering is explained as needing a bigger perspective—the bird's eye view—God's view, which is impossible for us to see. Underlying this is the assumption that all suffering is meaningful and has a deeper purpose. What seems arbitrary to us is a result of our inability to understand the deeper perspective of God.

This argument has many forms. The most common is the balcony and the road analogy.[31] Looked at from the balcony the many dangers and pitfalls of the road are easy to see, and the perspective from above is very helpful to the traveler below. From the road, however, the dangers cannot be anticipated or understood—they are encountered directly and often painfully. What we need is the perspective of the balcony to help us on the road of suffering.

Some would offer the argument that the task of the theologian is to bring the perspective of the balcony to the sufferers on the road down below.[32] While it attempts to understand how the task of theology might engage the experience of the road itself, this approach fails to take seriously the call to compassion in this endeavor. The deep involvement of compassion might complicate our theological understandings in the thick of suffering. The assumption that the theological clarity of the balcony will continue to persist on the road is unfounded. Speaking meaningfully about suffering is not simply a matter of articulating what one sees and knows to be true.

The matter of perspective is one that is familiar to the Christian view. We know that "now we see but a poor reflection as in a mirror; then we will see face to face" (1 Cor 13:12). We will always be limited in our perspective even if we give faithful attention to the Scriptures. God's perspective is unattainable for human beings, and, despite our efforts to see clearly, much of what we see and know is distorted by life in a broken world. What are the contributing factors to gaining this perspective?

Gaining true perspective on suffering would demand much of us. While the Scriptures invite us to gain the perspective of eternity, many Scripture passages could be cited to declare both our inability to see perfectly (distortion) and also to see through the eyes of faith (eternal perspective). We fluctuate between these perspectives in our earthly journey. Certainly all suffering cannot be explained in the perspective or tapestry approach.

The problem with this approach is the tendency to overlook and avoid the deeper realities of affliction. Explanations have the capacity to help the suffering, but they can also cause us to prematurely accept the conditions that gave rise to the suffering. The balcony perspective may be helpful in the articulation of the ultimate meaning of suffering, but it may also serve to alienate the sufferer even more as they find their suffering senseless and meaningless. In the face of ridiculous suffering, sensible answers are alienating and perspective is elusive.

Perspective is vitally important; as we will see, however, the resolved life in God's tapestry is another incomplete "answer" to the reality of suffering. We must use caution when explaining suffering in this way because of the tendency to omit facts that do not fit or to summarize a theological perspective that may in fact miss some of the deeper causes of suffering itself.

This leads us to a third common explanation, pedagogical suffering.

### Pedagogical Suffering

In this view, suffering is meant to educate us, to purify our intentions, and to mold and shape our inner being. Suffering is meant for the formation of our character and can be seen to have a positive educational effect on our development. The idea behind this "answer" is that all suffering is meant to have a pedagogical benefit or to catalyze some aspect of our moral development. In this view, suffering strengthens us, ennobles us, and repairs that which is faulty in us. God uses suffering, it is claimed, to teach us how to live in the manner most conducive to our flourishing.

The pedagogical interpretation that suffering is meant to teach us is one that finds ample biblical support. Sin has natural consequences and these consequences serve to restrain us from further iniquity. There are times, as well, when God will discipline us for our own good. These educational aspects of suffering can be attested throughout Scripture. A common text to support the pedagogical view of suffering is taken from the book of Hebrews, where we are advised, "No discipline seems pleasant at the time, but painful. Later on, however, it produces a harvest of righteousness and peace for those who have been trained by it" (Heb 12:11).

Here again, however, is the faulty assumption that all suffering can be attributed to God's discipline. The connection between our afflictions and the tragedies of life is often unrelated to any personal moral failure or educational, spiritual aim. The explanation that sees suffering as a teaching tool in the hands of God is not only inadequate but can be a cruel explanation for a child born with disabilities, for a car accident, or for an afflictive disease. The educational or pedagogical explanation of suffering is dangerous when it is used to justify all situations of suffering.[33] The idea behind this perspective is that suffering is always remedial or instructive. Suffering can lead us back to righteousness through the vale of soul-making.[34]

Suffering as educational or formational is certainly a theme that can be traced in the Bible. However, once again, we cannot be sure of the exact parameters of such an explanation of suffering. If God is using suffering to teach and train us, it is unclear when we should expect the training session to end. The educational aims of suffering are not clearly related to any particular interpretation of events, and it remains unclear when the remedial effects of suffering have achieved their purpose.

In his poignant book *Lament for a Son*, Nicholas Wolterstorff describes how painful these explanations of suffering are as "answers" to the reality of suffering. Wolterstorff comments on explanations given for the tragic death of his son Eric:

> The only thing that angered me in what people offered was a small book someone gave me written by a father whose son had also be killed in a mountaineering accident. The writer said that in his church on the Sunday before his son's death, they had read Psalm 18. He now interpreted verse 36 as speaking to him: "*Thou didst give me a wide place for my steps under me, and my foot did not slip.*" His son's foot had not slipped. God had shaken the mountain. God had decided that it was time for him to come home. I find this pious attitude deaf to the message of the Christian gospel. . . . I have read the theodicies produced to justify the ways of God to man [sic]. I find them unconvincing. To the most agonized question I have ever asked I do not know the answer. I do not know why God would watch him fall. I do not know why God would watch me wounded. I cannot even guess. . . . My wound is an unanswered question. The wounds of all humanity are an unanswered question.[35]

We turn now to a fourth common explanation of suffering, the idea of tragedy as a test of faith.

### Tragedy as a Test

The fourth common explanation of suffering is that tragedy is a test of faith. Suffering, in this view, is a test from God for those whom God knows will persevere. Genesis 22 is often referred to as a paradigm for understanding suffering as a divine test, "Some time later God tested Abraham" (Gen 22:1). At the root of suffering, in this approach, is a divine appointment *to suffer with a purpose.* This view understands suffering as a special calling. It is often offered to the afflicted as a way of understanding their suffering as a sacred task or even a privilege. God will only test those whom he knows will pass the test.[36] The affliction, however severe, is to be endured quietly and not resisted because it is seen as a special grace that God is giving to those whom he deems fit for the challenge. This explanation of suffering goes further than the pedagogical aims of the previous approach and offers suffering as a special calling or spiritual test that must be passed by those to whom the suffering is sent by God. The key assumption in this "answer" to suffering is that tragedy is not really tragedy but a spiritual test which has a divine purpose and that persons who suffer are singled out by God to pass through divinely appointed trials of suffering.

Suffering as a spiritual test can also find scriptural support. In the New Testament book of James, the faithful are instructed, "Consider it pure joy, my brothers and sisters, whenever you face trials of many kinds, because you know that the testing of your faith develops perseverance. Perseverance must finish its work so that you may be mature and complete, not lacking anything" (Jas 1:2-4). The book of Job can also be read as a test-of-life story. Job is commended for his patient endurance in suffering: "As you know, we consider blessed those who have persevered. You have heard of Job's perseverance and have seen what the Lord finally brought about. The Lord is full of compassion and mercy" (Jas 5:11). Yet, this is a very difficult judgment to make in the circumstances of life. Suffering is more chaotic than that, and seldom do we have any more than glimpses of hope in the face of unspeakable disappointments.

Tragedy as a test gives the satisfaction of explaining a deeper and hidden purpose in suffering that, once again, is known only to God. God knows not only the source of the affliction, but he knows that the outcome of the suffering will result in the test being passed. The problem with this view is that it tries to explain suffering in terms that make it a heroic journey rather than seeking compassionate understanding of the pain of the situation.[37] The answer, as in most of the truncated responses we have reviewed, fails to fit all the facts and imposes an interpretation that may comfort the one who speaks while alienating the suffering persons in their affliction.

In our journey with our disabled child, Chelsey, many have offered this explanation to us as a way to satisfy *their* own search for understanding God's ways in the harsh realities of life. People have often said to us things like, "God must think you are very special to give you this great challenge." We think it was meant as a compliment. It seldom occurs to people how painful such a theological "answer" can be. No one wants to be singled out for special suffering in order to prove fidelity to God. The tragedy-as-test approach fails to explain suffering's root and does not adequately answer the many forms and causes of suffering. While there is some biblical support for the thought that our faith can be tested, this does not explain the reasons for a situation of affliction in life nor should it be constructed as an argument to welcome suffering.

We turn to one final approach, suffering as a release from life.

### Suffering as a Release from Life

A final explanation of suffering is the view that suffering comes as "a release from life." The common approach of this explanation is the view that the afterlife is to be considered more important than the temporal suffering of grief in this life. According to this understanding, the focus of suffering should not be on the here and now but on the better situation in the life to come. If we remain faithful until death, we will experience the blessing of God after the troubles of this broken world have passed away.

This approach to suffering invites those who are afflicted to look past their suffering, or more accurately, to long beyond their suffering. The anguish, pain, and hardship of the present life are not to be compared with the glory of the future life that is to come. Suffering must be endured in this broken world, but it can be best endured, according to this perspective, if we only would be able to look beyond this life to heaven and the benefits of a life after suffering.

Again, scriptural support for this view may be easily found. The Apostle Paul admonishes the faithful, "For our light and momentary troubles are achieving for us an eternal glory that far outweighs them all. So we fix our eyes not on what is seen, but on what is unseen. For what is seen is temporary, but what is unseen is eternal" (2 Cor 4:17-18).

However, this explanation misrepresents some of the scriptural view of hope. The biblical call not to "grieve as those who have no hope" (1 Thess 4:13) is mistakenly taken to mean that we should not grieve at all. In this explanation of suffering, the call is to deny the anguish, pain, and extreme horrors of suffering by embracing the perspective of heaven on earth.[38] Once again, while the biblical call to hope is certainly a rich and explicit theme throughout the Bible, the problem with this view is that all suffering is to be accepted without grief, without protest, and without thought of the emotional anguish. This does not square with the biblical view of suffering.

This view is flawed in its inability to protest suffering and the root causes of affliction in this life. The challenge to this perspective on suffering is that we must make the distinction between the suffering that we can end and the suffering that is beyond our control. By easy acquiescence to suffering and placing all of the focus on the afterlife, we deny our responsibility to truly see the root causes of suffering and to work for their elimination.[39] It is imperative that we make this distinction and work for the abolition of the root causes of suffering. Even in this work we cooperate with God's expressed intentions in the world as God reconciles all things to himself. While there is a future hope for the people of God, this hope is not grounds for acquiescence and failed moral vision. We must act on the supposition that God wants our good now *and* in the future. The theological explanations that enable our premature acceptance of suffering weaken our moral resolve to work as agents of God's reconciling love in the world. This does not square with the biblical vision.

The view that suffering is resolved in the afterlife is also a truncated perspective on suffering. Here again, the wider lens that is required for a mature theology of suffering is undeveloped. In every approach listed above, there is an eclipsed or abbreviated perspective that only tells part of the story. To use these explanations as definitive understandings of the reality of suffering is very perilous to authentic faith.

## Conclusion

We can see that in all of these explanations there is the problem of deciding what is really going on. Some of these explanations are premature answers that thwart real actions of justice and mercy. To take these explanations at face value is to disallow something that Scripture itself does not disallow: the ability to ask questions in the face of affliction. The biblical text, viewed with a wider lens, invites those who suffer to lament the realities of their suffering and to protest the anguishing situation. While some of these "answers" or "explanations" may prove comforting on one level, they are also the source of deep alienation for the afflicted. They may bring hope to some while deepening the loneliness, the sense of abandonment, and the experience of forsakenness in the most afflicted. The tendencies to withdraw from suffering, to explain it away, and to defend God are all aspects that we must be aware of if we are to face up to the deeper reality of hope that the Scriptures offer us.

Biblical hope is not the neglecting of suffering or the premature resolution of suffering but rather the capacity to stand up to the presence of affliction with the help of God. Theological answers are possible, but we must always cushion our understanding with a movement toward authentic compassion. The biblical posture of hope is always in spite of and invites a firm trust in the God of hope. A mature theology of suffering will include the capacity to live up to the serious realities of suffering, affliction, and the senseless situation of the most oppressed. It will renew our awareness that "we now only see dimly as in a mirror," but it will also compel us to act in fidelity to that which we do see. It will call for a moral courage to live hopefully in the face of affliction while being careful not to explain away the situation of the most afflicted. It will lead us to a theology of compassion and one in which God himself is active in the realities of life in this broken world. A theology of suffering will lead us to the cross of the risen Christ and will give us clues to the dawning of a coming day when "the dwelling of God is with men, and he will live with them. They will be his people, and God himself will be with them and be their God. He will wipe away every tear from their eyes. There will be no more death, or mourning or crying or pain, for the old order of things has passed away" (Rev 21:3-4).

CHAPTER TWO

# Components of a Theology
# of Suffering

Suffering imposes a crucial test on the word-articulating efforts of theology. To speak of God in the midst of unspeakable suffering is to unfold one of the most elusive mysteries of Christian thought. Correctly conceived, theology has the enormous task of reflecting a constructive vision of God. A theology of suffering, in turn, bears the daunting challenge of articulating this vision in the context of overwhelming conditions of human tragedy and anguish. Although theology has always been done in the context of the world's brokenness, few theological works come to terms with the persistent threat that the existence of suffering poses to all God-talk and to the very belief in God. Theologians have noted that the situation of extreme suffering has become the functional dialogue partner of contemporary Christian theology.[1] If this is the case, we must take seriously the challenge of articulating a meaningful discourse about God in the midst of suffering. It is also crucial that our talk about God and suffering open up the question of a suffering God and how God's suffering is connected to the suffering of human persons. For a mature theology of suffering to emerge several core components are required. While not exhaustive, the following elements give shape to this book and outline the primary framework for the theology of suffering that will be expressed.

## Humility as the Fundamental Posture
## of the Theologian in a Broken World

A mature theology of suffering acknowledges the suffering of the innocent and is reluctant to overstate what one knows for sure. A creative
definition of theology offered by Gustavo Gutiérrez is "speech enriched
by silence."[2] The humility and spiritual depth required to do theology in
the light of the extreme situations of suffering must follow this pattern.
Establishing ourselves on the terrain of spirituality is the prerequisite
to authentic theologizing. The poet T. S. Eliot reminds us that "human
kind cannot bear very much reality."[3] Certainly, the concrete reality of
raw suffering will require a humble articulation of what we know.

The ambiguity of the situation of suffering requires that we be
grounded in a spiritual relationship with God. Good theology is not
accomplished through vague abstractions, but rather, through careful
integration of the biblical revelation in light of the personal and communal experiences of life in a broken world. While answers are tempting, we
are not seeking conclusions, but rather, entering into the mystery of God's
own presence and absence in the contours of life's darkest situations.
Suffering is not a subject to be explored from the "balcony" but rather
a theocentric way of speaking that engages the journey from the road.
As Dietrich Bonhoeffer states, "We have for once learnt to see the great
events of world history from below, from the perspective of the outcast,
the suspects, the maltreated, the powerless, the oppressed, the reviled—in
short, from the perspective of those who suffer."[4]

Christian ethicist James Gustafson expressed the importance of
both *perspective* and *posture* in mature theological reflection. Perspective
is drawn from the sphere of visual experience and suggests "the point
from which things are seen and observed determines what is seen and
what is not seen; which aspects of what is seen are outstanding, which
are shadowed and which are clear, what attracts attention and what is
subdued in attention."[5] Perspective is a basic aspect of the Christian
moral life.

Posture has come to suggest "where one stands in life."[6] It regards
our basic orientation as those who are loyal to Jesus Christ. Christian faith directs us to have, as we ought, a characteristic posture or
orientation toward the world. The perspective and posture of the person loyal to Jesus Christ is fundamentally a perspective and posture of
"hope and freedom."[7] "Christians are, can be and ought to be disposed
to be hopeful"—a hope grounded in a trust in the goodness of God who

makes all things new—and "Christians often are, can be and ought to be inwardly free," grounded in "God's care and love."[8]

Mature theological reflection requires utmost humility. Our penchant is to want answers and solutions rather than the harder work of staying with the questions. A theology of suffering requires that we remain clear minded as we enter into solidarity with those who suffer and view the world from the perspective and posture of those who are loyal to Jesus Christ.

## An Honest Appraisal of the Tears of the Most Afflicted and Oppressed

*"Again I looked and saw all the oppression that was taking place under the sun:*
*I saw the tears of the oppressed—and they have no comforter." (Eccl 4:1)*

To "theologize" about suffering requires first a full participation in the situation of the oppressed. A mature theology of suffering will "see" with new eyes the depth of suffering in all of its horror. This is more than merely identifying with the pains of others. Compassion is to "feel in the gut" the anguish, distress, inner torment, and frustration of those who are enduring unspeakable hurt. This capacity to truly "see" the situation of the sufferer has not always been achieved in theological explanations of suffering.

Consider the profound gap that surfaces between our experiences of suffering and the deeply held theological convictions about God's goodness and universal power that lie at the heart of the Christian faith. Christian theology has often accepted the premise of theodicy as the basis for this reflection. The theodicy (from the Greek *theos*, "God," and *dikē*, "justice, what is right") approach seeks to explain the apparent contradiction between God's love and God's justice. The theodicy approach frames God and suffering as a theological problem or riddle: "If God is good and all-powerful, why do suffering and evil exist?" The general solution calls for a rejection of one of the three assumptions present in this framing of the question. This approach is ultimately unsatisfying because it is removed from the complexities of suffering itself. A deliberate task of this volume is to develop a critique of the theodicy approach and expose the consequent common explanations of suffering that arise from this argument.

A theology of suffering must move beyond speculative thinking about God and suffering so that the reality of suffering as a lived experience is fully acknowledged. It is from this lived reality that we must learn to speak of God in the midst of suffering. It is important to restate one of the key premises of this book: *We must not approach suffering as a problem to be solved or as a riddle to be explained but rather as a reality to be confronted in cooperation with God's own expressed intentions in the world.* In this sense, a mature theology of suffering will take seriously the experience of personal and communal suffering and will seek to expound the implications of such situations for the doctrine of God.

At the heart of the proposal of this book lies an expansion of Jürgen Moltmann's seminal insight of the resurrection as God's protest against suffering.[9] I develop the concept of *compassionate protest* as the posture Christians must embrace in the face of unspeakable suffering. Participation in the kingdom of God means, in part, to enter into God's own protest against suffering and to recognize that the fragments of hope that exist in the midst of suffering point to a certain and defined future in the created order. A careful assessment of the situation of those who suffer will bring into focus the call to resist suffering and to avoid acquiescence to the structures of oppression, misery, and anguish. Hope resides in the confluence of resistance and mature acceptance.

## Being Grounded in the Reality of the Concrete Experiences of Suffering

Explanations for suffering often satisfy the questions of the comfortable rather than appease the anguish of the afflicted. The very experiences of extreme suffering provide the framework from which an authentic theology of suffering must emerge. In order to achieve this, this book deliberately brings into the conversation the complex situation of the suffering person, the anguished community, and the afflicted creation. The goal of this discussion is to protect against the tendency in Christian thought to underestimate the situation of suffering itself. Interactions with the concrete situations of affliction are supported by the conviction that any truly helpful theology of suffering must validate and enter into the painful experiences of the most afflicted. John Claypool outlines the excruciating situation of watching his daughter suffer. He writes,

> There were the times . . . when Laura Lue was hurting so intensely that she had to bite on a rag and used to beg me to pray to God to take away that awful pain. I would kneel down beside her bed and pray with all the faith and conviction of my soul, and nothing would happen except the pain continuing to rage on. Or again, that same negative conclusion was tempting when she asked me in the dark of the night: "When will this leukemia go away?" I

answered: "I don't know, darling, but we are doing everything we know to make that happen."[10]

A theology of suffering must provide the theological resources necessary to respond to the cry of the afflicted, "Where is God in all this?" Perhaps the most powerful contemporary articulation of the problem of God's absence or presence in the situation of suffering is Elie Wiesel's description of his painful memories of Auschwitz:

> Never shall I forget that night, the first night in camp, that turned my life into one long night seven times sealed. Never shall I forget the small faces of the children whose bodies I saw transformed into smoke under a silent sky. Never shall I forget those flames that consumed my faith forever. Never shall I forget the nocturnal silence that deprived me for all eternity of the desire to live. Never shall I forget those moments that murdered my God and my soul and turned my dreams to ashes. Never shall I forget those things, even were I condemned to live as long as God Himself. Never.[11]

The painful narrative in *Night*, together with other compelling experiences of suffering, is one means employed in this volume to remain grounded in the reality of suffering itself and to avoid any oversimplification of the horrifying reality of affliction. It is crucial that the concrete events, stories, and accounts of excruciating suffering be expressed. Our attempts to articulate a theology of suffering require that our reflections remain tangible and particular.

This method of moving from experience to theological reflection is crucial in a pastoral theology of suffering which will insist that a theology of suffering must begin from the real situations of the most afflicted. Bonhoeffer correctly suggests that "timeless and placeless ethical discourse lack the concrete warrant which all authentic discourse requires. . . . The words are correct but *they have no weight*."[12] Similarly, this volume maintains that any adequate theology of suffering demands that the experiences of the most afflicted, anguished persons and communities be acknowledged and reflected on as lived realities, rather than as illustrations of seemingly more important, if abstract, philosophical concepts. If these situations are not taken seriously as the lived realities of real people, the theoretical and doctrinal explanations devised by theological reflection fail the test of authenticity—the words have no weight to live up to the seriousness of the situation they describe. This is an exacting discipline of theological reflection that requires patience. The tendency to prematurely conclude or to offer theological reasons without truly attending to the depth and anguish of particular situations must be avoided in order for any mature reflection to come into view.

## Attention to the Transformative Power
## of Language

Patient waiting for the right words to form in the situation of the most afflicted can be thought of as a spiritual discipline. Our task must be to draw on language for agonies that cannot easily be expressed.[13] If the function of language is to express the relationship between things, then we must employ discourse that will convey the deepest significance of our experiences.[14] If we are to speak meaningfully of the multivalent experiences of suffering, we need to pay careful attention to how language is used to express the depth of these experiences. Words have power, and they evoke memory of the deeper realities to which they point. An authentic theology of suffering will search for language that describes a yearning for God in the experience of forsakenness. It will conceive the words that depict God's active agency and care for a world caught in the grip of brokenness. Every effort will be made to capture phrases that express the intentions of God's own presence in the situation of the most afflicted.

It is crucial for our task that we examine the role of language in religious thought. Words can function as either *signs* or *symbols*. Both signs and symbols "point beyond themselves to something else."[15] The difference is that "while symbols participate in the reality to which they point, signs do not."[16] The moment a word acquires a connotation that moves beyond its function as a pointing sign, it becomes a symbol. It is clear that we use words in both ways—sometimes as signs and other times as symbols. When used as symbols, as in liturgical or poetic language, words open up a hidden level of reality or "the depth dimension of reality."[17] Such powerful symbols have a corresponding "interior reality" in the soul. Thus, poetic language functions as a bridge between the interior experience of a soul and the exterior or depth dimension of reality: "Religious symbols open up the experience of the dimension of depth in the human soul."[18] It is the depth dimension of reality that is often unexpressed. In order to find transforming words for such profound experiences it is crucial to follow the path of theopoetic speech and the language of lamentation. The first movement of the soul in the experience of affliction is mutism, an inability to express the dimensions of suffering.[19] At the symbolic level, where words point to meanings beyond themselves, one begins to form a way of speaking about the unspeakable. Poetic language becomes a way to express the depth dimension (ontology) and the interior reality of the soul (experience).

The poetic word-form is familiar to much of the language of the Bible. The effort to express ultimate reality through symbol-bearing language is a common feature of the Scriptures. This volume will seek to enter into the language-bearing power of word-forms that articulate the anguish of spirit connected to the interior experience of suffering itself. The proximity of ontology and the unveiling of the eyes as a basis for speaking of ultimate reality is an important dimension of the pastoral theology of suffering proposed in this volume.

The approach taken in this volume is one that recognizes the proximity of ontology and an "opening" of the eyes as a basis for speaking about reality.[20] Much of our language in theology seems to have had the effect of lulling us to sleep, of "closing" our eyes. Detached observation, calculating analysis, and dry hypotheses fail to break through. What are needed are word-forms (symbols) that participate in the reality to which they point, word-forms which express the depth dimension of reality and open up the soul. In order to offer such meaningful expression, one must be immersed in reality. I would share Tillich's insight that only those who are "involved in ultimate reality," who have encountered "it as a matter of existential concern, can try to speak about it meaningfully."[21]

Suffering is not easily expressed. Many who suffer in silence yearn for an understanding person who will guide the reflection necessary to *word the void* and to give meaning to suffering through the use of language. Pastoral theology always seeks such "sensitive articulation."[22] If the condition of suffering is to be articulated, however, this will demand a participation in the conditions of suffering as a "suffering with," which is compassion.

This dual articulation of one's own suffering and the suffering of others involves the movement from mutism to lament (see chap. 4). Those who are immersed in the suffering situation are in unspeakable pain. "The first step . . . is then, to find a language that leads out of the uncomprehended suffering that makes one mute, a language of lament, of crying, or pain, a language that *at least says what the situation is.*"[23] The lament is a subversive prayer-form. The prayer of lament reframes the situation in ways that resist easy explanation or acquiescence. This is a form of protest or authentic resistance to simplified answers that are often recommended to persons to explain their suffering. The aim of the lament is not a full theological explanation of the suffering situation. It is more an experience-near language or psalmic language which gives authentic expression to the conditions of suffering in all of its dimensions. This lamentation is comprehensive because often suffering "threatens every dimension of life."[24]

## A Resistance to Easy Explanations of Suffering and a Deliberate Recovery of Mystery

One debilitating tendency that stands in the way of developing an authentic theology of suffering, especially in North America, is our tendency to attempt to "explain away" suffering. We commonly approach the situations of suffering with a deep desire to resolve the incongruities that they bring into our experience. The paralyzing effect of this tendency can be understood when we acknowledge the root idea of *explanation*, "to explain: from the Latin 'ex-planare,' to flatten, spread out, make level. A great bulldozer will push the mountains inside the abysses and everything will become a luminous plain under midday sun."[25] The attempt to explain suffering—that is, the mindset that suggests that the key lies in finding the "correct" explanation for all situations of suffering—is part of the problem in much of the Christian literature on suffering. Explanations often impose a greater suffering on the afflicted by alienating them from the community of hope. Such alienation leads to *the suffering in suffering*,[26] namely, loneliness, as was the case in the Old Testament experience of Job, which stands as the biblical epitome of suffering.[27]

However, explanations persist. We have a need to explain suffering, especially "the scandal of suffering in a God-made and God-ruled universe."[28] Moreover, although many people have confronted the situation of suffering in their personal and community life, most find it almost impossible to bridge the chasm between what they claim to believe about God and their experience of suffering itself.

The recovery of a sense of mystery in our articulation of suffering is part of the work attempted in this volume. Such reflection requires a respectful sorrowing with others who suffer. Often, the words that are meant to convey God's presence in the unspeakable experiences of suffering are structured more to defend God or to describe limited, human apprehensions. The retrieval of language that is less certain is required.[29] As our deliberation unfolds it is imperative to remain awake to the complexities involved when we speak about God and suffering. Theological speaking in this sense demands that we conform our expression about God in the face of the dismaying experiences of affliction in all their density.

## A Constructive Description of the Multidimensional Nature of Suffering

Analysis of the multidimensional structure of suffering itself is an important aspect for the development of a theology of suffering. This seems a rather obvious point, but it is often overlooked in treatises on the subject of suffering. It is crucial to clarify the dimensions of suffering and their corollary implications for theology. As stated in the introduction, this book will develop an understanding of the multidimensional description of suffering: physical pain, psychological anguish, social degradation, and spiritual desolation (see chap. 3).[30] In this way I attempt to elucidate suffering in all of its complexity, thereby offering a wider scope of reference in which to frame the development of a theology of suffering than is generally found in theological treatises on the topic. This analysis of the structure of suffering brings clarity to the dimensions of theological reflection required in order to live up to the deeper realities of brokenness and human anguish. While not all suffering contains all of the dimensions of pain, anguish, social degradation, and spiritual despondency, our ability to talk about suffering and God will rely on the understanding provided by this analysis of the multivalent structure of suffering itself.

The context of suffering must also be carefully developed. Attempts to understand the multidimensional nature of suffering must explore the personal experiences of suffering, the social dimensions and roots of suffering, and the wider scope of the situation of a broken world or "fallen" creation. Suffering takes place within the larger context of creation and in the sequence of events that come into the lives of persons and their communities. A theological analysis of God and suffering will require attention to this wider context and framework of where, when, and how suffering happens in the world.

The complex movements of suffering are not easily detected. However, attention to the deeper contours of suffering's multidimensional and multicontextual realities will provide the required precision of thought to open up the discussion of this all-encompassing theme. It will also stand in contrast to those approaches that fail to detect the compounding and multivalent dimensions of suffering. Without this deeper reflection, the theological analysis is not connected to the root elements of suffering as a whole.

## An Examination of the Root Causes of Apathy and Moral Indifference and Their Theological Implications

There is yet another important but often overlooked factor that must be taken seriously in the construction of a theology of suffering, namely, the avoidance of suffering.[31] We like to think of our immediate response to suffering as one of compassion, however, there is an underside to this—indifference and apathy.[32] We must take seriously the dynamics of aversion to suffering. The dearth of literature on this theme reflects the resistance to the experience of suffering itself that is so widespread today, especially in North America.

Moral indifference is rarely the result of a lack of concern for those who suffer but rather a result of "psychic numbness."[33] The fact that we understand some of the realities of suffering often comforts us and reinforces our indifference. We care about the plight of those who suffer, but there the mass scale of suffering shuts down our capacity to stay with suffering and to endure it. We often shut ourselves off from the deeper reality of suffering because of the expansiveness of the situations of anguish in our world. This insight will be more fully explored as a root issue in the theology of suffering.[34] We will uncover the compassion of God as the ultimate foundation for a theological reframing of indifference and apathy in our lives and in the communities of faith in which we participate. The compassionate community of God enacts God's own care and compassion in the brokenness of the world.

## A Careful Examination of the Implications of Suffering for the Doctrine of God[35]

A mature theology of suffering will delineate what suffering means for God.[36] This focus on God's own suffering provides the vantage point from which to engage the contemporary discussions on the theology of suffering. In contrast to much of the triumphalism of the *theologia gloriae* (theology of glory), this book aligns with those contemporary thinkers who are seeking to find theological significance in the renewal of the *theologia crucis* (theology of the cross). I will argue that the center point for understanding the suffering of God is the cross of Christ Jesus. Jürgen Moltmann's construct of "godforsakenness" in his theology of the cross continues to be a compelling orientation to the suffering of God in the Trinity.

However, this raises the deeper questions in contemporary theology about divine passibility. While the idea of a suffering God has gained significant ground in recent decades since Moltmann's *The Crucified God*, there are renewed debates about what it means that God suffers. The passibility of God is challenged in works such as Thomas Weinandy's, *Does God Suffer?*[37] Weinandy argues for God's impassibility and attempts to refute arguments for a passible God.

Recent discussions in the theology of the cross have opened up the idea of "willing vulnerability" as a fruitful concept which can navigate between total vulnerability and the active suffering of God.[38] This approach also seeks to develop a Trinitarian understanding of the suffering God, linking the paradigm presented in this book with current discussions in theology. There is a spiritual posture that is required for us to "formulate discourse on God in an authentic and respectful way."[39] We must first come to God in spiritual humility and openness. This volume seeks to explore the spirituality for the theology of suffering that would make contemplation and spiritual awakening to God's presence part of the task of doing theology. Theology requires the contemplation of the God who comes near to us in our affliction. Comprehending the vulnerability of God gives us language to explore the deeper questions of a God who suffers. A mature theology of suffering will orient us to the God revealed in the Bible as one who is "compassionate and gracious, slow to anger, abounding in love and faithfulness" (Exod 34:6).

## A Spiritual Vision That Emerges from a Theological Understanding of the Complexities of Suffering in a Broken World

Part of this reorientation to a God who suffers will also include a fresh look at the biblical picture of the suffering of all creation. A theology of suffering must place human suffering within this larger context and thereby transform the typical anthropocentric discussion into a creatiocentric theology of suffering. Crucial in the development of this perspective is the biblical theme of the "groaning of creation" (see chap. 8). Taking the Pauline paradigm in Romans 8 seriously leads to a strong eschatological focus for a theology of suffering. This sets the context of the suffering of creation as a groaning that anticipates the eschatological renewal of all things in Christ. The eschatological vision of God's reign even amidst the reality of brokenness will be explored. This calls for a spirituality that lives up to the deepest questions of affliction. This exploration will also include a revisiting and expansion of prayer as *absolute, unmixed attention*,[40] a hopeful posture in the face of unmitigated suffering.

## An Understanding of the Church as the Compassionate Community of God

Any thorough theology of suffering must engage discussion on the theme of ecclesiology and the role of the church in God's own reconciling action in the world. The church as the compassionate community of God is understood both theologically and practically as a foundation for a theology of ministry rooted in the nature of God as compassionate. This means exploring the biblical theology of the church as a community of persons whose vocation is to imitate God and to "suffer with" the afflicted. Foundational to this discussion is a renewal of a theology of compassion. I will explore the biblical and theological framework for a theology of compassion that will, in turn, inform the theology of suffering proposed in this volume. *Compassion is the action of moving into the suffering of others with active help.* It is not a distant pity or community sympathy but rather a radical moving into the reality of suffering itself. This compassionate movement is most completely expressed in the incarnation and suffering death of Christ. Understanding the church as the compassionate community of God will require a Trinitarian vision of the ecclesial mandate of the church. It will also require the renewal of a core commitment of compassion as the center of the moral vision of the church in the world.

## What Is Suffering?

There are occasions when the landscapes of normal life are eclipsed in such a way as to collapse previously held orientations.[41] Suffering disrupts our lives in ways that call for a new perspective and fresh understandings. Any thoughtful articulation of God and the experience of suffering will require a refined understanding of the nature of suffering itself. What is suffering? In one sense this is a very challenging task because the reality of suffering is ineffable and mysterious. Artists and poets throughout the ages have tried to give voice to the mystery of suffering. The ancient words of Job still poignantly portray the profound questioning that goes on in the hearts and minds of the afflicted person: "Terrors overwhelm me; my dignity is driven away as by the wind, my safety vanishes like a cloud. And now my life ebbs away; days of suffering grip me. . . . I cry out to you, O God, but you do not answer" (Job 30:15, 16, 20).

Suffering mystifies, and yet we feel a deep yearning to understand how the fragments and pieces of our broken lives fit together. This need to understand or to construct meaning in the face of even the most horrible conditions of life is fundamental to the human condition. The events and experiences of our lives must be linked through language to meaning, otherwise our lives are threatened by chaos and meaninglessness. This meaning-constructing activity is ongoing as our minds and hearts constantly process the significant events of life.

The mystery of suffering, however, goes beyond simply the ineffable experiences or the relationship of language to these. There are concrete concerns that emerge in the context of suffering. Many people who suffer wonder how they might gauge the severity of their situation. There is a need to create certain measures so that we can ascertain whose suffering is more acute. We are filled with comparisons, and yet, there are no easy ways to comprehend the nature of suffering. Two things must be said about this.

### All Suffering Is Serious

The tendency to compare suffering or to try to measure it against the suffering of others is a futile effort. Each situation of suffering must take into account the gravity of the situation that is being experienced at the time. For the suffering person, the situation of suffering, however it has come about, is serious. There is nowhere that one can turn away from it, because suffering, in whatever form it is encountered, is all-consuming.

This has important implications for those who are suffering and for those who are called to the ministry of compassion. All suffering must be taken seriously. The recognition that suffering cannot be quantified is crucial to our understanding of it. Rather than trying to gauge the seriousness of our suffering, we can take it for what it is: a disruption, a calamity, a deep and troubling event. In doing this we are able to locate the reality of suffering in the course of ordinary life, and this is very important. Further, taking all occasions of suffering seriously allows us to throw off comparisons that, aside from being unhelpful, often minimize and repress the actual situation in which we are living.

### All Suffering Pushes the Boundaries of Meaning and Sense-Making in Our Lives

Suffering eclipses our perspective. When we go through hardships, trials, and the anguishing situations of life, it is difficult for us to make sense of it all. Very often the essential meanings that we have constructed for our life disintegrate in the face of a severe crisis. Therefore the boundaries of meaning and the way that we make sense of our situation are pushed to expand into new territory. At the root of sorrow, then, is the experience of dis-integration. A disintegration of life—all meanings shift away, and what was once held as a deeply felt conviction can seem to melt away. People often think they are being weak because they are overwhelmed by the anguish of their situation. They wonder if their faith is not strong enough, and they are bewildered by the lack of meaning that comes with senseless suffering.

It is important to think about the gravity specific to each situation of suffering—to discern the root causes, the hidden aspects, and the breadth of the experience of suffering itself. This calls for an exploration of the dimensions of the situation itself. Elements of pain and physical ailment accompany suffering. There are often emotional costs to a situation of suffering that must also be accounted for. The social dimensions of suffering are acute and can add significant burden to an already impossible situation. Needless to say, the spiritual questions and turmoil that often go along with the other elements of suffering mentioned create anguish and uncertainty that is difficult to bear.

While suffering itself remains something of a mystery, we can learn to speak meaningfully about God and suffering only when we have more carefully discerned the contours of suffering. Theological reflection on the theme of suffering requires a careful examination of the reality of suffering itself. In theological works there are many notions of what suffering might be, and often there is a lack of clarity about the nature or definition of suffering. It is clear that treatises on the theme of suffering are not all using the same definitions or orientation to the concept of suffering itself. A thoughtful theological book on the experience of suffering must tease out all of the meanings and implications of what suffering is. Although the term "radical" has come to mean something negative and almost obscene, the original idea of radical means "from the root."[42] To be radical is actually to "go to the root of things." This chapter is an attempt to bring clarity to the reality of suffering itself in all of its dimensions.

How then are we to understand the nature of suffering itself? Suffering can be seen as a multidimensional disrupting experience of life. Dorothee Soelle argues for three key dimensions of suffering: physical pain, psychological anguish, and social degradation.[43] Simone Weil is attributed with the insight that where all three of these dimensions are present, the experience may be described as "affliction."[44] This is a very helpful interpretation of what suffering is, as it breaks the idea down into different dimensions. I will explore these various dimensions of suffering more closely along with the composite idea of "affliction." Before I turn to the description of each of these dimensions, I want to expand on this conceptualization of suffering by adding a fourth key dimension of suffering: spiritual despondency.

There are a number of implications here, but for brevity I will name only three key elements of this approach to suffering. First, this approach clearly grounds the conception of suffering in the concrete realities (events, circumstances, situations) of life in a broken world. I have intentionally not tied the approach to suffering in this volume with the broader philosophical questions of evil. This pairing of suffering and evil is often made in theological works on suffering without distinctions in the conceptions themselves.[45] The present volume, as a pastoral theological interpretation of the experiences of suffering, is focused particularly on the concrete realities of suffering in its multivalent detail. This view of suffering grounds our discussion in the soil of life itself. Without this perspective, talk about suffering may lapse into mere conceptualization without a grounded view of the situation or experience of suffering itself.[46] This is not to diminish the importance of the philosophical discussions of evil but to separate these from the more specific and concrete experiences of suffering in life.

Secondly, the proposed interpretation of suffering in its multiple dimensions has a richness and depth to it. This augments and deepens any one-dimensional understanding of suffering. There is sometimes a tendency to oversimplify the situation of those who are suffering by focusing on a single dimension: physical pain, psychological anguish, social degradation, or spiritual despondency. This often leads to a misinterpretation of the complexity of the situation of suffering itself that has embedded social, spiritual, intrapersonal, and physiological dimensions. The experiences of suffering are multivalent, and therefore a multidimensional interpretation of these experiences is required. In much literature on the topic of suffering it is generally assumed that everyone is relating to the same reality, when in fact suffering is not one single type of situation. This leads to many conflicting arguments about martyrdom, innocent suffering, meaningless suffering, persecution, and so on, without any orienting definition of what suffering or Christian suffering is.

Third, the confluence of several elements into one new category, "affliction," assists with the pastoral implications of the mystery of suffering in the lives of people. It is a contention of this volume that the deeper reality of suffering is multivalent and may be better described by the unifying concept of "affliction." This contributes to a "thicker" description of suffering that allows for the hidden dimensions to be brought into full view. For example, someone may be experiencing extreme physical pain as a result of an accident at work. However, the despair, internal doubting, spiritual questioning, and social import of this situation may not be as self-evident. These deeper aspects of suffering are often hidden. This may account for the preference of treating the obvious problem (attending to the physical alleviation of pain) while the concealed elements of affliction go undetected and unattended. In this sense every pastoral encounter with situations of suffering must take seriously the multifaceted dimensions of suffering in all of its complexity. This will challenge the assumptions we make about what is going on in suffering and also change the way in which we address the core question of this book, "Where is God in our experiences of suffering?"

To understand suffering in this multivalent way in no sense implies that the complex elements of suffering itself can be dissected and assessed independent of the other dimensions that are present in the reality of suffering itself. If anything, the approach taken here will seek to "complexify" and hold in tension the various competing elements that are sometimes present in suffering; the alleviation of individual pain may only make room for the deeper perplexities of social degradation or spiritual despondency. Therefore, while an attempt is made in the remaining portion of this chapter to focus on the various dimensions of suffering as a reality, our ultimate horizon will be to explore the matrix of the multidimensional experiences of suffering.

In order to ground the complexity of suffering as a multidimensional reality, I have elected to focus in this section on a key biblical text, Lamentations 3. Most scholars regard this text as the core or pivotal center of the book of Lamentations.[47] It is beyond the scope of this book to offer a full commentary even on this dynamic passage. In order to outline the four dimensions of suffering identified, I have elected to focus on the first twenty-nine verses of this pericope of affliction.

> I am the man[48] who has seen affliction by
>     the rod of his wrath.
> He has driven me away and made me walk
>     in darkness rather than light;
> indeed, he has turned his hand against me
>     again and again, all day long.

He has made my skin and my flesh grow old
    and has broken my bones.
He has besieged me and surrounded me
    with bitterness and hardship.
He has made me dwell in darkness
    like those long dead.

He has walled me in so I cannot escape;
    he has weighed me down with chains.
Even when I call out or cry for help,
    he shuts out my prayer.
He has barred my way with blocks of stone;
    he has made my paths crooked.

Like a bear lying in wait,
    like a lion in hiding,
he dragged me from the path and mangled me
    and left me without help.
He drew his bow
    and made me the target for his arrows.

He pierced my heart
    with arrows from his quiver.
I become the laughingstock of all my people;
    they mock me in song all day long.
He has filled me with bitter herbs
    and sated me with gall.

He has broken my teeth with gravel;
    he has trampled me in the dust.
I have been deprived of peace;
    I have forgotten what prosperity is.
So I say, "My splendor is gone
    and all that I had hoped from the Lord."

I remember my affliction and my wandering,
    the bitterness and the gall.
I well remember them,
    and my soul is downcast within me.
Yet this I call to mind
    and therefore I have hope:

Because of the Lord's great love we are not consumed,
    for his compassions never fail.
They are new every morning;
    great is your faithfulness.
I say to myself, "The Lord is my portion;
    therefore I will wait for him."

The Lord is good to those whose hope is in him,
    to the one who seeks him;

it is good to wait quietly
    for the salvation of the Lord.
It is good for a man to bear the yoke
    while he is young.

Let him sit alone in silence,
    for the Lord has laid it on him.
Let him bury his face in the dust—
    there may yet be hope. (Lam 3:1-29)

## Physical Pain

Emily Dickinson offers, "Pain has an element of blank; / It cannot recollect / When it began, or if there were / A day when it was not. / It has no future but itself, / Its infinite realms contain / Its past, enlightened to perceive / New periods of pain."[49] The description of misery described in Lamentations 3 includes notes of the pain of physical suffering. As the litany of painful experiences unfolds in the text of the Lamentations poem, we become deeply aware of the frailty of the human body to undergo such corporeal suffering. Notice the key phrases used to describe these in the text:

"My skin and flesh grow old" (Lam 3:4)
"He has broken my bones" (3:4)
"He . . . mangled me" (3:11)
"He pierced my heart with arrows from his quiver" (3:13)
"He has filled me with bitter herbs and sated me with gall" (3:15)
"He has broken my teeth with gravel." (3:16)

Penny and Tim Giesbrecht were persons of faith and were deeply convinced that bad things would not happen to good persons. They tell their story of their son's unspeakable pain in the book *Where Is God When a Child Suffers?*[50] Their little boy Jeremy stopped saying new words at two years of age. They thought it was a stage. As time progressed, the reality settled in. They discovered that their son was autistic, and further investigation showed that he was unresponsive to treatments. His incapacity to communicate or to share information made it very difficult for them to protect him at all times. At five years of age, Jeremy climbed up on the stove and his pants caught on fire.[51] In minutes he was engulfed in flames—burning his legs and 20 percent of his little body. The risk of kidney or respiratory failure in the first forty-eight hours of such a burn are extremely high as the body tries to cope with the strain of being pushed to its extremities.

The first dimension of suffering is physical pain. This pain is at times unbearable. The physical pain of suffering can be enormous. Pain is a very complex topic in and of itself. While we are narrowing this to one dimension of suffering, this is in no way to reflect the supposition that physical pain does not have its own cultural and physiological complexities.[52] While Philip Yancey points out the benefits of sensory pain as a gift from God,[53] it can also be a tremendous source of anguish as persons struggle through the physical trauma of injury, illness, sickness, and pain. Penny Giesbrecht details the horrendous story of her son Jeremy's burns:

> I looked down at my little son, his eyes reeling with fear. His cries were almost rhythmic as he panted for breath in between his screams. "EEEH! EEEH! EEEH!" I realized he had no idea what was happening to him.
>
> I could not be comforted. *We're good parents, God! Things like this don't happen to parents who watch their children! We prayed even today you'd protect Jeremy! Jeremy can't talk! Isn't that enough, God? . . .*
>
> We walked down a long hall. One side had doors opening into what looked like small examining rooms. The other was covered with huge blown-up pictures. Red angry skin covered by clear face masks stared at me. Bloody, open flesh gaped around a skinny child's legs. Long metal pins held a young woman's shaven head immobile in a frame.
>
> The strong smell of the Burn Center filled my nostrils. I felt as if I was going to be sick. Is this what our son's legs would look like? How could it be that only two hours ago we were in worship? *Dear God! It's Sunday afternoon. What are we doing in a place like this?*

Pain is not to be taken lightly. In this situation the painful burns brought the young Jeremy into critical intensive care. The anguish of seeing his seared, little body torments his mother as she watches helplessly in the halls of the hospital. There is no way to make the pain something other than what it is in this moment: suffering pure and simple.

Physical pain is a dimension of suffering that must be taken seriously. It has its own night—the darkness of ache, the hurt of physical torment, and the throbbing physiological distress of injury and illness in the body. These physical sufferings are difficult and agonizing in their own right.

## Psychological Anguish

Our Lamentations 3 text moves into another dimension of suffering, that of psychological anguish. Suffering cuts us off from emotional freedom. It drives us to despair, disconsolation, and takes away our peace.

Listen to the language of personal anguish that is described by the poet in this text:

"He made me walk in darkness" (Lam 3:2)
"He has walled me in" (3:7)
"I have been deprived of peace" (3:17)
"I remember the bitterness." (3:19)

The anguish of psychological suffering is a severe experience of trauma to the human heart. The human capacity to hope is suffocated by the traumatic and blinding realities of psychological torment. Anxiety, fear, grief, and psychic numbness all take their toll on the capacity for a human being to bear under suffering.

Susan[54] was a bright and talented young preschool teacher. She was cheerful, optimistic, and loved God deeply. Her recent engagement brought her much joy and delight. She was planning the wedding and was carefree. On a whim the young couple decided to take a ride in an ultralight plane. The young woman changed her mind at the last minute and decided not to go up on the flight. All of us who were close to her were horrified at the news when we heard that the plane crashed as it was landing, and the young man, together with the pilot, was instantly killed. The trauma, inconsolable grief, and anguish of this young woman were among the most severe I have ever witnessed in my twenty years of pastoral ministry. Every capacity to hope was threatened, and the extreme emotional anguish was unbearable to watch, much less for her to endure.

At the root of sorrow is the human experience of finitude. We all know that we are frail, weak, vulnerable, and anxious, but there, at the root of sorrow, is a dreadful realization of deep losses—losses too deep for words—or as the writer of Lamentations puts it, "A wound that is as deep as the sea" (Lam 2:13). Loss of control, loss of a preferred future, loss of "normal" expectations, and, at the deepest root, the loss of hope itself—these losses accumulate and pile up. After a short while these losses become unbearable, and the suffering person thinks that they will break apart.

Fear is a hidden element at the root of suffering. The fear of the unknown, the fear of pain, the fear of death, and the fear of a difficult future are all critical elements. When persons and communities experience suffering, a large part of that experience is the emotional element of fear—the fear of what will happen or the fear of what is already taking

place. This is so because we often fail to acknowledge the dreadful elements of suffering itself. Suffering is not only the experience of pain,
but it includes and is intensified by the emotional element of anticipated
anguish—fear is the dominant emotional response in suffering.

Life itself is intimidating; fear is the response to the unknown future
and the creeping suspicion of further pain. The fragile balance that we
achieve in our lives can swiftly be disrupted with a serious accident,
a bad diagnosis, or a broken relationship. It does not take much to go
wrong before things seem to be falling apart or unraveling, and this can
bring great distress.

Psychological anguish describes well the emotional dimension of
suffering. The painful emotional elements of suffering are difficult to
describe. Many persons who are entering into an experience of suffering
can attest to the "sinking feeling" of dread.

### Fear Is the Unqualified Expectation of Continued or Sustained Suffering

The uncertainty of the future is one key dimension of fear. All suffering
leads to a sense of the "bottom being knocked out." This is intimidating
for us as we place our trust in God. When the worst comes to us despite
our faith in God, fear and dread take over.

### Fear Is the Absence of Courage and Moves Us toward Despair

Courage is one of the great virtues of the human capacity to endure.
However, it is not easy to sustain in the face of suffering. The emotional
element of fear erodes faith and moves us to the edge of reality when
despair is the ultimate enemy.

Courage is needed to live into the emotional element of suffering as
psychological anguish. This involves moving away from the present fear
to the most dreadful fear.

This is the experience of despair or what Kierkegaard calls "the
sickness unto death."[55]

While we are hoping for the best, the emotional elements of suffering and psychological anguish push us to fear the worst. It is our natural
inclination to dread, to move into the future without hope, and to expect
calamity to continue.

Nicholas Wolterstorff, in his book *Lament for a Son*, speaks about his
anguish of spirit as he came to terms with the loss of his twenty-five-
year-old son, Eric, to a mountain climbing accident.

He was cut down at the peak of vitality and promise. He had finished his research and was ready to write. We found the outline on top of his notes. Friends who had visited him a week earlier said they had never seen him so enthusiastic. He was looking forward to climbing the Matterhorn with friends late in the summer and was getting himself into condition, running and doing practice climbs.

Is the death of a child any easier when vitality has wound down? If some disease had wasted him away, sapped his energy, made him weak, would death then have seemed a proper closure? But then all the pain would have been in seeing the winding down. Is it easier when good-byes have been said? We never said good-bye to Eric . . . . The son of a friend—same age as Eric—died a few weeks before Eric. The friend's son committed suicide. The pain of his life was so intense that he took the life that gave the pain. I thought for a time that such a death must be easier to bear than the death of one with zest for life. He wanted to die. When I talked to the father, I saw that I was wrong.

Suffering intimidates life. Dread and despair overtake us in the throes of anguish. There is no easy way to face the uncertainty and agony that come with tragedy in life. Such occasions sap our capacity for courage and leave us helpless in the face of creeping desperation.[56]

## Social Degradation

The third dimension of suffering in Lamentations 3 is "social degradation."[57] Dorothee Soelle argues that many Christian interpretations of suffering include the premature acceptance of suffering at the social level.[58] This is an important critique of much Christian literature, and I would agree with this assessment. A mature theology of suffering will revive the social dimensions of suffering and bring them into full light. The social dimension can easily be hidden from view or dismissed altogether, and yet it may be among the most painful aspects of suffering. Premature acceptance of the social elements of suffering distorts the call for prophetic resistance of the structures of oppression.

Notice the poignant descriptors in the poet's expression of social suffering:

"I became the laughingstock of all my people" (Lam 3:14)
"They mock me in song all day long." (3:14)

This dimension of suffering is related to how others perceive or respond [or fail to respond] to the situation of the afflicted. They may not have all of the "facts" but they offer their perceptions and thereby heighten the sense of isolation and rejection that is embedded in the experience of suffering. Often, suffering includes this social experience of being shamed, ridiculed, accused, or attacked. This forms yet another aspect of suffering in the lives of the afflicted. Not only do the suffering experience the blight of rejection, but often there is consent to the derision of the afflicted.[59] Therefore, this dimension of suffering includes the intentional and unintentional shaming, ridicule, and rejection of those who are afflicted.

It might be helpful here to identify shades of meaning intended when we are talking about social degradation. For our purposes, I have identified three types of social suffering which I see as inter-related, deepening experiences of social degradation: abandonment, rejection, and forsakenness:

> *Abandonment*: the experience of abandonment involves the deep disappointment of the withdrawal of support of others.
>
> *Rejection*: the experience of rejection involves alienation from the community. Here the companionship of life is refused. The loneliness of abandonment deepens with the isolation of rejection.
>
> *Forsakenness*: the experience of social rejection in which the anticipation of love and acceptance is fully disappointed and, in its place, one experiences scorn or forsakenness itself.

Suffering has this profound social dimension. While many aspects of suffering cannot be entered into by others, a mature theology of suffering will embrace the social responsibility of solidarity and prophetic engagement. We must become more acutely aware of the abandonment, rejection, and forsakenness that often accompany the situation of the most afflicted. While we are not "conscious" of any deliberate rejection of those who suffer, our theological categories may not allow for the obligation of overcoming the shame and rejection that come with many situations of suffering.

## Spiritual Despondency

The resilience of the human spirit upholds us in the seasons of our lives; however, there are experiences of suffering that erode our sense of well-being. Affliction has a fourth component, namely, spiritual despondency. To suffer in this spiritual sense is to experience the eclipse of hope itself, which leads us to experience a growing distance from God.

The accepted threefold description of affliction as including physical pain, psychological anguish, and social degradation has been an important contribution in works on the theology of suffering.[60] Expansion into this fourth dimension picks up on the biblical ideas of lament and complaint to God.[61] In fact, this dimension has particular import for the relationship of the suffering person with God. Here, suffering is actually inflicted by God, and God becomes the problem. Throughout the pericope in Lamentations the complaint is made against God. The problem is not just the reality of suffering but that God has inflicted this suffering. Throughout the text this complaint is made, accusing God:

"He has turned his hand against me" (Lam 3:3)
"He has besieged me" (3:5)
"He has weighed me down" (3:6)
"He has barred my way" (3:9)
"He dragged me from the path" (3:11)
"He has trampled me in the dust." (3:16)

At the root of the spiritual experience of desolation is the feeling that God has abandoned us and that God inflicts the suffering itself. The full dimensions of suffering are complete when the language of desolation is disclosed. To explore this more carefully I want to focus on several of the phrases that emerge in the depiction of suffering in this text that specifically make known the phenomenology of desolation:

"He has made me dwell in darkness" (Lam 3:6)
"Even when I call out or cry for help, he shuts out my prayer" (3:7)
"All that I had hoped from the Lord [is gone]" (3:18)
"My soul is downcast." (3:20)

These phrases capture what may be named the "eclipse of God."[62] Beyond the physical and emotional anguish of suffering is the desperate loss of light, hope, confidence, and trust. These losses are the equivalent to despair itself, so that the lament concludes with a statement of forsakenness, "My soul is downcast" (Lam 3:20). The social rejection of suffering is difficult to bear, but now, with the eclipse of God, the suffering person experiences the abandonment of God and declares, "All that I had hoped from the Lord is gone" (Lam 3:18). This is the ultimate low point in the affliction.[63]

Many who suffer in extremis experience this profound desolation of spirit. They hold up as best they can under the pressures of affliction, but the sense of God's withdrawal makes the situation unbearable. Their lasting hope in Yahweh has perished. They find themselves depleted beyond even the capacity to hope.

James Loney offers a poignant account of spiritual desolation from his experience of being held hostage in Iraq.[64] On March 1, 2006, day ninety-six of his captivity, he writes nine words in the notebook his captors had given to him: "no report due to illness—a day from hell." He describes his ordeal and its consequent eclipse of God in his life:

> All the sweat-soaked night before, lying on a mat handcuffed to Norman Kember and Harmeet Singh Sooden, I floundered helplessly in fevered waves of anguish. Held in the grip of a relentless nightmare, I felt my body being carved over and over into chunks, with each discrete piece of flesh and bone lined up in perfect anatomical sequence and tortured by a man holding electrodes in rubber-glove hands.
>
> I asked my captors for aspirin and anti-biotics but there was nothing they could do. Everyone was under curfew, they said. I wandered in a twilight world careening between despair and rage. God did not exist. God had died. There was no possibility of meaning or consolation. The only reality was suffering. At first I cursed the miserable circumstances of captivity. Then I imagined myself sliding into an abyss. I began to crave oblivion like a warm drug. If I wanted, if I let myself, I could just float away. . . .
>
> When after three days the curfew lifted, some Paracetamol was brought and my fever abated, God came back. In the days that followed, I began to reflect upon that period of absolute desolation. I was astonished, for always I had felt, even as a very young child, some sense of God's presence in my life. In my breath, my heartbeat, the light and breeze around me, even if only in a vestige of a whisper of a trace, always, always I felt, I knew God was there. But not during those three days. Not when I needed God most.
>
> I was confused. I used to think adherence to a spiritual practice—daily prayer, mindful living, loving service of others, facing myself honestly— would help alleviate my suffering when it came time for the *magnum curriculum* (great test). But none of that made any difference. It struck me that even Jesus, who of anyone did his spiritual homework, felt utterly forsaken by God in his last excruciating hours on the cross. Perhaps the dark night of abandonment is simply an inevitable season of the soul, something everybody has to go through at one time or another.
>
> With my life stolen from me, I saw clearly that as a free man I had lived as a wastrel, squandering freedom with the blind habit of taking it for granted. I began to think the real purpose of spiritual discipline was to help us live ordinary time well, not extraordinary time; to crack us open to the miraculous wonders of washing dishes, making a cup of tea, opening the curtains when you get up in the morning. But then Norm objected. That's fine if your ordinary time is reasonably comfortable, he said, but for lots of people ordinary time is extraordinary hardship. So much for theories.
>
> Finding meaning in suffering is perhaps the most difficult of all human tasks. How do you make sense of being locked up in a never-ending day (or week, or year) of hell, and the painkillers run out and God has died right when you need help the most? I don't know. I don't think I can make sense of it. The only thing I can say, beyond "no report," is that a window opened in me during those three days that God died: a window through which to see how much I need and love God, and how ineffably painful it is to be without him.[65]

Loney's story is difficult for us to pay attention to. The eclipse of God's presence for those three days was a frightening and unexpected experience. All his life he had depended on some sense of God's presence, and here, when he "needed God most," was the "dark night of abandonment." Loney describes this as a "period of absolute desolation." While it brought greater awareness of the sacredness of ordinary time and a heightened understanding of Jesus' own experience of godforsakenness, it was still an "astonishing" spiritual moment of the eclipse of God in his life. Persons who are experiencing affliction may not know how to put into words the similar moments of spiritual despondency in their lives. What Loney experienced and what is common to the root of suffering is the unexpected and turbulent dark night of the soul. The stabbing impact of the absence of God in the situation of the afflicted obscures any light and we are left in utter darkness. The comfort of God's nearness flies away and we are left with silent darkness.

At the root of affliction is the spiritual sense of being abandoned by God. This was at the core of Christ's cry on the cross, "My God, my God, why have you forsaken me?" (Matt 27:46). Spiritual despondency is related to the loss of hope that comes from experiencing God as absent or silent in our situation. We all have hopes that God will come as a rescuer to intervene in calamity. When he does not, when the worst happens, and when our sincere prayers are met with indifference, the experience of losing faith and spiritual despondency sets in.

One experiences the root of sorrow as the absence of comfort, the absence of courage, and, ultimately, the absence of God himself. At the root of suffering is a severe loneliness—the suffering in suffering. Anyone who has endured a terrible affliction will recognize the intense isolation and spiritual disconsolation that comes with suffering. There are aspects of the experience of suffering that simply cannot be shared. They must be endured in the place of absolute isolation.[66] At the root of suffering is the experience of compounded sorrows, unnamed losses, and many griefs. This in itself might be bearable, but the experience of God's indifference injects a painful loneliness that can only be described as the experience of godforsakeness.[67] Godforsakenness is the experience of having one's soul crushed by the weight of grief and the abandonment of God. Like Jesus in the anguish of Gethsemane, the brokenhearted have their souls "overwhelmed to the point of death."

God is not easily accessed in suffering, and the absence of God is the hardest thing to bear in the throes of affliction. In Lamentations 3 it is God who inflicts the suffering. In the experience of spiritual desolation,

God himself is the difficulty. God's goodness is questioned in the bleak night of despondency. In distress the human spirit languishes at the idea of being left alone by God, inflicted by God, and forsaken by God.[68]

## Conclusion

Conclusions are meant to close off the discussion.[69] Thinking through the components of a mature theology of suffering will require ongoing dialogue. The intent of this volume is not to close off the discussion but to open up a more thoughtful approach to the reality of suffering as it is experienced by the most afflicted. It is intended to serve as a resource to those whose ministry leads them into the abyss of suffering with the most afflicted.

Rather than offering premature or incomplete conclusions, this volume seeks to weigh carefully the reality of suffering itself. This leaves us simply with dared suspicions and hopes. Suspicions that God has purposed good for all persons despite the terrible reality of anguishing circumstances. Hopes that our own brokenness and inner anguish will be ultimately redeemed. Suspicions that God will be near to the brokenhearted even in the most horrible circumstances of life. Hopes that our sight will catch up with our faith. Furthermore, in the midst of our suspicions and hopes, we find ourselves being addressed—and even called—by God.

To believe the biblical promises of hope requires courage to face up to the mystery of suffering itself. It requires a confident assurance that the God who created this world is also the God who also suffers with us in the turmoil and uncertainty of the dark hours of life. The divine call is to share the journey of solidarity with the brokenhearted. As those who carry the name of the biblical God, we are called to walk by faith in the darkest corners of the earth. And we are called to wait for the consummation of creation in the completion of the divine promises. En route to that day, we travel as pilgrims, and as a pilgrim people we engage in the vocation of walking as faithful disciples in a broken world.

While these components offer a framework for development of this important theological theme, our "conclusion" leaves us in the realm of mystery. Ultimately, our goal cannot be to explain suffering away or to provide a definitive answer to the "why" of suffering. Instead, we are brought face to face with the mystery of the eternal God who suffers with us and who promises to bring creation to completion in the eschatological fullness of community.

Describing suffering is like describing the fractured light of a rainbow. There are too many colors that merge into one another to make clear distinctions. However, our theological vision is matured when we tease out the various dimensions of suffering in order to understand the full impact of affliction. Persons who suffer cannot easily name the nuances of their experiences of physical pain, psychological anguish, social degradation, or spiritual desolation. However, these dimensions are present in suffering, and they must be recognized in all of their terror and intensity. The biblical understanding of suffering does not hide these dimensions, but rather they are brought into full view. The biblical view of suffering, even as we have seen in the poem of Lamentations 3, is multivalent and complex. By recognizing the structure of suffering itself and naming its variations in our life, we have already taken an important step to understanding it better.

—  —  —

We turn now to the latter part of this volume, where I develop three constructive movements for a pastoral theology of suffering: the movement from silence to lament, the movement from indifference to compassion, and the movement from loneliness to community. The next three chapters move to a conceptualization of suffering in the form of a paradigm with three key movements. Each of the movements begins by the entering into the perspective of persons who are suffering. The starting point of a mature theology of suffering is to engage with those who are deeply embedded in the throes of an anguishing life situation. Rather than trying to "explain" their suffering, this paradigmatic approach situates the condition of suffering in the ambiguous tension that allows for multivalent experiences. The many and complex variations of the experiences of suffering cannot be fully explored, and, as has already been mentioned, patterns of suffering are erratic and unpredictable. The purpose of the paradigm, therefore, is to open up the experience of suffering in all of its dimensions. Ministry to and with the suffering person or community requires sensitivity to the various degrees of anguish experienced by suffering persons, and the paradigm serves to open this perspective up.

In the first movement I address the multifarious dimensions of suffering. Suffering makes us wordless. Mute suffering is the experience of the person whose suffering is so great that they cannot speak about it meaningfully. I explore in chapter 3 the progression of the movement *from silence to lament*. The movement shifts from inarticulate groaning to the expression of suffering as something to be bemoaned and even protested. The lament is the form in which this resistance is best expressed. The movement from mutism to lament is rooted in *the God who hears us*.

In the second movement another tension in suffering is explored. Suffering not only makes us mute and isolates us from the community, it also has the capacity to weaken our capacity to resist, resulting in acquiescence and apathy. Chapter 4 explores this second movement, the movement *from indifference to compassion*. Indifference can settle in without being recognized. This chapter is an attempt to explore the roots of indifference and apathy in the context of affliction thus making way for the dynamic process of compassion. A mature theology of suffering will be rooted in a biblical and theological orientation to the practice of authentic compassion. The movement from indifference to compassion is based on *the God who comforts us*.

The third movement indicates a shift in social posture in suffering. This is the movement *from loneliness to community*. Suffering not only makes us mute, but it isolates us and cuts us off from the vital, social relationships that would sustain and support us in the very experiences of suffering. I explore in chapter 5 how the suffering person can find, even in the depths of an anguishing situation, a shift in posture toward openness to God and others. There is a complex set of issues that foster isolation in suffering that need to be understood and overcome. A theology of community and the experience of spiritual communion will be explored in response to this profound sense of loss of social belonging that comes with suffering. The movement from loneliness to community is embedded in *the God who comes to us*.

## CHAPTER THREE

# From Silence to Lament

We begin with the word-slain existence of the most afflicted. This silence is rooted in the terrible loneliness of spirit born from the loss of meaning structures and theological answers that previously held great significance and nurtured the foundations of spiritual life. At its most severe the "whiteout" of affliction's unfathomable core cuts off the suffering person from the sustaining hope that abides in the words of meaning and life that had previously brought comfort and consolation. This brief depiction of mutism is consonant with the biblical tradition of faith-in-spite-of suffering's tormenting presence. Such a situation captures the essential losses of the soul: meaninglessness, helplessness, and the bleak sense of being cut off from the sustaining community of faith.

Suffering makes us mute. The harsh reality of affliction eclipses our perspective and disintegrates the meanings that once served to hold us together. This experience of deep silence in the situation of suffering is common because often the reality of suffering is so great that one cannot find words to express the pain, the anguish, and the hidden dimensions that abide there. Suffering is often so "great that it renders people helpless and speechless. One of the cruelties of suffering is that it is often 'language shattering.'"[1]

In this chapter we explore the articulation of affliction in its many forms. Part of this is an exploration of the role of language in the theology of suffering. However, the issues of this chapter go much deeper. The manifold experiences of suffering press up against our ability to disclose the meaning of what is going on. In this way the sufferer feels cut off from others, which leads to "the suffering in suffering"—loneliness. Mutism is a state of inexpressibility. This leads to the sense of being cut off from community. All suffering is difficult to bear; suffering that is borne alone is excruciating and nearly impossible to express.

## Exploring the Silence in Suffering

The ability to express the deepest experiences of the inner person are at the root of biblical faith. Consider the cry of Jesus on the cross, "My God, my God, why have you forsaken me?" (Matt. 27:46). This expressive lamentation allows the Son of God to utter his interior anguish in such a way as to bear his soul to the Father. The tradition of lamentation is rooted in the biblical witness. Lament is the expression of complaint to God that gives voice to the sense of abandonment by God in the experience of suffering. In the Bible the complaint in the context of extreme suffering is not masked but rather reflects a deeply held conviction that God must hear the anguished cry of his people. In most cases of lament in the Bible, the one who complains feels that the situation that has caused the suffering could have been avoided if God had been fulfilling his responsibility of meeting the covenant love (Heb. *hesed*). The suffering person cries out to God and expresses the volatile emotions common to the afflicted. However, before such lamentation is possible, there is a vast chasm of the inexpressible that must be crossed.

### Elements of Mutism

Mutism is the first response to serious suffering. Suffering is word-crushing, and the one who is suffering feels deeply that there is almost nothing that can be said. Afflicted persons feel a complex sense of personal abandonment and communal alienation that results in a particular kind of loneliness associated with voiceless anguish.

While it is impossible to pin down all of the elements of mutism in language-shattering suffering, perhaps an exploration of some of the common elements will assist to give explanation to this important dimension of our searching.

### The Paralyzing Effects of Affliction

Affliction cuts at the core of the human capacity to endure life. Keeping in mind affliction includes all of the dimensions of suffering: physical pain, psychological anguish, social degradation, and spiritual desolation,[2] the paralysis that comes with such life threatening experiences is complete and total, resulting in a psychic numbness that minimizes common capacity for articulation, speech, and self-expression. The paralysis of mind, heart, and soul deeply affect the ability to say exactly "what the situation is."[3] Somehow this incapacity to say what is happening is in itself deeply troubling and disconcerting. Not only has tragedy entered into the experience but new forms of isolation emerge that were not expected, keeping the suffering person locked in the world of their own anguish without remedy.

A Sense of Being Cut Off from the Normal Experiences
of the Community

Our socialization into roles in community normalizes around language. That is, our regularized participation in community depends on our capacity to communicate, to share feelings/thoughts/ideas, and to take part in the wider context of community life. Suffering cuts deeply into these associations and hinders the sense of belonging, identity, and meaning structures that come with such connections to the community. Suffering persons experience themselves as cut off from their identifying community, and this alienating moment results in a new hindrance—the hindrance to being able to relate to the normalized expectations of life in the community. Even small social graces seem to be difficult for the sufferer as they come to terms with earth-shattering losses deep at soul.

Feelings of Embarrassment, Shame, and Regret

Among the contributing factors to the mutism of the sufferer are the awkward self-recriminations that are often accompanied by feelings of embarrassment, shame, and regret. Acute suffering breaks down the inner confidence that we may have in life, leaving us feeling vulnerable.[4] These feelings may be unwarranted and unnecessary, but they are nevertheless very common to situations of deep suffering. There is a feeling closely associated with failure that accompanies even the most innocent suffering. The person may blame themselves for an aspect of the condition of suffering even if such culpability cannot be identified to be the source of the suffering. These prevailing and community-alienating feelings can thwart constructive self-reflection and further embolden the stranglehold of inarticulacy.

### Dissatisfaction with Words That Had, up to This Time, Sufficiently Explained the Presence of Generalized Suffering

While our theological explanations for suffering are incomplete and often loosely articulated,[5] they do represent our "embedded"[6] understandings of God in the circumstances of life. These fairly stable theological understandings are often assaulted at the root in the experience of extreme suffering and require profound reconsideration and often major reformulation. Deeply held theological convictions are not easily given up, and the resulting religious confusion may hamper one's sense of spiritual confidence and religious vitality. Persons who suffer in extremis often find that the explanations that have held them up in other situations prove to be helpless in the face of debilitating circumstances brought on by their plight.

### Profound Meaning Shifts That Occur in the Inner Being

Closely associated with the previous point is the collapse of meaning structures that often correspond with the experience of acute suffering. While some of these are theologically grounded, the meaning structures of our life are a complex aggregate of many processes that accumulated to define our understanding of the world (worldview). Our very relatedness to the world in which we live is predicated on meaning structures that allow us to "make sense" of the world. The experience of suffering can dislodge these core structures and may result in a vague sense of being "at sea." Our core meaning structures can be critically threatened in the world-crushing throes of affliction's grip, resulting in a crisis of the inner being. Our place in the world shrinks, our tidy explanation of the way things are gives way, and our capacity to endure the disintegration of our worldview requires a renewal of hope at the very nucleus of our inner being.

### Feebleness of Known Words to Communicate the Depths of Despair

Our life situations shape the words that we use to express reality.[7] This helps us to grapple with the situation of the most afflicted who discover that in the morass of their deepest agonies the "known words," words that they had come to depend on, fail to communicate the anguish of soul and the crisis at the foundation of their life. This begins the process of finding a new language or the "language of pain."[8] The discovery of the feebleness of words is a frightening one for the sufferer, as a previous capacity to say what is going on is given up in the seriousness of the life situation.

The winter storm whiteout is an example from nature of the seriousness of this situation. In whiteout conditions diffuse lighting from overcast clouds may cause all surface definition to disappear. It becomes impossible to gauge where the surface is. In polar regions the sea of white creates the illusion of a single white space, and the horizon cannot be judged in the context of unending white landscape. This situation modifies all capacity to perceive what the real situation is. To follow this metaphor through, the language of ordinary human experience blurs with the language of pain. It becomes impossible to have one's normal bearings. The entire meaning structure of one's life is invisible against the background of the situation of suffering, and the horizon of one's existence cannot be identified. The bearings for one's existence cease to have clarity and require the same radical self-protective instincts as one would exhibit in a winter storm. The loss of words is a like whiteout of soul in the context of the situation of the most extreme winter condition of the inner spirit.

"Groans Too Deep for Words"

The loss of language that meaningfully expresses the depth of forsakenness, anguish, and inner turmoil of spirit is further understood from the biblical metaphor of groaning. Research on pain has demonstrated the language-destroying power of physical suffering. Pain diminishes the capacity to attend, to breathe properly, and has a negative effect on the voice organs.[9] The suffering person may revert to a prelanguage state of groaning and sighs. To revert to the prior language of groaning and sighing, poets and artists have long understood the inexpressible anguish of soul that draws out from them expressive elements that have barely any structure. These seed elements are at the core of a theology of suffering. It is there, in the hidden dimension, at the root of suffering, that the groan idiom begins to draw out the darkness of suffering into the light of understanding.

> perhaps this wind
> is too severe?
> will God find me here
> hidden beneath
> the bleak whiteout
> in anguish—
> needful,

desiring life;
afraid to hope?
when will this agony
subside?
this sinking
that
slays my
words;
and crushes
my life. (PCZ)

We turn now to examine the shift from silence to *lament*. The biblical tradition of lamentation offers the recovery of meaning, the reestablishment of hope, and a revisioned faith-life for those who have encountered the cruel, language-shattering pangs of suffering. Suffering in silence calls up groans and sighs that, in time, lead to lament. Lament instills a hopeful reorientation to life with God in-spite-of suffering.

## Lament as the Renewal of Faith

### *The Goal of Lament Is Getting God's Attention or Getting God to "Hear" the Plea*

The fundamental aim of the lament is to seek help from God and to seek God's intervention in the situation of suffering.[10] Therefore some Old Testament scholars assert that the lament or complaint psalms should be classified more broadly under the category of "petition" or "plea for help."[11]

Our starting point, then, in analyzing the psalms of lament is to inquire about the help from the Lord that was sought by the sufferers. The nature of the petitions to God in suffering is of importance to our understanding of the lament literature in the Bible. Here we see the motivation, the intention, and the deepest desire for alleviation from suffering and for divine intervention in the causes of suffering.

Foremost among these petitions was the general petition for God to hear or heed the prayer. Getting God's attention was at the core of the petitions of lament in the Old Testament. The petitions of lament were aimed at getting God's ear. When troubles mount and the situation becomes desperate, the biblical injunction is primarily to get God's attention. Rather than assuming God is hidden and distant from their plight, the faithful of the Old Testament would cry out to God in their anguish with the hope of gaining the attention of God.[12]

### Lament Is Grounded in the Situation of Suffering

Lament is the expression of the depths of suffering. This expression of suffering allows the suffering persons to move beyond affliction's grip by at least saying what is happening in their situation.[13] This ability to say what is happening is a breakthrough for those caught in the throes of affliction as they move past the phase of inarticulate groaning. This points to an important theological clue about the nature of lament as reality-speech. Lamentation is a language that is grounded in a real situation. It is not the dry, abstract, removed language of esoteric reflection but is rather the raw, expressive, life-rooted language of the afflicted. Giving voice to suffering and saying *at least what the situation is* is crucial. The harsh reality of suffering must not be spiritualized, explained away, or softened in order to make it more palatable. In fact, the biblical tradition of lament is a concrete expression of the experience of suffering in all of its unrefined messiness.

In this way, the lament word-form gives us a way into the most anguished situations of those who suffer. The insistence on the concreteness of life experience is an important corrective to the tendencies we looked at in chapter 1 to explain suffering away in a category, to defend God, or to minimize the complexities of the suffering situation. In fact, the opposite is true in lament. The distress of life represents the core awakening of the anguished soul to the need for God in any given situation.[14] The lament, as we will see, exposes all of the concrete and ugly aspects of the suffering and touches on the four dimensions of suffering (see chap. 2).

### Lament Is Linked to Faith in God

The lamentation has an implicit faith dimension. The very stating of one's situation is a desperate cry to be heard by God. The suffering person moves from involuntary silence to lament in an effort to externalize the experience of suffering in such a way as to draw out the compassionate response of God. The hidden dimension of lament is faith. Articulating the anguish of our suffering is very difficult. At the root of life's darkest hour we must believe that God will hear our prayer and redeem our situation. The blind faith of lamentation is more than cathartic expression of pain; it captures the longing for a saving act of God in the distresses of life. It is, at the root, a prayer-form linking us with the only help that we can hope for in the despair of anguishing situations.[15]

This bruised faith of lamentation is poetically captured by Nicholas Wolterstorff's personal appropriation of Psalm 42 at the tragic death of his twenty-five-year-old son Eric:

> Faith endures; but my address to God is uncomfortably, perplexingly, altered. It's off-target, qualified. I want to ask for Eric back. But I can't. So I aim around the bull's-eye. I want to ask that God protect the members of my family. But I asked that for Eric.
>
> I must explore The Lament as a mode for my address to God. Psalm 42 is a lament in the context of faith that endures. Lament and trust are in tension, like the wood and string in bow. My tears have been my food day and night, says the songwriter. I remember, he says, how it was when joy was still my lot, how I used to go with the multitude, leading the procession to the house of God, with shouts of joy and thanksgiving among the festive throng.
>
> Now it's different. I am downcast, disturbed. Yet I find that faith is not dead. So I say to myself, Put your hope in God, for I will yet praise him, My Savior and my God. But then my grief returns and again I lament, to God my Rock; Why have you forgotten me? Why must I go about mourning, oppressed by the enemy? Again faith replies: Put your hope in God, for I will yet praise him, my Savior and my God. Back and forth, lament and faith, faith and lament, each fastened to the other. A bruised faith, a longing faith, a faith emptied of nearness: As the deer pants for streams of water, so my soul pants for you, O God. My soul thirsts for God, for the living God. When can I go and meet with God? Yet in the distance of endurance I join the song: by day the Lord directs his love, At night his song is with me—a prayer to the God of my life.[16]

The lament form still enables those who are struggling with the deepest pains of life.[17] Writing to articulate the depths of personal anguish at the loss of her twenty-one-year-old son, Ann Weems demonstrates the complex embedding of faith in lamentation in her "Lament Psalm Twenty-two":

> I don't know where to look for you, O God!
> I've called and I've called.
> I've looked and I've looked.
> I go back to my room
> And sit in the dark
> Waiting for you.
> Could you give me a sign
> That you've heard?
> Could you numb my emotions
> So I wouldn't hurt so much?
>
> I walk in circles.
> I rock in my chair.
> I pour a glass of water.

I look out the window.
I walk to the kitchen.
I open the refrigerator;
There's nothing I want.
I close it again.
I turn on the TV.
The voices are too loud,
I mute the voices;
I turn off the faces.
The silence is my friend;
The silence is my enemy.
I go upstairs.
I lie on the bed.
I get up again.
I walk to the window.
No sign of you!
I'm dying, O God, without you.

O God of wonder,
You can change it all.
You can distract me
From thoughts of death.
You can fill my days with purpose.
You can make the nights shorter.
You can let me find you.
Don't hide from me any longer, O God.

O God,
you reveal yourself to those
who call upon your name.
Blessed be my God
who does not fail me![18]

In both of these wounded parents there is an expression of trust in a God who hears the complaint without an explaining away of the root cause of suffering or its disorienting effects. There are certain anguished experiences in life, such as the loss of a child, that cut through one's very sense of being. The search for meaning in the midst of indescribable agony of spirit is *both a reaching out to God* and *a questioning of God's ways in our life*. Lament is linked to faith in God but fastened to the reality of suffering at the same time. Hence the faith dimension that is expressed in the lamentation is "a bruised faith, a longing faith, a faith emptied of nearness" where there is no sign of God's presence even if it is eagerly sought.[19] This faith endures in the context of unfulfilled promises with the hidden expectation that somehow God will show up. Lament occurs in the context of the gap between the hope for God's intervention and the distress of being left by God alone in one's suffering. Lament expresses the dissonance of lived reality with the promises of a God of love.[20]

The lament is the most life-giving and meaning-restoring word-form of the Bible. In the lamentations of the Bible, we discover a language that moves from the depths of forsakenness to the renewed spiritual center of trust even in the most serious situations of life. Lamentation and the renewal of faith are intimately linked.[21]

Lament Reforms Our Relationship with God

The movement from silence to lament parallels other recent efforts in Christian theology to recover the permission to express pain, misery, anger, rage, and inconsolable grief that is resident in the Bible in the form of lament prayers. Our practice of prayer in the church has often neglected the harsh realities of affliction and rendered the suffering person voiceless. It is important to recognize that this shift requires not only a recovery of the tradition of lament but a reformulation of our theology—our understanding of God. At the heart of the lament word-form is the *desperate expectation* of God's intervention. We see, in the examples of biblical lament, that the radical hiddenness[22] of God in the experience of suffering calls forth the outrage, disappointment, and anger toward God that is often censored from our worship liturgy. There is a concealed belief that to speak to God with anger, resentment, and rage is irreverent and therefore off limits to authentic faith. Lament breaks the protocol of accepted engagement with the living God.

This is one of the key aspects of the movement from silence to lament. It is the daring declaration of the conditions of *godforsakenness* to the only one who can truly absorb this dark reality—namely God. God's own covenant fidelity is at stake in every anguished cry of those who feel forsaken by God. Even more than this breaking of the prayer protocol, the prayer of lament as witnessed in the biblical tradition alters our very conception of God.

God must hear. This is the root conviction of the biblical witness of lamentation. Recall our earlier insistence that the laments in the Bible confirm the critical importance of getting God's attention. The theology of the laments is that God will turn his ear and will open to the petition of those who are suffering. The implicit assumption about God is that if we have God's attention we will secure God's help.[23]

God is the one who hears the anguished soul-cry of the afflicted, who is affected by our suffering, and who ultimately *suffers with us*. This conception of God as the one who hears, sees, and is affected by our suffering is at the root of the theology of suffering. A mature theology of suffering will convey the biblical sense of God's responsiveness to the afflicted. This theological portrayal is carefully depicted in the opening chapters of Exodus as the plight of Israel rises up to God. Compare the language of groaning and then crying out to God with the reciprocal actions of God's hearing and seeing: "During that long period, the King of Egypt died. The Israelites groaned in their slavery and cried out, and their cry for help because of their slavery went up to God. God heard their groaning and he remembered his covenant with Abraham, with Isaac, and with Jacob. So God looked on the Israelites and was concerned about them" (Exod 2:23-25).

## From Silence to Lament in the Book of Job

When the severity of Job's suffering is recognized, the first response of those around him is *respectful silence*—there is nothing to say because the suffering is so severe. The first phase of Job's suffering is a period of silence in which the situation is so acute that his friends are speechless, burdened with the weight of Job's distress. The depths of his misery overwhelmed his friends who had come to comfort him and to sympathize with his losses. "When they saw him from a distance, they could hardly recognize him; they began to weep aloud, and they tore their robes and sprinkled dust on their heads. Then they sat on the ground with him for seven days and seven nights. *No one said a word to him, because they saw how great his suffering was*" (Job 2:12-13, emphasis added).

In the book of Job we have multiple theological discourses and soliloquies that represent various views of the source or cause of Job's suffering. Of key importance to our study are the laments in the book of Job as Job seeks to express his own alienation from the theological "answers" of his friends, his deep anguish of spirit, and the physical dimensions of suffering's weight in his life. Job is bold in his assertion of innocence and his reliance on God as the *go'el* (Heb.)—the Redeemer—who can be trusted despite agonizing losses and acute suffering. However, Job is far from easily persuaded that God is acting in his interests. The affliction experienced by Job is recounted in his lamentation in chapters 16 and 17. In this lament we see, once again, the multidimensional nature of suffering as Job decries the experiences of physical pain, psychological anguish, social degradation, and spiritual desolation. Taking a more careful look at these dimensions will help us to understand the full gamut of the experience of suffering as expressed in the lament—that it threatens every dimension of life.

### Physical Pain

"Yet if I speak, my pain is not relieved; and if I refrain, it does not go away" (Job 16:6)

"My gauntness rises up and testifies against me" (16:8)

"Without pity, he [God] pierces my kidneys and spills my gall on the ground. Again and again he bursts upon me; he rushes at me like a warrior" (16:13-14)

"My face is red with weeping, dark shadows ring my eyes." (16:16)

Job is familiar with pain. The torments of physical suffering weaken him and diminish his capacity to hold fast under the mounting pressures of his broken life. He is able, even in his feeble condition, to articulate this pain and to name the effects on his physical body. A key aspect of lament is developing the capacity *to say* what is going on in one's suffering. At the most fundamental level, it is to name one's pain and not to hide any aspect of the effects of suffering. I emphasize this aspect of naming what is going on because of its importance in the development of a theology of suffering. Very often our theologizing moves to statements about life that are not grounded in the situation that we are in. This shift to localize our articulation of theological statements in the context of our painful situation is a crucial element in the theology of suffering. The biblical narrative of Job offers precisely this approach—pain must be named.

### Psychological Anguish

"My eyes pour out tears to God" (Job 16:20)

"My spirit is broken, my days are cut short, the grave awaits me" (17:1)

"My plans are shattered, and so are the desires of my heart" (17:11)

"Where then is my hope? Who can see any hope for me?" (17:15)

Lament also includes psychological anguish and the emotional outpouring of this dimension of suffering. Persons who are suffering need permission to "pour out" their "tears to God." While this dimension of suffering often goes unrecognized, Job is deeply aware of the losses that diminish his hope and destroy his confidence. Here the lament picks up on this dimension of suffering by naming the kinds of inner anguish that accompany suffering: a broken spirit, shattered plans, unfulfilled desires, and the eclipse of hope. The emotional sophistication of these statements clarifies the situation in which Job has found himself. Rather than allowing the anxiety of suffering to remain nebulous and undefined, Job laments the inner sense of loss and anguish. To be able to say that one's spirit is broken or that hope is now out of reach is to claim the one thing that the suffering person has—true inner anguish. Lamentation is, in part, the articulation of inner sorrows and a careful enumeration of the losses that have taken root in one's soul.

### Social Degradation

"Miserable comforters are you all. Will your long-winded speeches never end?" (Job 6:2-3)

"Men open their mouths to jeer at me; they strike my cheek in scorn and unite together against me" (6:10)

"Surely mockers surround me; my eyes must dwell on their hostility." (17:2)

One dimension of the lament that often is missed or profoundly neglected is the social dimension of suffering. In his lament Job articulates his experiences of oppression by others and the social ostracism of his affliction. I have been arguing in this book that the multidimensional nature of suffering must be expressed in its fullness. Here we see that the lament incorporates the experiences of social degradation. The mocking, jeering, and scorn of others torment Job. Those who offer their "long-winded speeches" about Job's guilt especially affect him. Such theologizing increases and heightens Job's suffering. The lament picks up on the social degradation that inflicts further sorrow on the person who is suffering.

Suffering includes this social dimension of derision, scorn, and ostracism. Very often these aspects of suffering are more hidden or less obvious to the untrained eye. Social rejection can happen in many ways. At the root is the separation of the community of concern from the person(s) who have experienced great affliction. To name one's social losses is part of the fabric of authentic spiritual lamentation. Job is unhappy with the cold hostility and blind ignorance of social derision that is embedded in the long-winded speeches of the "comforters" about theology. Scorn and spite alienate the suffering person and expose the fabric of indifference at its root. This expands the scope of the lament to include the social isolation in one's affliction.

*Spiritual Desolation*

"Surely, O God, you have worn me out; you have devastated my
  entire household" (Job 16:7)
"God assails me and tears me in his anger and gnashes his teeth at
  me" (16:9)
"God has turned me over to evil and thrown me into the clutches of
  the wicked" (16:11)
"He [God] shattered me; he seized me by the neck and crushed me.
  He has made me his target; his archers surround me." (16:12)

At the spiritual core of the lament is the need to cry out to God. The experience of spiritual desolation is the unbearable sense of being abandoned
by God. Here, in the lamentation of Job, we hear the anguished spirit of
one who feels forsaken, assailed, and shattered by God. Not only does
God feel far away, but God is experienced as the ultimate source of the
suffering. Notice Job's language: "God, you have devastated my entire
household," "God assails me," "God crushed me," "Surely, O God, you
have worn me out." This dimension of suffering can be termed "spiritual
wounding."[24] Spiritual wounding occurs when we cannot find a reason
for our suffering and, in our desolation, we feel alienated from a loving
and caring God.

Lament therefore moves beyond mutism to express in full the experience of suffering. The lament includes all of the four dimensions of
suffering and *dares to say how bad the situation really is*. This is an important corrective to the spiritualization that often takes place in the face
of suffering. Spiritually truncated responses often fail to take seriously
all of the dimensions of suffering or place emphasis on only one of the
dimensions to the exclusion of the others. Saying "how bad things really
are" is at the core of the lamentation. Expression of suffering is a central
affirmation of the Hebrew attitude toward suffering. Rather than deny
our experience of suffering or offer a reduced view of its complexity and
multivalent force, the Hebrew attitude is to embrace the totality of our
experience with trust in God.[25] The movement from silence to lament is
rooted in this tradition. Rather than glossing over the profound effects
of suffering or blending them into some composite concept of general
suffering, the biblical text encourages the full disclosure of affliction
in all of these dimensions. Suffering, as we find it in the laments of the
Bible, offers full disclosure of the depths of affliction.

## The Heart-Cry of Godforsakenness

The cry of Christ on the cross is a central depiction of this movement from silence to lament. Jesus' own response to the agony of cruel treatment was mixed with silence and lament.[26] A key turning point for the theology of lament in the Bible is this focus on Jesus' own agonizing experience. The importance of this heart-cry of *godforsakenness* is taken up as a key theme in the *theologia crucis*. Jürgen Moltmann suggests this to be a defining center of Christian theology when he states, "The death of Jesus on the cross is the centre of all Christian theology. It is not the only theme of theology, but it is in effect the entry to its problems and answers on earth."[27] The concept of godforsakenness that we see in the cross of Christ at Golgotha is at the center of this theology of the cross.[28]

The nature of the cry of Jesus at Golgotha is the root of lament in the Bible because of the significance of forsakenness as an event "in God," and, speaking in Trinitarian terms this means those who experience themselves as forsaken "are already taken up by Christ's forsakenness into the divine history and that we 'live in God,' because we participate in the eschatological life of God by virtue of the death of Christ."[29]

Lament or the cry of godforsakenness is rooted, therefore, in the cry of Christ on the cross. The laments of all who experience themselves as forsaken by God are taken up in the cry of Christ.[30]

## Contours of the Movement from Silence to Lament

Having explored the reality of mutism and the biblical understanding of lamentation, we are now in a position to outline the important contours of this movement and its implications for pastoral theology.

*The Subtle Shift from Silence to Groans and from Groans*
*to Words Must Be Regarded by Those Who Attempt to Minister*
*to the Most Afflicted*

Pastoral theology has always emphasized the importance of listening and attention in the pastoral situation. However, the explorations of this chapter develop a more fully orbed paradigm of pastoral attention. Mutism—the harsh, empty chasm of wordless existence—is at the core of the experience of suffering. People cannot express what they are experiencing. They cannot say what their suffering really is. This loss of words, or experience of eclipsed meanings, is a terrifying dimension of suffering.[31] In this voiceless, speechless state of agony, the sufferer cannot easily move to speech. We must recognize that the spiritual wounding that comes with suffering obscures the meanings that people otherwise would associate with their lives. Suffering eclipses these meanings and makes articulation difficult or even impossible for a period of time. While inner meanings may still be attached to the situation, the expression of those meanings will likely come first in groans that are too deep for words. Pastoral care involves the reestablishment of these inner meanings by nurturing the expression of anguish and disappointment. Rather than giving "answers" to suffering, the pastoral, theological response is to acknowledge the reality of suffering, allowing persons to express "how bad the situation really is."

We must also recognize where a suffering person is on the continuum between silence and lament. The mute stage of suffering is severed from the normal rhythms of life, and here, in the void of wordlessness, the suffering person turns in on himself or herself. It is an extreme and agonizing gap that leaves one unable to speak, unable to share, unable to express the depths of anguish of the soul. The inability to say how bad things are is a painful kind of loneliness that is experienced in affliction. Not only are the dimensions of suffering acute, the capacity to say what is happening is cut off and the afflicted feel themselves to be godforsaken.

At the groaning stage, there is still a high level of separation from normalcy. Here, however, there is a beginning effort to "sigh" how bad things really are. The groan is the trembling sound of emerging lament. Groaning conveys the deep sorrow, regret, and inner pain of one who has been struck down by life's calamities. Here, as we listen to the emerging anguish of a suffering person, we hear an echo of the groaning creation. It is part of the journey toward healing and articulation. To groan inwardly is to seek out a *go'el* (Heb.)—one who will come to help. While the isolation of suffering continues, something new is afoot in the inner being—a desire to cry out, to speak out, and to at least say how bad things really are.

The lamentation is the next phase. Here emerging questions are asked, complaints are stated, and the radical reorientation to life begins to take form. Lament is a form of trust—"a bruised faith" but a faith that has learned to say what the situation is. In the lament we find the signs of a renewal of faith because we will only call out to God if we expect God to hear our cry. Furthermore, the forming of the lament is an expression of one's reconnection with reality.[32] Lament, in this way, forms a pathway for community to be born through renewed attention to the reality of suffering.

### The Lament Stage Cannot Be Skipped or Substituted

One of the most enduring insights of her important volume *Suffering* is Dorothee Soelle's insistence that the stage of lament cannot be skipped. In her description of the psalmic language of the factory worker, Soelle captures a crucial principle in the theology of suffering. She writes,

> It is clear that the phase of expression cannot be skipped as though one could immediately proceed to surmount the suffering through action. In that way the needs of the sufferers themselves would be skipped as well. . . . A phrase like "Believe me, folks!" is a modern day psalm. . . . I think of his language as "psalmic language" not so much in respect to a literary genre as to specific elements of language, such as lament, petition, expression of hope. . . . The repeated phrase, "Believe me, folks!" occupies exactly the same place occupied in the ancient psalms by, "Hear me, O God; hear my supplication."[33]

This insight shapes a pastoral theology of suffering by insisting on the expression of all the dimensions of suffering in psalmic language that ultimately is addressed to God. The idea that our suffering is meant to be endured quietly in patience is challenged by this principle of expression and articulation of the experience of affliction. While the ability to say how bad things are is temporarily eclipsed by suffering, the ongoing aim of a pastoral theological response to suffering is to tease out the groans, the inarticulate sighs, and to assist in the full expression of suffering.

### The Four Dimensions of Affliction Must All Be Addressed
#### The Articulation of Suffering in Its Entire Dreadfulness

The biblical elements of lamentation face up to the reality of suffering in all of its complexity. Suffering must not be minimized or truncated but fully acknowledged. The tendency to leave out parts of the experience of suffering or to abridge the full experience of suffering can weaken our understanding of what is really happening in a situation. There must be a deeper resolve, in every pastoral encounter, to fully disclose and comprehend all of the dimensions of suffering. This is hard to sustain because the human spirit cannot bear the full weight of affliction without moving away or withdrawing. The articulation of affliction in lament must be nurtured and cultivated with an increasing capacity to bear up or to take on board all of the complexity of multivalent suffering.

In particular the hidden dimensions of suffering are almost universally missed. While physical pain and emotional turmoil are attended to, the hidden reality of social degradation, isolation, and exclusion must also be considered. The spiritual roots of suffering as godforsakenness are serious and must be taken into account. While our tendency is to move away from suffering, the biblical call of the movement from silence to lament is to express, to say how bad the situation is, and to find a community of solace and concern in the midst of the complexities of affliction.

### *Wordless Moments Can Be an Important Phase of Ministry to the Suffering*

We have seen that the groan of despair may be one of the most elemental expressions of suffering. There are extended times where words may not be helpful to those who are suffering. Silence is an important ally to solidarity with the afflicted. At times there are no words to express the inconsolable reality of affliction. Therefore a fundamental pastoral response requires the ministering person to discern whether this is a time to speak or a time to be silent (Eccl 3:7b). This amounts to a recovery of the ministry of *wordless empathy* by entering into the excruciating reality of the suffering of others. Rather than giving voice to our understandings of what is going on, we must search more carefully for the deeper aspects of the situation and offer our tears as expressions of solace. Wordless consolation is at the heart of authentic pastoral response to the reality of affliction.

### *The Power of Symbol to Express the Deeper Contours of an Indescribable Interior Experience*

The interior experience of suffering is impossible to fully convey. One of the key problems for any pastoral theology of suffering is to understand how to enter into the abyss of suffering in a meaningful way.[34]

Liturgy and ritual have the capacity to move beyond the word-forms to the underlying reality of suffering—entering the ineffable. Advocates for the renewal of the lament word-form have helped us to see that liturgical symbols may empower suffering persons to be known even in the depths of their being. The movement from silence to lament must include the symbolic opening of the depths of the human experience of anguish to God. The power of the symbolic allows us to enter into the suffering of others with spiritual depth.

*The God Who Hears Us*

God attends to the cry of the afflicted. The expression of our condition of sorrow and anguish will result in meaningless suffering unless it is met by the compassion of God at the very root of our distress. While the experience of suffering can be so acute that the person actually experiences themselves as "godforsaken," the biblical revelation is that God cares about our suffering, that God hears our cries, and that God attends to our lamentation. To lament is to give voice to suffering—to actually *say how bad things really are*. Not only that, but the lament form is clear that we are able to say this to God. The lament form is a hope-word—dared complaints to one who alone can help us and rescue us in all our turmoil.

The biblical perspective is that God will give us God's attention. God will "give ear" to our complaint. God will hear. God sees our suffering, he hears our cry for help, and he listens from his holy hill. Psalm 3:4 declares, "I call out to the Lord, and he answers me from his holy mountain." God is not unconcerned or distant, but God is one who comes near to those who suffer and hears their lament. The biblical revelation is clear that God attends to our lives. Psalm 18:6 says, "In my distress I called to the Lord; I cried to my God for help. From his temple he heard my voice; my cry came before him, into his ears."

This notion that *God suffers with* God's people is rooted in the Exodus, "Then the Lord said, 'I have seen the affliction of my people who are in Egypt, and have heard their cry because of their taskmasters. I know their sufferings, and I have come down to deliver them out of the hand of the Egyptians'" (Exod 3:7-8).[35]

The movement from silence to lament is a movement of hope in God. It is founded on the promise of God to hear our cry, even in the most desperate circumstances. In Psalm 34 we see the confident assertion of God's attention. In verse 4 the psalmist states, "I sought the Lord, and he answered me; he delivered me from all my fears." Later, in verses 15 and 17, this assertion is reaffirmed, "The eyes of the Lord are on the righteous, and his ears are attentive to their cry; The righteous cry out, and the Lord hears them; he delivers them from all their troubles." Whatever our distress, we are invited to call to God and to rely on God's attentive listening to our cry. Psalm 55:16-17 illustrates this confident hope; "As for me, I call to God, and the Lord saves me. Evening, morning and noon I cry out in distress, and he hears my voice." In fact, even before we call out to God in our misery, the Scriptures declare that God already hears, as we read in Isaiah 65:24: "Before they call I will answer; while they are still speaking I will hear."

At the root of all lament is the cry of godforsakenness. Here the lament is taken up in the cry of Christ at Golgotha, where all human suffering is contained in the mysterious solidarity of the cross of Christ. God not only hears our cry, our cry wounds God in the cross of Christ and is taken up by Christ in suffering love.

## Conclusion

Suffering must be expressed. However, the word-crushing power of affliction eclipses our capacity to communicate the reality of suffering. Suffering makes us mute. We cannot say how bad things really are, and it is often impossible to declare our lament. The groans that are more like the cry of an animal are the beginning of "sighing" our sorrow. The groan gives expression to our inner suffering and participates in the cry of godforsakenness that comes to the ear of God who attends, who hears, who knows our suffering, and who takes up this suffering in himself in the cross of Christ. Suffering makes us mute, but we resist suffering and declare our pain to God. The process of lament is a bruised trust—reaching out to God despite the sense of God's absence in our affliction. The lament is a leap over the abyss of the dark night of the soul with a plea for help to God. Lament is pregnant with the hidden expectation that God will show up. The full disclosure of affliction in all of its dimensions is at the core of the lament word-form. This stage of lamentation cannot be skipped, for it is the full expression of our suffering in psalmic language that cries out to God. In lament we expect God to hear our supplication. The cry of the godforsaken is the attempt to move past mutism, a tradition that goes back into the ancient faith of Israel and that is ultimately rooted in the cry of Christ at Golgotha. The Bible gives us permission to *say how bad things really are* and to move beyond silent acquiescence to articulate our pain. The disintegration of meaning that comes with suffering is slowly restored in the movement from silence to lament. The language-shattering experience of suffering gives way to the groaning of the inner spirit and ultimately to God in the cry of abandonment. This cry is taken up into the mystery of the suffering of God.

CHAPTER FOUR

# From Indifference to Compassion

In the previous chapter, we examined the crucial movement from silence to lament. If we are to think theologically about the reality of suffering and how to overcome it, we must find a language "to at least say what the situation is"[1] and eventually to declare *how bad things really are.* Discovering the language of lament is an important step enabling the afflicted to cry out to God who sees our plight and hears our desperate cry for help. Even though this articulation may begin with silent sighing or a difficult groan, we have seen the power of the lament to express the anguishing situation to God. We turn in this chapter to consider a second movement in a paradigm for a theology of suffering, *the movement from indifference to compassion.*

The ethical implication of human solidarity results in the biblical call to compassion. As we will discover, however, this call to compassion is not so easily established as a reality in our lives and in our faith communities. Before compassion can become an embedded practice, we must come to terms with the complex reality of indifference, of entrenched apathy, and of the subtle resistance to companioning with the most afflicted.

On one occasion, after a critical four-hour surgery, my daughter Chelsey suffered extreme lung failure. At that time I wrote this reflection in my journal. It captures some of the complexity of the theme we are exploring in this chapter, namely the penchant to move away from suffering rather than toward it:

> I am surprised how the pain and suffering are so easily forgotten. I ask myself whether this
> is a great grace or a defect of soul? I suppose that we cannot bear the sustained reflection

*on suffering and that the lapse in memory allows one to repair a sense of balance, com-*
*posure, and a readiness to engage life. At the same time I wonder if we are not too easily*
*led back into moral indifference thus reinforcing the natural penchant to avoid suffering.*
*If we could, somehow, allow our sufferings to compel us to move near to the affliction of*
*others with active help—this would facilitate our growth in love. Such love is the aim*
*of the mature Christian life.*

### 3 O'Clock in the Morning

like a bird caught in a snare,
I pace.
awake in fear; afraid to sleep.
how will I find
my way home tomorrow?
everyone has left—
doctors, nurses, staff—
they're all gone. . . .
I am alone.
it's 3 o'clock
in the morning
and these
haunting walls
are about to close in on me.
it's late;
it's dark;
and I am filled
with terror. (PCZ)

The question of indifference explores why good people fail to act in the face of extreme situations of affliction. Indifference is the "failure either to see, to acknowledge, or to act on behalf of another."[2] Indifference is a central concern for a mature theology of suffering because it forces us to come to terms with an enigma in human interaction at the places of serious affliction: the failure to see, the failure to acknowledge, and the failure to act.

When we encounter the suffering of others, we do not readily enter into that suffering as much as we might think. In subtle ways we fail to acknowledge the full implications of the situation. This has also been described as the condition of "apathy," which comes from the Greek word *apatheia*, "which literally means non-suffering, freedom from suffering, a creature's inability to suffer."[3] There are many ways in which we can become deconditioned from attention to suffering—our own or the suffering of others. This inattention in turn leads to the condition of apathy.[4] We can distance ourselves from the reality of suffering itself, which disempowers us from acting on the causes of suffering. This tendency to avoid suffering at all costs is a natural tendency. Apathy and indifference are more natural to us than compassion. We must acknowledge, at the outset, our avoidance of suffering, which is intimately tied to our resistance to compassion.[5]

A beginning point for us as we explore the movement from indifference to compassion is to recognize how apathy and indifference are operative in our lives. It is imperative that we acknowledge our natural tendency to avoid suffering and to move away from situations that involve us in the suffering of others. Before we can develop a theology of compassion we must look more carefully at the reality of indifference as a root problem in a theology of suffering. Before we are able to articulate a careful theology of suffering we must expose the underside of the ethics of indifference. We turn now to explore how apathy is cultivated in our personal and communal lives. If we can recognize the roots of indifference itself and understand how this works in our lives, we can establish the foundations for a theology of compassion.

## The Roots of Indifference

Suffering is unattractive and threatening. We are repelled by, not attracted to, the situation of those who suffer. Understanding this is an important step to overcoming indifference. However, before we move to a concrete explication of the themes of compassion, I turn to an exploration of the roots of indifference.

### Indifference as Our Natural Response to Suffering

Indifference may be hard for us to recognize as our natural response to suffering. We prefer to think of ourselves as caring human beings, and, in many ways, we give ourselves credit for much more compassion than we are really enacting. It is important, from a biblical and theological perspective, to come to terms with our apathy. It is hard for us to acknowledge that fundamentally caring persons avoid, move away from, and even ignore the suffering of others.

Upon reflection we may discover that it is uncommon for us to explore carefully the contours of this indifference. Suffering repels our inner being, and very often we participate in an unconscious despising of the afflicted.[6] This is crucial for our understanding of the movement from indifference to compassion. We need to see at the beginning of our efforts toward compassion that there is an unconscious move away from those who suffer. This subtle despising of the afflicted can be reinforced and, despite feelings of empathy or pity, may result in the avoidance of the reality of the situation of those who suffer. The life of love commended in Scripture, though fundamental to the biblical vision of the ethical response to suffering, is less common than we would like to think. The radical call of love asks more of us than we are prepared to commit.

Consider 1 John 3:16-18 as the basis of an examination of indifference. "This is how we know what love is: Jesus Christ laid down his life for us. And we ought to lay down our lives for one another. If anyone of you has material possessions and sees a brother or sister in need but has no pity on them, how can the love of God be in you? Dear children, let us not love with words or tongue, but with actions and in truth."

The three aspects of indifference are embedded in this text: failing to see the need, failing to acknowledge the situation, and failing to act in love. Failure to see is an aspect of moral vision. Indifference here is aligned with a faulty perspective. We are preoccupied and cannot see the suffering of others. We are distracted and our inattention causes a moral blindness to the suffering of others. We are shortsighted, looking only at the immediate circumstances of our lives; this failure to see the wider horizons of suffering is another way in which indifference is reinforced in our daily lives.

Failure to acknowledge is the response of the heart to the suffering of others. While we may see the need, we do not let it impact our lives in such a way as to move us to action. Failure to acknowledge may include reducing the situation of suffering to only one of the dimensions we explored in chapter 2. Or, failure to acknowledge may include a denial of the facts, a refusal to accept the situation that is being expressed to us. Here, too, more indifference is reinforced by subtle nonacknowledgments that keep us at a safe distance from the reality of suffering.

Failure to act is the volitional dimension of moral indifference. While we may see and acknowledge, the failure to act impedes our compassionate activity by resisting the costly engagement of compassion. Love acts on the understood need. The engagement required of true compassion is costly and demands our full participation in the situation of suffering itself.

Indifference and apathy are more engrained in our habitual response to the ongoing situations of suffering all around us than we first imagine. Recognition of this fundamental posture of indifference is a key starting point for the renewal of moral vision that is required deep at soul.

## The Subtle Reinforcement of Indifference

Moral indifference is reinforced in subtle ways. We tend to talk ourselves out of compassion and pay attention to stories that actually reduce our commitment to involvement in the alleviation of the causes of suffering. Stories and narratives are powerful tools that shape our inner disposition and responses to suffering. Recent studies in moral ethics demonstrate that morally numbing narratives can have a detrimental effect on our moral vision and our capacity to see suffering clearly.[7] These stories or narratives of indifference can become part of our social embeddedness in a given cultural location. In this view we acquire indifference in the same way we acquire language, by our participation in ideas, rituals, narratives, and stories that foster or legitimize indifference.[8] This acquired sense of indifference is not something that we establish directly or self-consciously. Rather, this is subtly reinforced by the stories to which we attend, the rituals we practice, and the foundational assumptions about life that are operative in our dominant narratives.

When it comes to suffering, the subtle reinforcement of indifference can happen in an innocent way. If we fail to see the full impact of the sufferer's situation, we can make the unintentional conclusion that "it must not be all that bad." The ways that we frame the seriousness of suffering establish the moral importance, the inner motivation, and the volitional effort that such a situation deserves. The failure to see, acknowledge, and act is rooted in the narratives we tell ourselves, which may be truncated expressions of the real situation. It is crucial to understand that the narratives we embrace about the seriousness of a situation are operative in shaping our moral vision and our response to that situation. Therefore, the first step to compassion is not only becoming more aware of the suffering around us but unlearning the settled indifference that takes root in our hearts and that has been reinforced by stories and narratives that reinforce this lack of sympathy.

## Indifference Is Rooted in Pain Avoidance

I have already stated that the avoidance of suffering is quite natural. Our physical existence in this world is such that we are keenly aware of the possibility that pain will come with injury. Consequently, we are prone to self-protection and the avoidance of any situation that would cause us suffering. Pain avoidance is a natural aspect of human life. When this avoidance becomes a settled disposition in our participation in life, it is a small step to moral indifference. We justify not getting involved in human suffering because it jibes with our prior sense of self-protection. To get involved in pain "on purpose" seems a nonsensical action. It moves against the tide of normal human response.

In most situations of indifference there is even an advanced sensibility that we are doing good for ourselves and those we love by not entwining our lives with needless suffering. The moral sensibilities are not at all alerted to a problem because we are avoiding pain and pain avoidance has come to be settled in our inner being as a good thing.

### Theologically Propped up Indifference

Indifference can also be justified by our theology. In the Old Testament, the narrative that describes Jonah's deep resistance to bring the good news to Nineveh was rooted in a theologically justified indifference. While he understood the clear imperative of his mission to herald news of God's mercy, he actively resisted this assignment and found within his inner spirit a justification for his indifference. This theologically justified indifference can be boldly intransigent and resistant to change. Once we have sufficiently convinced ourselves of the moral high ground we are on, we can see the suffering of others as deserved suffering and excuse our nonparticipation in the conditions to alleviate suffering. There are several ways in which this attitude to the suffering of others can be theologically propped up. These views tend to reinforce the premature "answers" to the problem of suffering as described in chapter 1. I would like to explore at least four views of theologically legitimate indifference.

### "Justice Prevails"

This view suggests that leaving things alone is justified in that God will ultimately prevail and God's purposes will stand. In this perspective, justice has its own seasons and times, and it is not up to us to interfere with the scales of just reward. In the end, at the right time, God will intervene. The theological justification for this view is that God is sovereign and nothing happens outside of God's control. If suffering is happening, then there is a reason that is beyond our capacity to understand. We should accept suffering as part of something bigger that is unfolding before us. In the end, justice will prevail.

### "You Reap What You Sow"

The more callous view suggests that most suffering is deserved suffering and is the consequence of some guilt on the part of the sufferer. This perspective is theologically supported by the retribution theory. If you act righteously, you will reap reward. If you do evil, you will suffer the consequences. Getting involved in the alleviation of suffering, in this view, is tantamount to condoning sin. The suffering is a direct consequence of some previous situation, and the situation which called for punishment has resulted in the affliction. Proponents of this perspective may even go back three or four generations to discover the root of the evil that has brought this predicament upon the current suffering person or situation. Reaping what you sow has a clean view of suffering—nothing happens by accident; there is only suffering that follows a previous action of iniquity.

### "Everything Happens for a Reason" / "Everything Has Its Time"

A more sympathetic but equally noncommittal perspective on the suffering of others is that suffering is happening for a larger reason that we cannot see. This view does not quite equate previous sinful actions with suffering, but it does take a passive perspective on the suffering that is going on. The theological rationale behind this analysis is that God is working out a bigger purpose that we cannot possibly see or understand. While we take pity on those who suffer needlessly, this view maintains a distance from the sufferer by offering prayers of sympathy but not actions that alleviate suffering.

In tandem with this view is the perspective that there is a "time for everything" (Eccl 3:1) and that we should accept suffering as a transient aspect of some greater purpose that is unfolding before us. Suffering cannot be avoided, and therefore, in this view, the suffering that is taking place must be acknowledged as "the way things are" for now. There will come a day when wrongs will be righted and when unfair suffering will be resolved. For the moment we are not able to see such resolution and our lot is to simply endure and wait for God's ultimate purposes to be revealed.

### "We Are Not Responsible for Other People's Mistakes"

This view is similar to the first view, but it theologically justifies nonparticipation in the alleviation of suffering. The view is that some consequence is taking place that is the result of a misdeed, a sin, or some unknown. Since we are not to judge nor to prematurely conclude the reason for a situation, this view suggests that we each take responsibility only for what we can humanly endure—namely, our own situation.

The responsibility for the suffering of others cannot possibly be borne by us. This must be left between the person who is suffering and God. God will bring about the assistance needed to alleviate the suffering person. Our work is to quietly take responsibility for our own situation and leave the ruling of the universe to God.

In all these ways our root indifference is theologically propped up by an incomplete view of the reality of suffering in a broken world. Much like the incomplete "answers" to the problem of suffering, theologically supported indifference must be overcome by clarifying the complexity of the situation of suffering itself.

### Indifference as a Conditioned, Communal Response to the Overwhelming Odds of Alleviating Suffering

Indifference is a social condition. It is not something that is held as a personal distance and withdrawal from the suffering of others but rather something that is embedded in the social fabric of the larger community in which we participate. Suffering is overwhelming. It is massive, oppressive, far-reaching, and constant. While we fabricate many ways in which to distance ourselves from suffering, there is an inevitable coming to terms with the abiding presence of affliction in the world. This is an overwhelming prospect for all of us who share the human condition. When we find ourselves engulfed by the sea of human misery, it is a common reaction to withdraw, to shore up our hope, and to anchor ourselves in the more hospitable environment of apathy or nonfeeling. It is easier to be indifferent than to face up to the unspeakable pain of a broken world.

Again, the point of this is not to substantiate the source of our indifference but rather to expose it. Once we have been able simply to reestablish the existence of suffering itself, we are putting ourselves into the human terrain of compassion, where we can work toward the alleviation of the conditions that cause suffering. Solidarity and communal action grow out of a deeper awareness of the reality of suffering in our world.

### Implications of Indifference

Those who suffer feel themselves to be cut off from help, alienated from the community, and isolated in their situation. They do not feel God's presence, and they experience themselves to be despised by others, even if this is an unconscious response to suffering. The shift from indifference to compassion will require more, therefore, than heightened awareness of suffering. It will require a new understanding of the roots of apathy—to the preference for nonsuffering that is our natural life orientation.

Indifference, rooted in settled convictions and reinforced by morally numbing myths, can cripple the compassionate response of God's people to the situation of suffering. We can become numb to the deeper reality of affliction and leave the sufferer alone in their abandoned darkness. This leads to loneliness—the suffering in suffering. Therefore, we must overcome indifference by reassessing the roots of indifference and learning the ways of compassion. I now turn to a description of the nature of compassion and how compassion is cultivated in the pioneer community of God.

## Theology of Compassion

The theological center of a theology of suffering is rooted in the conception of God as compassionate. Biblical studies have demonstrated that God's compassion can be understood as a "controlling metaphor" in the Old Testament.[9] The implications of this are highly significant for a mature theology of suffering. Among the most critical texts where this characterization of God occurs is the covenant renewal with Moses in Exodus 33–34: "Then Moses said, 'Now show me your glory.' And the Lord said, 'I will cause all my goodness to pass in front of you, and I will proclaim my name, the Lord, in your presence. I will have mercy on whom I will have mercy, and I will have compassion on whom I will have compassion.' But, he said, 'you cannot see my face, for no one may see me and live'" (Exod 33:18-20). Also, in Exodus 34:6 we read of God's compassion: "And he passed in front of Moses, proclaiming, 'The Lord, the Lord, the compassionate and gracious God, slow to anger, abounding in love and faithfulness.'" This revelation of God's character as compassionate has significant implications for a theology of suffering. God's own compassionate nature is disclosed in this text with at least four elements that instruct us.

### God's Compassion Is Restorative

God remains true to God's self in the revelation of compassion as the true expression of covenant fidelity. God will always restore Israel and us because of the creative nature of God's love. God's redemptive action in Christ is reconciling the world. This action restores a life of fullness, and, because of the compassion of God, we can experience the restoration of harmony.[10]

### God's Compassion Is Rooted in His Covenant Love

The covenant God made with Israel is at the base of God's compassionate response even in times of betrayal by Israel. God will always restore the nation to himself. To be true to compassion is to be true to God's very being.

### God's Compassion Overcomes Wrath

Compassion is not a winking at sin, nor is it divine sympathy with the brokenness of humanity that is prone to wander from covenant fidelity with God. Rather, the compassion of God takes up all of the iniquity and resolves this in forgiveness.[11]

### God's Compassion Is Limitless

In Jesus' parable of the Good Samaritan, the Samaritan sees that the man on the side of the road is in need of help and he stops with active help. This is the essence of the compassionate response: *to move into the suffering of others with active help.* We tend to think of compassion as roughly equivalent to sympathy (feeling with) or pity (feeling for another). However, compassion is a much more radical expression of solidarity with the afflicted. Compassion involves a commitment to enter into the suffering of others. To be compassionate is not a simple gesture of concern but rather a deep engagement with the suffering of others.[12]

The Greek word for compassion most often used in the New Testament is *splagchnizomai* and means literally "from the bowels" or "to be wrenched in the gut." When used of Jesus' life and ministry, this word, *splagchnizomai*, explains the deep yearning and care for the person in their suffering. It is a compassion from the gut, a profound entry into the suffering of others that depicts God's very character as compassionate.

The messianic vision that Jesus demonstrated was one of compassion for the people. He was not indifferent to the spiritual, physical, emotional, and social suffering of those with whom he came into contact. He was alarmed by it, motivated to help, and always reacted to these situations with a gut response of concern, help, and mercy. The messianic vision of Jesus was to participate in compassion. It is here, most completely, in Jesus that we see what true compassion really is. It is not sympathy, but rather a deep yearning and care for the person, the community, and the situation of the suffering.

Jesus, "seeing the multitudes," recognized them as "sheep without a shepherd." He had *compassion* on them (Mark 6:34). The compassion moved Christ to embrace the role of shepherd on their behalf—to lift his rod and staff in active help, to make a difference with life-giving words, to bring hope, and to sustain the physical journey with food and water. The participation of Jesus in the situation of the suffering is the most compelling Christian reason for active compassion. If this was the central activity of the Lord in his messianic vision, it also becomes the paradigmatic framework of ministry for those who are his disciples. Compassion is not one option among many moral options in the Christian life; it is the central concern of the heart of God for the lost, the broken, the helpless, the shepherd-less, and all those who suffer.

Compassion is important because those who suffer need help. They are being probed, jabbed, and tormented by their affliction. They are trapped in poverty, homelessness, economic injustice, and oppression. Left to their own situation they will die. Those who are suffering experience threat in every dimension of life. The only way that the situation will change is if someone takes the responsibility to help. Compassion involves movement toward suffering—to come to the aid of the oppressed. Compassion acts in such a way as to free the suffering from their oppressors and to give them a better chance for transformation. This is the call of compassion—to move with active help toward the "people and places where suffering is most acute."[13]

It is true that suffering is more acute in some places than others. Further reflections on this theme invite us to consider the context of suffering itself and the conditions that lead to the acute affliction of others. This is a complex question, but the mature Christian response is that we will not tolerate or stand by idly while innocent people suffer. We will move with compassion to those places where suffering is acute with the intention of helping. Compassion is needed because those who suffer need help.

Suffering, in this sense, is the central calling of the pioneer community of God. It is possible to miss how radical this statement is. For a very long time, the church has prioritized its vision around other activities, mostly those of proclamation: we preach, teach, and tell people how to live. This, however, is a truncated vision of participation in the *missio Dei*. The mission of God is compassionate intervention in the conditions of suffering. The call of the church is to alleviate suffering, to eliminate the causes of suffering, and to move with compassion into the situation of the oppressed with God's care. The call of the church to compassion is rooted in Jesus' own self-identity and missional participation.

A mature theology of suffering will explore the range of these human needs. Furthermore, it will call for discernment regarding the participation of the church as the community of God's compassion in the world. We must understand the direction in which compassion is moving us. However, the central issue to get clear in our minds is that compassion is at the very center of the *missio Dei*. As the people of God called to share this mission, we are commanded to imitate the deep yearning and gut-wrenching concern for others that characterized the heart of Jesus.

Compassion is a key theological concept upon which the theology of suffering must be developed. The root idea of the composite word "compassion" is "suffer" (Lat. *pati*) and "with" (Lat. *cum*). Compassion means, *to suffer with*. This expresses well the movement of the compassionate person toward the suffering of others. This action of compassion, defined as suffering with, is rooted in the actions of God as we find them expressed in the Scriptures. At the center of God's own activity is the movement toward humanity and the ultimate concern for the plight of suffering humankind. God, as revealed in the Bible, is a God who moves into our story, into our world, into our situation, and brings active help. Compassion is expressed most fully in the coming of Christ and the cross of Christ. Here God reveals himself as one who moves into the very situation of conflict, anger, rage, alienation, injustice, hatred, and brutality. The incarnation and the cross, therefore, are the defining expressions of God's own compassion. God comes to us.

## The Dynamic Process of Compassion

The contours of our examination of compassion have yet another dimension, namely, the "dynamic process of compassion."[14] This process must be seen to include:

1. A disposition of solidarity toward the neighbor's suffering[15]
2. The action of entering into the context of that suffering as one's own[16]
3. A commitment to overcoming the cause of the suffering itself.[17]

This understanding of the theology of compassion moves it from a static idea to a dynamic process. Each dimension builds on the previous one to give us a working understanding of compassion in the theology.

### A Disposition of Solidarity toward the Neighbor's Suffering

The first movement of compassion is "a disposition of solidarity."[18] "Solidarity" is a word that can be overused in Christian theology. However, it has an important place in helping us to enact a process of true compassion. The character of our life ought to imitate the character and disposition of Christ. This results in a particular way of being in the world and in a particular way of seeing the world (posture and perspective). The adoption of this posture is a moral way of being in the world facilitated by absolute, unmixed attention (prayer). By nature we are self-absorbed and filled with self-interest. When we align our intentions with the intentions of God through prayer, we have a change of posture and perspective. We move from self-interest to the interest of God, from self-concern to participation in the concern of God. A disposition of solidarity is not simply the act of the will—that is, choosing to be selfless. Rather, it is the active adopting of the heart and concern of God as our own. We "put on Christ"—and this involves the virtues of compassion and love as the ultimate extension of God's own heart for the suffering world. This is what Paul meant in his instructions to the church at Colossae:

> Therefore, as God's chosen people, holy and dearly loved, clothe yourself with compassion, kindness, humility, gentleness, and patience. Bear with each other and forgive whatever grievances you may have against one another. Forgive as the Lord forgave you. And over all these virtues put on love, which binds them all together in perfect unity. (Col 3:12-14)

### The Action of Entering into the Context of That Suffering as One's Own

The context of suffering is not something that can be neglected, avoided, or ignored. Compassionate response means carrying out a helping response in a specific context where suffering is happening. The elements of context require our full attention: systemic oppression, economic frameworks, and resources of the community—these are all aspects of compassion. The owning of the context or the full participation in the context is what makes compassion different from the other virtues of kindness, sympathy, and care. These virtues, while important, do not necessarily require the same full participation in the context of suffering as compassion. Kindness can be extended to others without moving into the context itself; care can be shown regardless of our participation in the community of suffering; sympathy is, by its very definition, a feeling toward others in need without a full engagement of the context. Compassion, on the other hand, is a full engagement in the context of the suffering. This activity is what makes compassion a more complete expression of God's heart for the suffering. At the root of compassion is the action of entering into the context of suffering as one's own.

There is a corollary aspect to this statement. The statement implies, correctly, that compassion means reframing our vision of suffering. Suffering is not simply "out there" for us to actively reduce; it is "ours." We share in that suffering. We own it. It is "our suffering." When we begin to realize that the context of suffering is "our suffering," we become invested in the ministry of compassion. Authentic compassion requires that we have fully embraced and owned the situation of suffering as our own.

If we took time to unravel the implications of this for a theology of suffering, we would be able to see that the move from indifference to compassion requires a total commitment from us. The suffering child in an impoverished economic situation is our child's suffering. The oppression that gives rise to torture of innocent detainees is our oppression. The conditions that allow people to be exploited, hurt, taken advantage of, and hindered from full participation in life are the conditions that we are subject to. Compassion means owning the suffering of others as our own suffering.

### A Commitment to Overcoming the Cause of the Suffering Itself

The commitment to overcoming the cause of suffering is a third and vital aspect of true compassion. Without this commitment, we have something more like sympathy or empathy. Christian theology reminds us that "to be radical . . . means to seize a matter at its roots."[19] Compassion is not content to deal with the symptoms or the external realities of suffering alone. There is a deeper search for the roots of suffering.

Commitment to overcoming the causes of suffering will require that we pay full attention to all the dimensions of suffering: physical pain, psychological anguish, social degradation, and spiritual desolation. It will also mean that we radicalize our investment in compassion as an imitation of God.[20] Before we summarize the movement from indifference to compassion, I would invite a closer examination of the idea of the compassion of God and the implications of this for compassionate ministry.

## The Compassion of God

*The compassion of God is the structure of all human compassion—it offers the pattern for reconciling activity as we seek to be helpful to those in desperate need.*

God is revealed as the God of compassion. It is in our alignment with God's own character that the reality of compassion is lived out. The community of faith, aligned with God's own purposes, will be a community of compassion, and the actions of this community will reflect God's own posture of coming near to those who suffer.

*The Holy Spirit* (paraclete) *is the one who comes alongside us. God does not abandon us in our need, but God, through the work of the Holy Spirit, is active in our suffering.*

The power to live a life of compassion is enabled by the Holy Spirit. We are not capable of living this life in our own human strength. It is a divine enablement that allows us to enter into the suffering of others with active help. The parable of the Good Samaritan was Jesus' radical reorientation to a life of mercy, which is the calling of the pioneer community of God. The lived reign of God revealed most closely in the life, death, and resurrection of Jesus is the life that we, the church, are called to live and enabled to construct as we align ourselves with the *missio Dei* and are enabled by the power of God in us.

*"Have this attitude in yourselves which was also in Christ Jesus" (Phil 2:5).*
*Compassion is costly and incarnational.*

The radical call of the incarnation is also the call of the church in the world. We must take seriously the call to displacement that this calling implies. The attitude of Christ was one of selfless service and sacrifice. The incarnational mission is one in which we will imitate the action and the attitudes of Christ, who did not regard equality with God something to be grasped, but emptied himself (Phil 2:6-7). The compassionate community of God links with the selfless movements of Christ in the world. Therefore compassion is not the action of the powerful to the powerless but the vocation of the Christian community to enter into the suffering of others with active help. We follow our displaced Lord into the places and actions of displacement in a broken world.[21]

The discipleship of God's people requires a reorientation to the ministry of compassion. While the world continues to influence our values and judgments about what is important, the perspective of compassion reframes our purpose, our aims, and our *telos* in the world.[22]

The formation of the pioneer community of God includes the cruciform calling of compassion. In imitation of the compassion of God (Luke 6:36), God's people are called to the creative activity of reconciliation in a world of hurt, suspicion, selfishness, and disregard for others. This countercultural mandate shapes the people who bear witness to God's own compassion in the world.

## The Movement from Indifference to Compassion

The movement from indifference to compassion is one of the pivotal progressions in the theology of suffering because of the reorientation from our natural tendencies to avoid, to withdraw from, and to be repelled by the conditions of the most afflicted. In theological terms, compassion is the very movement of God, who enters into the condition of human suffering through the incarnation and whose reconciling love is fulfilled in the costly humiliation of the cross.

The importance of this movement in the development of a mature theology of suffering cannot be overstated. At the core of the biblical mandate is a call from God to *participate in the suffering of others with active help.* This is the call of compassion, and this call is at the root of our life together with God. Nevertheless, fulfillment of this mission from God will not be easily embraced. Everything in the human predicament causes us to flee suffering, to avoid the risks of compassionate involvement, and to despise the afflicted. The natural tendency of the human spirit in the face of unmitigated suffering is to flee, to run away, to withdraw, and to find ways to reinforce a justified indifference. We must constantly reorient ourselves with the spiritual capacity to stand firm in the face of the multivalent reality of suffering. The pioneer community of God has a profound vocation to share in the *missio Dei*, which is compassion. In the following pages I wish to propose several dimensions of this corporate calling to compassion.

### Compassion Is Rooted in the Revelation of Yahweh as the Compassionate God

The compassion of God is inclusive and unconditional. This controlling metaphor establishes compassion as the essence of who God is and the root idea of God's program in the created order. God is revealed to Moses as compassionate in the theophany of Exodus 33–34, and here God's name, which is a revelation of God's essential being, is explicitly identified with graciousness and compassion.[23]

Whatever else we learn about God in the biblical revelation, the core idea of his mercy and compassion defines the nature of God. A theology of suffering must carefully link with this revelation of the God of the Bible. The scriptural picture of God is a composite of ideas and metaphors. However, in a controlling metaphor, the true essence of God's character is revealed. Throughout the biblical revelation and in the course of divine providence, this characterization of God is upheld and shapes the discourse of theological reflection on the theme of suffering. God is a God of compassion. The community that God is making in Christ shares in the compassionate mission of God in the world. This is essentially our character as the people of God, who bear God's name and who represent God's mission in the world.

### Compassion Is the Calling to Participate in the Alleviation of the Causes of Acute Suffering

Suffering is the vocational center point of compassion. To move with active help toward those who are suffering is the essence of compassionate ministry. We should be critical of theological interpretations of suffering that cause us to acquiesce too easily to the root situation or that might instill a *premature acceptance of suffering*. If we are to fulfill our ministry as God's compassionate people, we must resist suffering, protest its incursion into our lives and the lives of those we love, and work to alleviate the root causes of suffering. The primary calling of the church is to the ministry of compassion that moves us into the very situations of acute suffering with solidarity for those who are afflicted. Solidarity is more than speaking out against injustice—it is a posture of identification with those who suffer and a deep commitment to overcome the causes of suffering in whatever form.

Solidarity may be an overused concept in Christian ethics. However, it represents a posture of the church toward suffering. In this volume I have identified this posture as "compassionate protest." This means to participate in God's own protest of suffering by aligning ourselves with the spiritual posture of resisting suffering, moving into the place where suffering is most acute, and actively seeking to overturn the root causes of suffering in the world. Compassion is a holy work of cohesion rooted in the reconciling love of God in the world.

The implication of compassion is that each member of Christ's pioneer community will participate in the ministry of comfort, consolation, and hope-giving by willingly entering into the difficult and dark spaces of affliction wherever it is found.[24]

### The Downward Path of Compassion as Servanthood

The movement from indifference to compassion demands a kingdom orientation or, perhaps better, a kingdom disorientation. If the path of Christ revealed a self-emptying and giving of himself, the vocation of the church as the compassionate community of God will share in this path of downward love.[25] However, downward mobility is not an easy calling. We not only resist solidarity with those who suffer but we are repelled by the difficult work of love that enters with compassion into the suffering of others.

Compassion is far from a natural calling, as we have seen. Only God's Holy Spirit enables this life. The spirit of God makes compassion possible. It is impossible without God's enabling to act in true compassionate, downward service.[26] Servant leadership is a much-vaunted theme in Christian literature. However, this servant leadership is not one of gaining power and control. Rather, it is a sacrificial and cruciform service that suffers with others in their anguishing situation. The radical nature of compassionate service is a concrete challenge to the church in the twenty-first century.

### God's Compassionate Community as a Community of Creative Justice

Edward Farley, in his book *Divine Empathy*, tries to articulate the connection between God's compassionate activity in the world and the cooperation with God that is formed by just communities. In Farley's view it is virtually impossible to co-opt God into a human paradigm of empathy or compassion. Therefore, in Farley's approach, we must surmise from the actual experiences of the world that we know what it means that God is compassionate.

The divine *pathos* in Farley's approach is discernable as a justice that overcomes suffering. This paradigmatic approach moves beyond God's "permissive will" (God does not only allow suffering but participates in the tragic) and locates the center of divine activity as the creative engagement with suffering. Farley depicts divine-human collaboration in the phrase "others-together-in-peril." In this collaboration God participates in the creative resistance to the world as we know it.[27]

### Compassion Finds Its Full Expression in the Incarnation and Cross of Christ

The innocent suffering of Jesus as fully God must be considered as the basis for a theology of compassion. Compassion is fully revealed in the action of Christ to divest himself of "equality with God" (Phil 2:6), and to enter into the conditions of human suffering. We must come to understand the theological significance of Jesus' innocent suffering at the cross as a basis for a theology of compassion. Here, at the cross, God enters most fully into solidarity with the innocent suffering of the afflicted.[28]

### Compassion as the Radical Protest of Suffering

I have been inspired by the provocative theological assertion that "the resurrection is God's protest against suffering."[29] In this sense, as the people of God, we can never come to terms with the "necessities of this world"[30] or the reality of suffering. Jürgen Moltmann explains that for the Christian "the resurrection of Christ is not merely consolation in suffering; it is also *the sign of God's protest against suffering.* That is why whenever faith develops into hope it does not make people serene and placid; it makes them restless. It does not make them patient; it makes them impatient. Instead of being reconciled to existing reality they begin to suffer from it and to resist it."[31]

Building on this seminal insight, I have come to think of the Christian vocation as compassionate protest and to think that at the root of compassion is a profound resistance of suffering. We live in a broken world and in a groaning creation. This means that suffering will come. However, we do not acquiesce to this suffering, and even our patience has a measure of resistance to it. Suffering is something not to be accepted but to be resisted, protested, and overcome. Compassionate protest lives in the tension of a broken creation that is being renewed and that will ultimately be reconciled by God. In the time before the consummation, we live and wrestle with the anguished situation of suffering, and we work with God's power to alleviate it wherever we find it and in every way possible.

### The God Who Comforts Us

"Praise be to the God and Father of our Lord Jesus Christ, the Father of compassion and the God of all comfort, who comforts us in all our troubles, so that we can comfort those in any trouble with the comfort we ourselves have received from God" (2 Cor 1:3-4). God cares for the world God has created. God comforts us in all our troubles and in the deepest sorrows of life. God is the Father of compassion and the God of all comfort. The consolations of divine love are the fulcrum of the good news. When we suffer we certainly need the companionship of others who will act in solidarity with us and help us to overcome the causes of our suffering. The compassion of God's pioneer community is of tremendous solace in the hour of great need. However, the deepest and most profound reality that suffering produces is our need of God's comfort and God's love.

The cross is the sign of God's protest against suffering. Here the divine consolation finds its true insignia—the very love of God poured out for us. Suffering is sometimes unspeakable, and the very reality of the broken creation crushes our spirit. However, God is making all things new. Despite the apparent success of evil, God is at work for the reconciliation of all things to himself.

## Conclusion

Many people suffer in silence without any hope of their situation improving. We do not have to look far to see that there is suffering all around us. Some of this suffering is caused by natural disasters, some of it is caused by human hatred, and much suffering is caused by the root reality of a fallen creation. In every case, the suffering person finds their plight to be unbearable without human and/or divine compassion. The troubles of these broken persons are further worsened by indifference: the failure to see, to acknowledge, or to act on behalf of others. This indifference is reinforced by morally numbing narratives—ways of construing reality that often ignore the facts of suffering and fail to see the root causes of that suffering.

The God of the Bible is revealed as the compassionate and gracious God. God's very nature is compassion, and God has entered into the suffering of the world through the incarnation, death, and resurrection of Jesus. This coming near of God to the world that needed reconciliation was more than a symbolic gesture of divine sympathy. This was a radical engagement with the very roots of suffering. Compassion is a controlling metaphor that describes God's very nature and being. The compassion of God brought about the reconciling action of the cross of Christ, and all those who claim the Christian vocation share in this ministry of radical protest of suffering and actions of compassion. Our common vocation as the church is to enter into the suffering of others with active help.

Compassionate ministry imitates God. It moves in the path of downward service and actions of godly love to alleviate suffering and to work for the abolition of the causes of suffering. Compassionate ministry requires a reorientation of the church as the pioneer community of God. We must recognize that the world has shaped us in its mold. The restoration of the ministry of the church involves renewing our commitment to the *missio Dei* and embracing the restorative purposes of creative love as we cooperate with God the Spirit toward the renewal of all creation. Until that day, we suffer with the afflicted and share their burdens with the comfort we ourselves have received from God.

## CHAPTER FIVE

# From Loneliness to Community

To suffer alone is to bear an infinite agony. The vast chasm that separates the suffering person from a sense of belonging can be described as the inner experience of loneliness. There is, in all suffering, a deep-seated occurrence of cut-off-ness. The afflicted person feels alienated and dislocated in the world. This experience is not simply another aspect of suffering but rather the troubling sense of being cast off. Desolation of belonging is intrinsic to the experience of suffering. Those who feel abandoned are trapped by a hidden desertion. In this chapter we will explore the nature of this loneliness that is at the root of the experience of suffering. This dark cavern of aloneness hinders the sufferer from any sense of being acknowledged, seen, or understood.

There is in this third movement from loneliness to community a deeper reflection of the absolute darkness that often accompanies the experience of suffering. Being alone in one's affliction is another way to describe the hidden dimension of suffering as loneliness. In this way, all suffering is inaccessible to others. We suffer in a way that cannot be articulated or described with any accuracy. This remote place of isolation is painful to bear and makes loneliness the suffering in suffering.[1] In this chapter we will explore the movement from loneliness to community, which is the next movement in our paradigm for a theology of suffering.

# Loneliness
## *The Suffering in Suffering*

The deep chasm between the experience of suffering and the comfort of the community is the experience of loneliness, the suffering in suffering. One of the hardest things to bear in suffering is the loneliness and sense of abandonment that accompanies affliction. At the root of suffering is the agonizing experience of hidden loneliness. Persons who suffer find themselves cut off. They perceive themselves as not truly seen, acknowledged, or understood. Loneliness as the suffering in suffering inhabits all four of the dimensions. These dimensions can be described as experiences of "being cut off."

### *Cut Off from Health (Physical Pain)*

The pain of physical suffering cannot be easily described. A headache or a backache can be identified as a localized pain, but the actual experience of the pain itself is inaccessible to others. We may be able to relate to pain that we have had, but this still is a different reality for the sufferer. Our own experience of pain may pale in comparison to what we are witnessing in the suffering of others, thus reinforcing their sense of loneliness and abandonment in physical pain. At the core of our being is a need to be understood, and the failure to really know the depths of physical anguish diminishes the hope of the suffering person.

Peter (not his real name) had been working in a sawmill his entire life without incident. However, on this particular day, something went awry on the conveyor belt, and before he knew what had happened, the two-foot-diameter circular saw that he was manning had ripped into the large bone of his leg. When I visited him some days later in the hospital, he had already endured several painful skin grafts as the doctors worked to save his leg. The physical pain was unbearable. During my visit with Peter, he braced himself from pain by pulling on the steel hospital bed rails that he had bent with his bare hands by the sheer force of his suffering. It is impossible to describe the inner torment of such agonizing pain to others who come alongside the suffering.

### *Cut Off from Meaning (Psychological Anguish)*

Psychological anguish includes the experience of being cut off from previous meanings that once had oriented one's life. Meanings that held sway before a crisis experience no longer provide the same consolation and hope that they once did. The anguishing situation breaks down these previously held meaning constructs and leaves the person feeling cut off from orienting convictions that were once deeply held. Suffering disorients and breaks down our settled convictions about the goodness of life. Being cut off from meaning can be a frightful experience for the suffering person. The inner loss of meaning disrupts our equilibrium, and our thoughts become more and more sorrowful.

Sorrow can expand deep at soul in such a way as to obscure the understandings of faith. Previous convictions that held us up in trouble fail us under the heavy weight of affliction. When we open the door to the darkness of isolating anguish, perspective on life diminishes with it. Words that once held significance for our spiritual sense of balance now break down as the complexity of sorrow becomes heavier and harder to bear.[2]

### Cut Off from Social Belonging (Social Degradation)

Loneliness as the suffering in suffering is most deeply felt in a sudden break of community. One's sense of belonging and companionship is often shattered by the difficult experiences of suffering. The loneliness of being cut off from immediate social ties is an agonizing experience. Loneliness is one of the most universal aspects of suffering.[3]

A mature theology of suffering will incorporate this dimension of social alienation, forsakenness, and abandonment. Persons who are suffering in extremis may well be surrounded by a caring community and still experience this suffering in suffering or loneliness. The universal need to be understood requires the posture of true compassion. However, as we have already seen, the response of compassion is seldom forthcoming in our communities of faith. Instead, those who are suffering often experience further derision, alienation, and rejection. The distance between the situation of suffering and being understood drifts wider apart.

### Cut Off from Communion with God (Spiritual Desolation)

The spiritual dimension of the suffering in suffering is also difficult to describe. Here the sufferer experiences him/herself as abandoned by God or "godforsaken." The terrifying effect of feeling cut off from God's presence or any sense of God's nearness is at the core of spiritual desolation. The spiritual agony of the "dark night of the soul" is difficult to bear.

Roger Helland gives the account of the sorrowful years that he and his wife endured after a critical accident occurred at their family home:

It began on Monday afternoon, 3 April 1995. My wife was baby-sitting the three little sons of Tom and Judy Tearoe, friends of ours. I was at home preparing for a talk I was to give that evening to recently arrived students at a ministry school. Gail was cooking an early supper. Judy worked as a nurse at the hospital. As usual, on his way to work, Tom dropped the boys off at our place for the day. Our youngest son, Micah, was six. Andrew, their firstborn son, was turning six that month. They would play together after Micah would come home from school until Tom came to pick up Andrew and his younger brothers on his way home from work.

We have a four-foot rock retaining wall in our front yard that overlooks a grass area alongside the street. The boys decided to have a contest to see who could jump the farthest off the wall. After our oldest son Joel jumped, Andrew went next but landed prostrate. Then Micah jumped. Andrew didn't get up. Because he lay motionless and started to breathe funny, Joel ran into the house to tell us. Andrew was unconscious and not breathing. Later he appeared to have no pulse. Panic set in. We phoned 911 while I performed CPR on him. He did not respond. His face turned blue. We knew this was serious. We prayed.

The fire department and paramedics arrived and tried to revive him without success. They rushed him to emergency. Five minutes later Tom arrived at our home to learn of the accident. We all drove to the hospital. Judy, who was on her nursing shift, was called to meet us in the waiting room. The emergency team got Andrew's heart beating, but on his way to the operating room he was pronounced dead. Only ninety minutes earlier he was playing at our home. We were all stunned and grief-stricken. He had a freak accident. Later we learned he immediately went unconscious and died of a neck and spinal injury. Why did God not prevent the accident or spare his life? It wasn't fair. The boys were playing. This family was innocent. The loss was unbearable. . . .

For two years after his death, we wrestled with God. We walked in a daze that stifled our ability to think clearly and that confined our emotions to unimaginable despair. . . . Every morning we awoke heavy and tired with a pit in our stomachs coupled with disorientation and no motivation. Daily, we attempted to control a volcanic rumble, lying just below the surface, which in a moment, in a memory, could erupt into waves of lament or anger. . . . We were shaken.[4]

Shaken by the tragic death of this little boy, Roger declares the struggle as a "wrestling with God" and "unimaginable despair." This grief-stricken family had no warning of how their lives would be disrupted by suffering. In the wake of tragedy, they struggled to piece together their shaken faith. Spiritual desolation is the experience of being cut off from communion with God. Suffering disrupts the feeling of intimacy with God, and one no longer knows where one stands.

These accounts of suffering do not fully describe the unfathomable inaccessibility of suffering. The loneliness at the heart of the experience of suffering must be endured without consolation because of the fact that suffering is always beyond our capacity to fully express. While we cannot fully enter into the suffering of others because of this hidden barrier, it is important to reflect on the implications of the loneliness that accompanies all human suffering. I would like to articulate some implications of loneliness as the suffering in suffering.

### Suffering as an Experience Is Inaccessible to Others

One hindrance to the communitarian sharing with the suffering of others is the fact that, as described, suffering is often not accessible to others. While we can empathize and carry the burden of suffering to a degree, we must always recognize that the deeper experience of suffering entails a loneliness of not being entirely understood. The suffering person will always have some element of the aloneness that comes from having to bear the suffering internally without being able to fully describe the details of this experience to others. It is important that we recognize the suffering in suffering. To acknowledge this loneliness is one of the key elements of a pastoral theology of suffering.

### Suffering Can Be Shared but Only in Limited and Analogous Ways

I have argued that the church is the pioneer community of compassionate protest. This depiction of God's compassionate people is important, but it is equally important to realize the limitations of human community. We are not able to fully experience the suffering of others, despite our intentions to alleviate that suffering. Suffering can never fully be accessed, but it must be borne with a willingness of the Christian community to enter into the pain, the distress, and the anguish with active help. This may seem something of an impasse in Christian ministry. However, it is actually more helpful to recognize, at the outset, the limitations of access to the mystery of each person's unique suffering. In this sense, suffering can only be shared in limited and analogous ways. There is a community in suffering—a sense of shared loss. However, there is also a veil that separates each experience of suffering. We can never fully know the infinite loneliness that is being carried by another—even someone close to us. We must always be mindful of the sacred space in which the deepest secrets of the soul abide.

This awareness of the inaccessibility of suffering will call for greater openness to mystery in the life of the church. This is not to excuse our constant effort to understand and to come near those who are suffering. However, we must also create safe space for persons to explore the spiritual anguish in their search for the nearness of God. The church must proclaim God's presence even in the darkest night of affliction.

*Loneliness Continues Even with the Consolation of Others*
*and the Participation of Companionship in Suffering*

The suffering in suffering (loneliness) is inescapable. In other words, this reality will always be in play somehow in every situation of suffering. The importance of this cannot be quickly dismissed. For the community of concern to enter into the ministry of consolation will require sensitivity to the deeper loneliness and sense of abandonment that accompanies all true suffering. The loneliness that accrues in the heart of the suffering person is the gnawing feeling that *no one really understands* or can enter into the deepest feelings of anguish that are experienced deep at soul.

The reality of this inaccessible suffering should not enable the withdrawal of the community of care. Rather, this calls for a reorientation of our ministry with the suffering. We must draw from our human experiences of suffering and, with the sensitivity of shared loneliness and shared grief, gently come near with news of God's nearness to those who suffer.[5]

*Abandonment Is the Spiritual Experience of Being*
*Alone in One's Suffering*

In her modern-day psalms of lament, Ann Weems articulates the experience of God's absence in suffering:

> One day you were here, O God,
> and then you disappeared
> like a magician
> doing tricks
> on a stage.
>
> One day we were talking,
> and suddenly you turned
> silent.
> And I spoke only
> to the wind.
> Have you gone so far away
> my voice can no longer reach you?

Surely you're not
rejecting me
when I am so desolated!
Surely you remember
that I've always
belonged to you!

When I was a child
I flew into your arms
and settled there.
I had no secrets from you.
Now like a baby
abandoned
on a doorstep,
I have awakened
in a strange place
where you do not live.
This is a godless land,
and I do not want
to be here.

Please reappear, O God,
and listen for my prayers!
When you hear me,
your compassion
will fly on the wind;
you will remember
your own
and I will leave
the horror
that I've lived in,
and my feet will walk
next to yours
once more![6]

Weems describes the "horror" that she must live as rooted in God's absence. "One day we were talking, and suddenly you turned silent." Her experience feels to her like "a baby abandoned on a doorstep." This helplessness is combined with a feeling of abandonment and rejection. God has withdrawn to a place where her voice "can no longer reach" and where God's voice is now suddenly "silent." Weems experiences this as "a godless land" or "a strange place where you [God] do not live." At the root of the suffering in suffering is the experience of abandonment by God.

## Abandonment
### *The Root of Loneliness*

If loneliness is the suffering in suffering, then a mature theology of suffering will reflect more carefully on the experience of Christ at Gethsemane as a way of understanding this root concern. At Gethsemane the agony of abandonment foreshadows the experience on the cross of godforsakenness. Christ is left alone and experiences the profound sorrow of this aloneness. In Jesus' experience of being left alone, we find the core meaning of abandonment and social isolation in suffering. Jesus' experience in Gethsemane is the archetype of abandonment—he was abandoned by his companions and left alone in the anguish of soul at the very place where such companionship and friendship was most needed.[7]

The suffering of abandonment and the loneliness of rejection are at the core of the suffering in suffering. Abandonment intensifies the experience of suffering by cutting us off from companionship, the nearness of human comfort, and, ultimately, the sense of communion with God.[8]

The core experience of being abandoned by others, but also by God, is at the root of the darkest aspect of suffering, which leads to a great loneliness. Those who are truly afflicted know the brokenness of spirit and profound sorrow that accompanies this loneliness. The Gospel of Mark records Jesus' experience in Gethsemane in these words: "My soul is overwhelmed with sorrow to the point of death" (Mark 14:34). This overwhelming sorrow and distress of soul must be acknowledged at the root of all suffering. Since we are created for community, this pointed loneliness cuts deep and weighs down the suffering person with inconsolable grief.

### *Yearning for Community*

Reflection on this hidden loneliness in suffering reveals three yearnings of the afflicted: the longing to be seen, the yearning for a community of belonging, and the need to be understood.

### The Longing to Be Seen

Part of the loneliness at the center of suffering is the sense that one has been forgotten and that the long night of affliction is no longer in view of others. Suffering alone is, in part, a yearning for others to acknowledge and understand the seriousness of the situation that is being confronted. It is not merely a matter of being brave or courageous in the face of severe affliction but that this affliction must be faced without the support of companionship.

Each situation of suffering is unique, and every grief has its own contours.[9] This is why suffering is so impenetrable. Yet, below the surface is a human longing. It is the deeply embedded desire to be seen. Our reflections on suffering must include something of the theology of seeing. To acknowledge another in the situation of great anguish is to share in that suffering by our intent seeing. If indifference is the failure to see or to acknowledge, a mature theology of suffering will foster moral vision for those who suffer and recognition of the depths of their affliction.

## The Yearning for a Community of Belonging

Lonely suffering also includes a yearning for a community of belonging. The social need of belonging has long been assumed and has been integrated in several social psychological schemes, including that of Abraham Maslow, who placed belonging in the middle of human needs after basic safety needs have been met. Only recently, however, has extensive research supported the hypothesis that people have a deep-seated need to belong. In 1995 Roy Baumeister and Mark Leary conducted research to test their "belongingness hypothesis."[10] After extensive research and testing they make the following summative conclusion about belongingness: "At present, it seems fair to conclude that human beings are fundamentally and pervasively motivated by a need to belong, that is, by a strong desire to form and maintain enduring interpersonal attachments. People seek frequent, affectively positive interactions within a context of long-term, caring relationships. . . . The desire for interpersonal attachment may well be one of the most far-reaching and integrative constructs currently available to understand human nature."[11]

Belonging is especially important for those who are experiencing affliction. The sense of social degradation that comes with affliction has an alienating effect, causing the suffering person to feel excluded, neglected, or shunned. In this situation, there is a heightened yearning to belong and to feel accepted by others who can accompany the suffering person on their long and difficult journey.

## The Need to Be Understood

Suffering, as we have seen, is a word-crushing experience, and the first response to suffering is mutism, the inability to say anything. This situation of inexpressible anguish also cuts off the suffering person from the sympathy and understanding necessary to support them in their greatest hour of need. People who are wounded by life have an essential need to be understood. The complexities of suffering are numerous, and part of the suffering in suffering is the isolating experience of not being able to say (or sigh) how bad things really are. A theology of suffering will mimic the patterns that emerge in the lament psalms, which include cries of dereliction, complaints against God, and the expression of disorientation. We often limit persons to expressing their anguish in theologically acceptable ways. This increases the frustration and sense of despair resident in all affliction. Pastoral theology must renew the practice of lament, encouraging the sufferer to pour out their complaint to God.[12] While the experience of affliction alienates and breaks down our sense of belonging, the expression of complaint and lament in a hospitable environment of trust heightens the possibility of spiritual reorientation.

These yearnings depict in concrete terms the kind of community that the suffering person needs. In other words, there are certain aspirational aspects of authentic community that parallel the profound loneliness of the afflicted. In the next section of this chapter we will explore the elements of authentic community that are required as we seek to address the suffering in suffering in our faith communities.

## Trinitarian Patterns of Community

The spiritual calling to be a community that is determined by the life of the Trinitarian God has been called for in many theological writings on the theme of Christian community. To set the context for this discussion, I will explore some of the key theologians who have espoused this view and then extrapolate from their writings the relationship to the core issue of this chapter, namely loneliness as the suffering in suffering. To be an authentic spiritual community for those who suffer will demand not only imitating the Trinitarian pattern of relationship but also recognizing the deeper alienation and brokenness that comes with suffering alone.

The Trinity is often used in pastoral theological discussions as the formative idea for the authentic spiritual community.[13] However, such reflection may be deficient in extrapolating the significance of this for ecclesial understanding. The concept of the Trinity as a social entity is not sufficient to warrant a renewed theological apprehension of the nature of the church as the compassionate community of God. Deeper reflection is required as to the nature of the community that might be formed in the locus of Trinitarian perichoresis.

I would like to begin with the theme of the "eschatological community"[14] as an integrative motif for Christian theology. Combining the motif of the kingdom of God with contemporary explorations of a theology of community is an important development in recent Christian theology. The authentic Christian community emerges when God's rule and reign are present.[15]

As an integrative motif of Christian theology, the "eschatological community" moves the center point of authentic community into the realm of the future. The full realization of our enjoyment of communion with God is proleptic—it belongs in the future that God is making.[16] The theological focus of this community is fixed in relationship to God as the "social Trinity," therefore, "community is not merely an aspect of human life, for it lies within the divine essence."[17] The essence of authentic community, therefore, is participation "in Christ" as we share the divine life and live with expectancy of the fulfillment of God's purposes in history.[18] This sets the platform for the articulation of a compelling vision of the Trinitarian formation of the community of God. The authentic formation of the spiritual community of persons "in Christ" is shaped by God the Spirit into the perichoretic pattern of love enjoyed by the Trinity. This Spirit-directed shaping brings the faith community into true communion with the Triune God.[19]

Contemporary explorations of this theme of communion in theology offer important implications of a more robust Trinitarian ontology for a description of the *being-in-communion* of the church. We must clarify what we mean when we speak of the church as imitating the Trinitarian pattern. Trinitarian approaches to ecclesiology invite deeper reflection on the ontology of the church as the pioneer community of God. Following recent arguments in this discussion in theology, I would like to focus on four clarifying ideas that serve our purposes here.[20]

### Relationality over Sociality

The doctrine of the Trinity implies that "God is neither a collectivity nor an individual but a communion."[21] This relational description of the Triune God orients us to who God is in God's essential and inmost being.[22] The shift to the language of communion is an important one in Trinitarian theology as this shapes theological discourse about God's essential being. The move away from a social concept of the Trinity to a relational one allows us to consider the importance of the theology of communion itself. Communion that is enjoyed by the perichoretic life of the Triune God is also, by the Spirit, available to the community of God in which we may participate through the reconciling love of God in Christ.

### True Community or Koinonia

The idea of *koinonia* is a term of relationality.[23] The church is the true community of God when we enter into the communion that God is in God's essential being. The identity of the church as the true community of God is less a form of social belonging and more a result of authentic communion with God.[24]

### "Echo of the Godhead"

The church is called to be a temporal "echo" of the eternal community that God is. Theologians who espouse this position express the view that the church is oriented to the being of God through baptism and the Eucharist—the sacraments of incorporation and communion with God. This echo of the Godhead animates the reality of the church as the community that represents (re-presenting) God's presence in the world. The spiritual communion that makes up the reoriented church also has a forward momentum of sacred presence in a broken world.[25]

### The Church as an Intermediate Community, Oriented to the Being of God

However, although the church is a "community rooted in the being of God,"[26] it remains highly fallible and therefore only functions as an echo of the life of the Trinity when it is "enabled by the Spirit to order its life . . . to the life, death and resurrection of Jesus."[27] The church is "the concrete community of the last times."[28] This qualification of the nature of the church in the world clarifies that, while we share in communion with God, the communion of the Triune God enjoys a perfect union that we cannot fully enjoy until the eschaton. I turn now to address how these Trinitarian patterns of communion assist our exploration of the core issue of this chapter, namely, loneliness as the hidden reality in the experience of suffering.

If the Trinity is the ontological center point of all true communion, then the experience of forsakenness, while deeply disturbing to the afflicted person, is taken up in the sufferings of Christ. The ideal community, therefore, is not one in which the elements of brokenness are totally absent, but one which can "take on board" the suffering of the world. This is essentially the approach taken by a theology of the cross. A mature theology of suffering will probe carefully how the suffering of the world can be incorporated in God's very being.[29]

Loneliness must be taken up into the suffering of God. This is the heart of the effort that Jürgen Moltmann attempts in *Crucified God.* Moltmann states it this way: "What happened on the cross was an event between God and God. It was a deep division in God himself, in so far as God abandoned God and contradicted himself, and at the same time a unity in God, in so far as God was at one with God and corresponded to himself."[30] Though criticized for the way his theological scheme works out, Moltmann here attempts, through a theology of the cross, to locate both the basis of authentic Christian community in Christ and the center of God's own suffering in the exchange between the Father and the Son. Moltmann explains this exchange of God's own suffering and its implications for the suffering of humanity, "The Son suffers in his love being forsaken by the Father as he dies. The Father suffers in his love the grief of the death of the Son. . . . It is the unconditional and therefore boundless love which proceeds from the grief of the Father and the dying of the Son and reaches forsaken men [sic] in order to create in them the possibility and the force of new life."[31] The role of the Holy Spirit is not outlined in this explanation, but Moltmann is clear that this suffering love can only be authored by the Spirit of God. As he explains in *The Way of Jesus Christ,* "The sufferings of Christ are also the sufferings of the Spirit, for the surrender of Christ also manifested the self-emptying of the Spirit. The Spirit is the divine subject of Jesus' life history; and the Spirit is the divine subject of Jesus' passion history. This means we must even add that Jesus suffered death in 'the power of indestructible life' (Heb 7:16), and through this power 'of the eternal Spirit' (9:14) in his death destroyed death."[32]

Consider this summative paradigm, "God is with us; God is for us; we come from God."[33] The movement from loneliness to community is ultimately a movement toward God. For the suffering person the alienation and loneliness of suffering is unbearable unless there is an indication of God's own involvement in the conditions of suffering. God is with us in solidarity with our sufferings and anguish. God is for us and intervenes on our behalf through the sufferings of Christ. Our ultimate destiny is rooted in God's new creation; we come from God.[34] When we awaken to God's solidarity, to God's saving action, and to God's ulti-mate renewal of all things, we reframe the loneliness of suffering into the ultimate framework.

The church is to enact this paradigm and live in compassionate pro-test against suffering. God suffers with us, but God is ultimately making all things new. This proleptic future is one in which the church resists suffering and acts in compassion—to share in the suffering love of God in the world. The mandate of the eschatological community of God is to work for justice as we await the final consummation of God's reign of peace. We see in this approach the importance of resistance of suffer-ing as a core aspect of the theology of suffering. We do not acquiesce to suffering, but we resist it and protest it. The compassionate community of God has a new orientation. This community bears the marks of resis-tance that "echo" the divine protest of suffering at the resurrection.[35]

## Moving toward Authentic Spiritual Community

Suffering pushes the boundaries of our human capacity to cope with life. At its worst form, suffering alienates, disrupts, and breaks down our sense of belonging to the point where we feel alone, forsaken, and forgotten. The quest for authentic spiritual community must come to terms with the root of loneliness, the suffering in suffering, and move us toward genuine communion with God.

The move from loneliness to community must begin with recogni-tion of our fundamental human loneliness. While there is much talk of togetherness, community, and belonging in our world, the deeper reality is that suffering isolates us.[36]

The first step to overcome this loneliness is not by creating ways of belonging but rather by transforming the loneliness itself into soli-tude. This entails paying attention to our "inner necessity"[37] and our true "vocation."[38] This recommendation may seem trivial, but it concurs with deeper perceptions about finding intimate communion with God in the midst of our brokenness. Our inner yearnings to belong, to be seen, and to be understood must find their ultimate expression in a common search for communion with God, which is the life of prayer. Prayer, in this context, needs to be reframed. It is not simply a pious activity of the righteous, but rather a reaching out to God (Acts 17:27), who hears our sighs, our groans, and our laments. Suffering pushes the boundaries of our relationships with others and God; prayer restores our connec-tion with God, "for in him we live and move and have our being" (Acts

17:28). Suffering cannot separate us from God (Rom 8:39), but it can disrupt our communion with God. Prayer is the foundational movement of the spiritual life that restores our communion.[39] It is important that we understand this as the fountain of authentic community. Consider Simone Weil, who understands the center of the spiritual life to be fixed in "waiting patiently in expectation"[40] for God and prayer as the movement of God into our situation.[41] This ties to our core theme of the spiritual response to the loneliness in suffering. Henri Nouwen's articulation of this bears repeating in full here when he states,

> Absence and presence are never separated when we reach out to God in prayer. The spiritual life is, first of all, a patient waiting, that is, a waiting in suffering (*patior* = to suffer), during which the many experiences of unfulfillment remind us of God's absence. But it also is a waiting in expectation which allows us to recognize the first signs of the coming God in the center of our pains. The mystery of God's presence, therefore, can be touched only by a deep awareness of his absence. It is in the center of our longing for the absent God that we discover his footprints, and realize that our desire to love God is born out of the love with which he has touched us.[42]

Prayer is reaching out to the near God (Acts 17:27). In this next section I would like to draw four foundational precepts from the pastoral theology of Henri Nouwen.

### We Are Not Primarily for Each Other but for God

The word "community" usually refers to a way of being together that gives us a sense of belonging. Nouwen offers a distinction in authentic spiritual community stating that it is not simply "togetherness" but a specific kind of togetherness. Nouwen states, "We discover each other by following the same vocation and by supporting each other in the same search. Therefore, Christian community is not a closed circle of people embracing each other, but a forward-moving group of companions bound together by the same voice asking for their attention."[43]

Overcoming the experience of bitter aloneness and godforsakenness is a matter of searching for God's own presence. By naming this as the focus of our searching in times of suffering we reorient the search for true community as a listening or attention to God's voice. In the tradition of the psalms, we are invited to seek God's voice and presence in the darkest moments of life. There, in that very searching, we will discover "a group of companions bound together by the same voice asking for their attention." This redirection of energy is an important aspect of cultivating authentic faith communities. Nowhere more poignantly than in our suffering do we require the voice of God comforting and bringing consolation to our deepest losses, our personal anguish, and our profound sadness. Here, in the midst of crying out to God, we discover that we are not alone. We encounter others who, on their own search for God, sojourn in the same path of true communion, and here, too, we find that God is near.

### The Basis of True Community Is the Divine Call

If true Christian community is "waiting community," the basis of this authentic community goes beyond the normal sense of being together. True spiritual communion is rooted in God and in God's call to us, even in the darkest moments of our lives. When we substitute the weaker version of community as belonging, a sense of shared complaint, or some other aspect of human belonging, we lose this deeper connection of authentic spiritual community rooted in the divine call.[44]

Rooting authentic Christian community in the divine call protects it from being simply a way of being together. It opens up the possibility of resurrection—of divine response. In this way Christian community is something that is authored by God for the purpose of spiritual liberation and true freedom. It is this true salvation that is required if we are ultimately to address the experience of godforsakenness at the root of all suffering. While we depend on the spiritual support and encouragement of other sojourners in the spiritual life, we ultimately search for God's own response to our suffering. It is here, at the root of things, that we find the spiritual community of common searching for our home in God.

### "The Wisdom of the Bell Tower"

There is a third implication of Nouwen's approach for the theology of community, namely, what he terms "the wisdom of the bell tower." He writes,

> There is a great wisdom hidden in the old bell tower calling people with very different backgrounds away from their homes to form one body in Jesus Christ. It is precisely by transcending the many individual differences that we can become witnesses of God who allows his light to shine upon the poor and rich, healthy and sick alike. But it is also in this encounter on the way to God that we become aware of our neighbor's needs and begin to heal each other's wounds.[45]

God's invitation to all persons, regardless of their situation in life, is to enter into communion with himself. This central calling is at the heart of the Christian message of reconciliation and is the basis for a theology of communion. Authentic Christian community begins with God's invitation for all, regardless of their life circumstances, to come to him. From this basis of divine reconciliation, we form community with others, especially those who are suffering, and we become a source of compassion as we fellowship with them. The radical hospitality of the bell tower invites those who are suffering out of their forsakenness and isolating anguish into the fellowship of fellow strugglers who themselves have been rescued by God. Authentic Christian community is born of God for the purposes of reconciliation of all things to himself (2 Cor 5:19).

*Prayer Is Generative of Authentic Christian Community*

Authentic Christian community is born in prayer. Prayer unites us with God who calls us and forms us into a community.[46] The compassionate community of God is authored in sacred communion with God who is with us and for us and in whom all things consist. True spiritual communion cannot be entered into by simple mechanistic approaches of social belonging. At the root of the spiritual experience of loneliness, abandonment, and forsakenness is the need *to belong to one another in God.* Suffering can leave us bewildered, distraught, and forlorn. Human belonging cannot save us in these depths of despair. We need to discover the possibility of union with God who rescues, redeems, and saves us in our plight. Here, in the darkest corners of life, we find hope renewed for a new beginning. We join the pilgrim community of faith. We throw our depleted lives on God. Here, too, we discover a group of companions who, in their own sufferings and loneliness, have also cast themselves on the same comforting God. Together we walk toward a new horizon—the horizon of the inimitable persistence of hope.

## The God Who Suffers with Us

The question of authentic spiritual community is at the core of this chapter. If the suffering person is to overcome the suffering in suffering (loneliness), there must be some way in which the experience of solidarity and communion are mediated to the anguished situation of the most afflicted. The starting point for any serious reflection on such a community must essentially be God. Communion with God is the center of all authentic Christian community, and our life together in Christian community is a response to the divine call.

However, in order for this community to be realized, we must ask what suffering means for God. In the sufferings of Christ we have a paradigm for the suffering of God. Solidarity, vicarious power, and rebirth are the divine dimensions in the sufferings of Christ. These demonstrate God's own participation in suffering.

The church, however, is not separated from God but participates in communion with God. The church is the "echo of the Godhead" and enacts the mandate of reconciliation, though imperfectly, through communion with God. Our participation in the divine life of the Trinity is both a proleptic hope and a reality for which we labor. In this way we share in God's life—through prayerful communion and by resisting suffering wherever and however we can. We do not acquiesce to suffering nor do we abandon those who, for whatever reasons, are experiencing the abandonment of human fellowship and the abandonment of God. The church is called to be the community of compassionate protest, enacting the divine mandate and living hopefully into the future.

The Spirit of God authors the movement from loneliness to community. The Spirit enables and empowers the church to enact its mission in the world as the pioneer community of the living and Triune God. Or to state it once more in the words of Stanley J. Grenz, "The indwelling Spirit leads and empowers the church to fulfill its divinely mandated calling to be a sacrament of Trinitarian communion, a temporal, visible sign of the eternal, dynamic life of the triune God."[47]

# CHAPTER SIX

# The Suffering of Creation

The multivalent and complex reality of suffering calls for a biblical understanding of the reality underlying suffering. In the New Testament, this may be best described with the Pauline statement regarding "the groaning of creation" (Rom 8:22). Eschatological hope presses forward to a future expectation of God's intervention in the reality suffering. The larger context for the exploration of suffering, however, is not individual suffering or even the suffering of the community—the larger context is the brokenness of creation itself. While not a complete explanation of suffering, this crucial biblical formulation of the foundational understanding of suffering in a broken world is important for the development of a mature theology of suffering. Yet the question remains as to how a good creation that is created by the hands of God who is also good could be languishing in this way. This is a particularly difficult theological question. The tendency is to embrace the "answer" to this question without exploring the implications of this answer. However, the waiting hope of the redemption of all creation is at the heart of the biblical picture of the reality of life in a broken world. I have stated throughout this volume that suffering must not be considered a riddle to be explained, but rather suffering should be understood as a reality that must be confronted in compassionate protest. The suffering of creation must be met with a posture of expectancy in God's redemption of all things.

The courage to face up to the reality of suffering is not fatalism but mature acceptance that looks long into the future—as we await the day of the full realization of God's restoration of all creation. There is an unresolved tension here between the expectation of God's reconciliation of all things and the lived reality of life in broken, frustrated creation.

## The Groaning of Creation (Romans 8)

For a deeper understanding of the reality of suffering in the world I turn to an exposition of Romans 8. Here the Apostle Paul develops a theology of creation and, in particular, focuses on the role of the Spirit of God in bringing assurance to beleaguered believers in the face of life's deepest afflictions.

### The View of Suffering in Romans 8

In Romans 8 the Apostle Paul makes several statements about the reality of suffering as it is experienced in life. At the root of this, Paul lists seven forms of affliction in verse 35: trouble, hardship, persecution, famine, nakedness, danger, and sword. Biblical scholars take note of the significance that Paul himself experienced these and is using his own example as the basis for expressing the lived realities of life in a groaning creation. This "catalogue of difficult circumstances" is a feature of Stoic literature. However, the Apostle Paul, drawing from his own experiences of suffering in the world, uses this catalogue of suffering to describe the situation for all believers.[1] His depiction opens up the multivalent dimensions of suffering in the widest context of the groaning of creation.

If verse 17 is seen as the controlling idea of suffering in this pericope, then the specific instances of affliction mentioned serve to *move from the abstract to the concrete*. While not inclusive of all experiences of affliction, the list serves to identify the disappointments and hardships of life in a creation that is frustrated from its first purposes. If we take the sevenfold depiction of suffering identified in Paul's statement in verse 35 as only a category, suffering becomes simply a philosophical summation of difficulties in a broken creation. If, however, we take it seriously as the reality of brokenness in a frustrated creation, we begin to see that the biblical depiction of suffering is not a philosophical category but a confluence of situations and realities to be confronted in compassionate protest. The picture that Paul describes in Romans 8 once again reinforces the understanding that suffering cannot be taken as a simple idea but rather as a composite idea of many experiences intertwined and rooted in the reality of a broken world. Paul's sevenfold list of suffering in verse 35 opens up the discussion of suffering rather than trying to summarize or contain it. The following brief analysis of the catalogue of suffering used here by Paul will help to frame a deeper biblical understanding of the reality of suffering in a broken and groaning creation.

Trouble, Affliction

In Romans 8:35 Paul picks up this theme of trouble or affliction that has already been mentioned in 2:9 and 5:3. In Romans 2:9 the emphasis is on the retributive nature of affliction as the consequence of doing evil. The affliction referred to is the end result of doing evil as opposed to those, who in the power of God's Spirit, do good. Paul emphasizes that God does not show favoritism (2:11) but rather rewards the faithful and punishes those who "reject the truth and follow evil" (2:8).

In Romans 5:3 the emphasis turns to focus only on believers who "rejoice in our sufferings" knowing that "perseverance" in the face of such afflictions produces patience in the Christian life—the formation of inner character rooted in the hope of God's outpouring of love evidenced by the giving of the Holy Spirit (5:5).

Therefore, when Paul uses this term in Romans 8:35, he has in mind the reality of afflictions that are caused by human sin and the distress that is caused by injustice toward those who have entrusted their life situation to God by faith. The trouble that we experience in life (2 Cor 1:4) is responded to by the very comfort of God and is the basis for pastoral consolation and comfort of others in their afflictions (2 Cor 1:3-4). The presence of trouble and affliction in its many forms is part of life in a broken world and is one aspect of the "sufferings" of Christ in which we share (Rom 8:17).

Hardship, Distress

Paul uses this same term to describe his own apostolic hardships in 2 Corinthians 12:10. There he states that the anguish or distress of soul experienced for the sake of Christ demonstrates God's power in his weakness. Part of Paul's view of suffering is the reality that there will be "difficulties" endured for the sake of Christ that are commensurate with participation in the gospel. Paul encourages believers to hold fast in their experience of such difficulties, as the future outcome rests not in their weakness but in God's sustaining power.

Persecution

The term for "persecution" used in Romans 8:35 is the same term used in Acts 8:1, "On that day a great 'persecution' (*diōgmos*) broke out against the church at Jerusalem." Opposition to the gospel, both in the first century and today, leads to persecution. The persecution is apparently for religious reasons, which is the fundamental meaning of the word in this context.[2] In the Pauline view, the reality of suffering includes persecution for one's faith. This oppression and violence by others is one of the troubling aspects of life in a broken world.

The groaning of creation includes, in the Pauline vision, the suffering that is inflicted on others by human cruelty and evil. Suffering has causes that can be traced to the actions of injustice, hardship, distress, and persecution by persons against other persons. This tragic sense of life is part of the picture of suffering created here by Paul.

Famine

Famine or severe hunger is the next element of suffering in Paul's list. Famine is the lack of food and the consequent suffering that comes with such want. This idea is fully expressed in Stephen's speech to the Sanhedrin in Acts 7, "Now a famine (*limos*) came over all Egypt and Canaan, and great affliction with it, and our fathers could find no food" (Acts 7:11). The lack of food and the scarcity of human sustenance are aspects of the brokenness of creation depicted in Paul's taxonomy of suffering.

The need for food to sustain us is part of the very fabric of human life in this world. The lack of adequate food is a painful existence for those who suffer in this way. In every generation from biblical times to the present, the problem of lack of sustenance has described a harsh reality of life for many.

Nakedness

Coupled with hunger is the reality of "nakedness" (*gumnotēs*). The deprivation of food is now accentuated by the lack of basic clothing to protect from the elements. This situation of suffering, nakedness, depicts the absolute want experienced by the poor who cannot even clothe themselves with the basic garments essential for life.

The depiction of suffering here is one of poverty and the functional desperation in all of life. The hopelessness that accompanies this condition of scarcity is at the root of suffering. The poverty depicted here can be seen to describe the physical, the emotional, the social, and the spiritual picture of absolute misery.

Danger

Danger (*kindunos*) is a general word, but in the only other instance of this word in the New Testament, Paul identifies the types of danger that he personally had endured in his ministry in 2 Corinthians 11:26: "I have been in danger from rivers, in danger from bandits, in danger from my own countrymen, in danger from Gentiles; in danger in the city, in danger in the country, in danger at sea; and in danger from false brothers." There are many dangers in the world. Some of the hostilities are dangers inflicted upon us by others—in Paul's case those who, for various reasons, would oppose his ministry. Other dangers are contextual: at sea, in the country, in the city—dangers that we are all susceptible to in life.

Sword

The word used in Romans 8:35 for sword (*machaira*) indicates violence and war.[3] The closest use to this in the New Testament is the litany of heroic perseverance listed in the book of Hebrews:, "They were put to death by the sword" (Heb 11:37). Perhaps unsure of his own impending demise, Paul reasoned that among the sufferings of humanity to be endured for Christ's sake there might even be a martyrdom of dying by the sword. This ultimate sacrifice of one's own life for the cause of the gospel was a threat for the persecuted church, and Paul, undeterred by the disappointments and tests of life, includes the sword as one of the possible threats against Christian fidelity.

The catalogue of suffering here is consistent with the theology of suffering I have been arguing for. In Romans 8, Paul expresses the multivalent suffering that touches every dimension of life. This is important for the purposes of this volume to set the context in which we interpret suffering. The biblical picture is one of realistic acknowledgment of pain, anguish, persecution, danger, trouble, sword—all of the elements of suffering in a broken world.

It is in this theology of creation, or more particularly, the "fallen creation," that the Apostle Paul locates the understanding of hope as an eager expectation of the reconciliation of all things in Christ. The Pauline theme of broken or frustrated creation is expressed in Romans 8 in a threefold groaning: the groaning of creation (v. 22) and the groaning of hopeful believers (v. 23) are met by the groaning of the Spirit (v. 26).

These corresponding groans set the table for a mature theology of suffering, which, while acknowledging the reality of a frustrated creation (v. 20), also aspires to live into the hope of a reconciled creation rooted in the "love of God that is in Christ Jesus our Lord" (v. 39).

We turn, therefore, to explore the paradigm of this threefold groaning as a basis for a theology of suffering that refuses to acquiesce easily to the causes of suffering and that also refuses to let go of the eager expectation of a reconciled reality rooted in the love of God.

## The Threefold Groaning
### *Paradigm for a Biblical Theology of Suffering*

> "We know that the whole creation has been groaning as in the pains of childbirth right up to the present time. Not only so, but we ourselves, who have the firstfruits of the Spirit, groan inwardly as we wait eagerly for our adoption as sons, the redemption of our bodies. For in this hope we were saved. But hope that is seen is no hope at all. Who hopes for what he already has? But if we hope for what we do not yet have, we wait for it patiently. In the same way, the Spirit helps us in our weakness. We do not know what we ought to pray for, but the Spirit himself intercedes for us with groans that words cannot express. And he who searches our hearts knows the mind of the Spirit, because the Spirit intercedes for the saints in accordance with God's will." (Rom 8:22-27)

This key pericope gives us a deeper perception of the reality of suffering in a broken world. While we cannot explore all of the theological dimensions of this text and the implications for a theology of suffering, I wish to explore the paradigmatic expression of Paul around the key idea of "groaning." This threefold groaning of the creation, the adopted children of God, and the Spirit is an important insignia for the basis of suffering and hope in the New Testament.

### *The Groaning of the Whole Creation*

> "The whole creation has been groaning as in the pains of childbirth."
> (Rom 8:22)

The first instance of groaning in Paul's trilogy indicates a very broad context—the groaning of "the whole creation."[4] However, there is yet an even wider view—the eschatological renewal of all creation that the creation awaits. There is an intentional juxtaposition of the created order that groans with the created order that expects God's renewal. Suffering and hope combine here in the metaphor of "travail"—the agony that leads to new life.[5] The new birth of the creation is an eschatological image that Paul is using to ignite the hope of believers. The creation is distorted and there is a distress in the fabric of the created order that is in view in the Pauline picture of the world as we know it.[6] There is a contrasting element in the picture being presented to us of the created order as in that state of "present suffering" and, at the same time, anticipating "future glory."[7] This groaning and anguish is rooted in the situation of the material creation and expresses a desperate context that requires the reconciliation of God.[8] Further reflection on this verse brings to mind both the reality of creation's brokenness and the hope or expectation of a travail with ultimate purpose.[9]

Therefore, "creation can do nothing but wait and hope—and groan."[10] This does not explain in full the reality of suffering but expresses the biblical viewpoint that the creation has been broken and is groaning for a rebirth. This points us to the renewal of creation in the eschaton. Barth links together the reality of suffering and hope when he states, "We know that everywhere this hope-ful distress and this distress-ful hope are linked in one all-pervading unity."[11]

A theology of suffering must indicate the widest context in which that affliction is to be understood in order to provide meaning and hope. In the biblical view, however, this understanding is intentionally ambiguous—it is both hopeful groaning and unresolved waiting. As we discovered in the lament literature of the Bible, the lament implies a God who hears. The implication of hopeful groaning includes the elements of rescue, redemption, and the saving intervention of God. At the core of the lamentation and the groaning that gives rise to it is the anticipation that God will hear and that God will act. Here, using the widest lens possible, the Apostle Paul orients us to the reality of suffering in the created order. This orientation includes four key elements that shape a mature theology of suffering.

Suffering Includes a Travail toward Newness

The creation has been frustrated and distorted and bound (Rom 8:20-21). However, embedded in reality itself is a breaking forward—"as in the pains of childbirth" (Rom 8:22). This travailing toward a distinct newness is as much part of the created order as the frustration to which the creation was bound by the fall. The implication for a theology of suffering is that suffering cannot be acquiesced to nor can suffering be resolved in the frustrated creation itself. This tension may be best understood as a descriptive conceptualization of the reality of suffering rather than an explanation of the reason for suffering. When we mistakenly make the "fall of creation" the reason for suffering, we lose the tension that is imbedded in the biblical worldview—suffering is part of reality but is in an incomplete understanding of reality as it will be.

### To Understand Suffering Requires an Orientation from the Wide to the Widest Lens

One of the common explanations that was challenged in chapter 1 was the perspective of "the resolved life in God's tapestry." In this view the idea is that suffering can be best explained as the underside of the tapestry—from a human perspective we see only the knots and loose strings of a random set of problems; from the other side of the tapestry God sees a harmonious weaving with purpose, intention, and beauty. The one element of this approach that is worth salvaging is the element of perspective. However, the perspective presented here by the Apostle Paul reorients our viewpoint to a both/and—a wide and wider perspective. We both see the underside of the tapestry (the wide view of a frustrated creation) and glimpse the true anticipation of the reordering of creation (the widest view of the eschatological renewal of all things). This may be seen as "eschatological imagination,"[12] which embraces, as part of the point of view, the promises of God yet unrealized in the groaning creation. Suffering, in this view, may be seen with eternal perspective (the widest view) without being explained away. The reality of a broken creation impedes life, disrupts wellness, and continues to be frustrated by its fallenness, yet, a new dawn is emerging that can already be glimpsed.

### The Groaning of Creation Calls Us to Be Careful Stewards of Nature

The creation has been subject to frustration "not by its own choice" (Rom 8:20). This implies the importance of the ongoing care of creation as a stewardship of humanity who shares in this broken creation. Creation's dilemma is exacerbated by the choices that lead to the continuation of disruption, destruction, and pollution of the globe. In this sense, a mature theology of suffering will also have a constructive ecological ethic.

The anticipation of the renewal of creation implies a moral posture of cooperation with God toward the end that nature be cared for and nurtured. This is part of a biblical vision for the natural environment and the ecosystems of the earth. The renewal of concern for the earth is

an invitation to see beyond creation's brokenness and to act in cooperation with God's own intentions of the restoration of all things. This concern should motivate new ways of seeing the earth and our stewardship
of it. Furthermore, it should inspire affirmation of all of God's creation.
The groaning of creation is a call for justice and a deep awareness of the
interdependence of the material world and humanity.[13]

Suffering Will Include Dark Periods of Waiting

The picture being conveyed to us of a frustrated creation, which groans
for liberation and freedom, is one that includes the experience of dark
periods of waiting. Perhaps this assists with the recalibration of hopefulness in the face of unspeakable suffering. Suffering and hope are
intimately tied together in the pericope. However, hope is not radiant
sunbeams of illumination but rather small fractures of light in the heavy
darkness of a frustrated created order. This depicts for us an orientation
toward suffering—one of patient waiting without clear illumination. It
is my contention that a mature theology of suffering will not ignore the
reality of a broken creation but will also not acquiesce to the existence
of suffering as something to be endured. It is, rather, a dark waiting with
hidden expectation of a new birth of the entire created order. This posture of waiting in darkness, in frustration, and without resolved clarity
represents the widest lens of a theology of suffering. In suffering we are
*at sea yet tethered to a promise.*

### The Groaning of the Christian Community

*"We ourselves, who have the firstfruits of the Spirit, groan inwardly." (Rom 8:23)*

The second "groaning" in the Pauline trilogy is the inward groaning
of the Christian community: "Not only so, but we ourselves, who have
the firstfruits of the Spirit, groan inwardly as we wait eagerly for our
adoption as sons, the redemption of our bodies" (Rom 8:23). Paul uses
this same language of the communal groaning of God's people in a similar way in 2 Corinthians 5:2-4: "Meanwhile we groan, longing to be
clothed with our heavenly dwelling. . . . For while we are in this tent,
we groan and are burdened, because we do not wish to be unclothed
but to be clothed with our heavenly dwelling." Together with the groaning creation, those who await their full adoption as God's children also
groan and are burdened.[14] Here we begin to understand the basis for
our unsettled anxiety in a broken world. We suffer and this suffering

causes us to groan. While some commentators do not see the necessity of a physical (i.e., voiced) groaning, I am convinced that the groans should be understood as both voiced expressions of lament (groans) and inner sighs of the burdened spirit. There is nothing in the text to suggest that these groans must only be silent. The reality of the broken creation startles us and wounds us. Our burden in this broken world is that, while our faith in Christ has given us a foretaste of the redemption to come, we must live with darkness, death, and the pain of life in a broken world. We participate in the frustrated creation and bear the marks of its burden in our bodies, in our souls, and in our bruised faith.[15]

This links the suffering of the creation with the other sufferings described in Romans 8:18 as "our present sufferings."[16] Paul does not excuse the believing community from the reality of suffering but rather indicates that we too are caught up in a larger drama that is still unfolding.[17] The "glory to be revealed in us" (Rom 8:18) is yet unseen. Caught in the tension between the reality of a suffering world and the hope of a redeemed creation, we suffer and we sigh. We wait with unease, with unspoken prayers, and with moans of anticipation of a new order. The implications of this second groaning are important for a mature theology of suffering resulting in two key insights.

### Believers Are Not Exempt from the Reality of Suffering in a Broken World

The idea that faith in Christ shields us from suffering may not be an explicit claim, but it can become a misplaced orientation to the reality of suffering. Paul here, and in the passage in 2 Corinthians 5, shares the wider biblical perspective that the experience of suffering is common to all humanity. The biblical picture actually offers the view that suffering can intensify because of our faith convictions (persecution for righteousness sake), and that, indeed, suffering cannot be avoided simply because of our trust in God.

The conviction that we do not bear our suffering alone grows out of a spiritual communion with God and with the people of God, who share in the compassionate ministry of Christ in the world. This posture of suffering "in hope" is an important part of a theology of suffering. This acceptance of the reality of suffering, however, must not be construed as acceptance of the conditions that give rise to suffering. To be human in a broken world is to suffer. The difference between the believing community and the nonbelieving community is not the experience of suffering but the capacity to endure with hope. All of us have responsibility to resist suffering and to work for the elimination of the conditions that give rise to affliction in the world. There is a fine line between the premature acceptance of suffering and the mature acceptance of the reality of suffering in a world that is expecting renewal. We must be careful not to condone or consent in any way to the unjust conditions that give rise to suffering in the world.

## The Christian Community Must Practice Its Sighing and Groaning

Recent efforts to renew our understanding of the relationship of beliefs and practices in practical theology have helped us to see the importance of this symmetrical relationship.[18] Beliefs inform practices and practices shape beliefs. The practices of sighing and lament are undeveloped in the church. These practices, however, are embedded in a way of being and knowing. The anticipation of God's intervention in creation while patiently waiting in the dark gives rise to a new practice in the church— the practice of groaning. This ought to be rehearsed in every situation of suffering. I will expand this in the final chapter, but I note it here because of the relatively diminished view of lament that persists in liturgical practices of worship in the church. The tendency in triumphalistic approaches to worship belies the conditions of suffering to which we are all subject. If the common reality of a broken and groaning creation also persists in our lives together as we groan and are burdened by suffering, this practice should take a more central role in our faith communities. The shaping practice of sighing together would enable a mature theology of suffering. The theopoetic has been called "the language of silence" for the poets "all look for words which only grow out of silence."[19] The theology of suffering emerges from sighing. Theopoetic comprehension involves the inarticulate expression of an inner knowing—*we sigh what we see*. The artists and the poets have always known that the reality of suffering cannot be said—it is an immense and "difficult river."[20] Theology is "the Word spoken before the void, 'We do not even know how to pray.'"[21] The renewal of the practice of moans, groans, and sighs will enable the faith community to stand in the ambiguous tension of experienced suffering and the glimpse of glory. The practiced groan will equip the faith community with a hope that sustains the afflicted in the burdens and distresses of life.

### The Groaning of the Spirit

*"The Spirit himself intercedes for us with groans that words cannot express."*
(Rom 8:26)

Here, then, is a third "groaning" in the paradigm—the intercession of the Spirit "for us" with "groans that words cannot express."[22] A mature theology of suffering will explore carefully the implications of this third groaning mentioned in the Pauline paradigm. Here something new begins to form in the theological imagination of the apostle who envisions God's own participation in the activity of groaning. At the very least, this expression of the Spirit's inarticulate groaning must be understood as the passionate expression of God's own invested interest in the world.

God continues to be invested in the created order, and this expression of passionate concern elicits something ineffable—a groan, a yearning, a deep utterance of divine disquiet. The very act of creation has been called "the beginning of the passion of God."[23]

Two implications of this third 'groaning' require reflection.

### The Suffering of God Expressed in the Spirit's "Groans That Words Cannot Express"

Many commentators back away from the possibility that this text implies that the Spirit grieves as we do about creation and turn this passage toward the issue of a believer's prayer that is supported by the Spirit. But the deeper possibility exists in this text that the very suffering of God is in view here. The Spirit's groans are of a different order than the groaning of creation and the groaning of believers who wait for the fulfillment of all things. The Spirit anticipates in a different way that God is making all things new. These groans enter into the mystery of God's own reconciling love in the world.

The grief and suffering of God the Spirit are revealed here and elsewhere in the biblical vision. The creation groans in its disruption and anguish, but the Spirit keeps hope along. Despite suffering, the Spirit persists in the enabling and interceding action that frees and sustains us even in the bleakest experiences of life. Especially here, God alone can "help us in our weakness."[24]

The Activity of Prayer as a Cooperation with the Spirit
in the Situation of Suffering (Rom 8:26-27)

Sighs and groans of the suffering are met with the groans of God the
Spirit who "intercedes for us with groans that words cannot express"
(Rom 8:26).[25] In our helplessness and affliction we do "not know what
we ought to pray for" (Rom 8:26). Suffering reframes our view of prayer
in that suffering makes communication impossible. This requires, therefore, an intervention of the Spirit. The Spirit himself intercedes for us.
Suffering eclipses all language and makes us mute. But even more than
this, silent anguish that comes with affliction cuts us off from God. The
spiritual communion is severed by our helplessness. Prayer in the situation of suffering is not initiated by the sufferer but by God the Spirit
who "searches the heart" and "intercedes for the saints" (Rom 8:27).
This moves us into the realm of divine protest against suffering.[26]

## Conclusion

This brief excursion has significant implications for the task of the current book. By exploring the pericope of Romans 8:19-27, we are given
a posture and a theological apprehension about the reality of suffering.
Paul's paradigmatic trilogy of groanings helps us to discern some new
elements of a mature theology of suffering. This analysis provides the
stimulus for some concluding precepts that will move toward the greater
aims of this book, namely, to develop a mature theology of suffering.

### *Hope Contains the Unknown Longings of the Inexpressible*

Paul reminds us that "hope that is seen is no hope at all" (Rom 8:24).
There is a hidden dimension to hope and the renewal of all things in
God. The Spirit intercedes for the saints, particularly those who "groan
inwardly" under the effects of the broken creation. Hope springs from
this divine accompaniment. We yearn and long for something we do
not even know fully. The language of hope is rooted in God and God's
infinite love.[27] These expressions of the inner soul cannot be articulated,
especially when we have been brutalized by life. Therefore, the inner
yearning of spiritual intimacy with God requires God's own Spirit to
intercede for us according to God's will.

### *There Can Be No Simple Explanation of Suffering*

The groaning of the Spirit reaches for the ineffable. The groaning of
creation and our sufferings in this world cannot be easily articulated or

understood. There is a deep mystery to life in this broken creation. We must learn to become accustomed to ambiguity, unresolved anxiety, and the deeper feelings of the "not yet" of the created order. Suffering cannot be explained with simple correlations or a matrix of human logic. We must come to terms with the reality of suffering as a mystery.

Even though the creation is a broken one, we are mystified by the reality of how bad things really can get. We can have a theology of the fall of creation, but when suffering hits home it defies our comprehension. We are crushed by the weight of suffering and its debilitating effects in our life. This is, in part, the force of the Spirit groaning on our behalf with inexpressible sighs. Suffering mystifies and "radical suffering" changes our point of view completely.[28]

### Suffering Is Not to Be Glorified but Endured with Patience

The Bible speaks of suffering as a reality to be confronted and endured. There is a biblical sense of "in spite of" that is of the essence of the hopeful spirit in the face of suffering. Suffering must not be magnified or made to be an object of our deepest concern. Rather, we are to live with hope and trust in God who redeems us and who comes to us in our greatest affliction. The hope that we carry in our hearts is a hope that God will also be our *go'el*, our liberator, and come to the dis-ease of our life situation. We wait eagerly for that day. We hope for that day. We resist suffering and protest its agonies in our lives while we endure with great patience and with the comfort that comes from God to our lives.

The mature Christian life is a responsible "living into" the realities that we have come to know. We cannot simply sit back and wait for God to act in the future. A theology of renewed creation ought to motivate us to ethical concern for all of creation and move us to cooperate with God in our divinely given mandate to steward the earth.[29]

### Suffering Is Painful and Anguishing—It Must Never Be Minimized

Life in this broken world can be profoundly alienating and lonely for the afflicted. Many persons who are experiencing the pain and suffering of this anguished world are not comforted by platitudes and simplistic answers to the suffering. Rather than trying to "explain" suffering, we are called to bear one another's burdens and resist the root causes of suffering. Compassion is the deepest calling of the church. Suffering repels us and often, in response, we withdraw and leave the suffering alone in their anguish. The gospel calls for a reversal—a supernatural move toward, rather than away from, suffering.

The Spirit of God intercedes for us. We must cooperate with the Spirit of God in sharing the weight of suffering and lifting the burden of the suffering in suffering—loneliness. The promptings of the Spirit of God will move us in the direction of authentic compassion and toward the reconciliation of all things in God.

### Suffering Will End in the Eschaton

Suffering will end. The deep expectation of a mature life with God is rooted in the ultimate completion of God's purposes. There is an uneasiness with the heavy reality of suffering in this world as we know it. However, the scriptural vision is one that depicts an ultimate freedom that is rooted in God. The glory "that will be revealed in us" will outweigh "our present sufferings" (Rom 8:18). There is a deep expectancy in the Christian life that rests on the ultimate completion of God's purposes. While we wait in hope, we long for the day when all suffering will end.[30]

### The Reality of Suffering Requires Us to Walk in Faith toward God, Even if It Means Walking in the Dark

We sometimes speak about suffering as a dark night of the soul. But what does it mean to walk in the dark toward God? Suffering eclipses our hope. We find ourselves struggling in the lonely night alone. This is a difficult place to enact our trust. The courage to trust God despite the evidence of God's absence is a demanding task. Resolute trust in God in the midst of suffering requires valiant courage.[31]

The exploration of the paradigm of the threefold groaning in Romans 8 amplifies our conception of a mature theology of suffering. This text reinforces a key understanding that suffering is not a problem to be solved or a riddle to be understood but a reality to be confronted with compassion in cooperation with God's intentions. Clarity about the nature of this reality is opened to us in the Pauline paradigm of the groaning of creation, the groaning of God's people, and the groaning of the Spirit who intercedes for us. The implications for the theology of suffering call for a mature theology of hope, which introduces the theme of the next chapter, the subtle persistence of hope.

## CHAPTER SEVEN

# The Subtle Persistence of Hope

Hope is part of the fabric of human existence, yet the subtlety of hope's persistence requires deliberate reflection. Circumstances of the most afflicted often do not reveal the presence of hope at all. The anguished situations of the distressed and suffering are often bleak and full of darkness. Hope is usually depicted as a light in the darkness. My suggestion is that hope is subtler, more nuanced, and more hidden than this metaphor suggests. In this chapter I wish to present the view that hope is veiled as a persistent dimension at the root of suffering. The stalking darkness of the plight of persons who are in serious affliction must be our true starting point if we are to uncover the subtle persistence of hope. It must be more than an unfounded assumption that hope exists in these anguishing situations. How can we get to the root of the situation of affliction to discover if hope really resides in such a condition?

Christian theological approaches to suffering will often claim that hope always triumphs over despair, but thoughtful understanding of the complexities and torments of the situation of the afflicted calls for a more hesitant *yes*. Hope endures, yes—but a faded hope; a wrinkled hope; a hope mixed with sadness. Lament? I am reminded of Elie Wiesel's account of Juliek in the experiences endured at Buchenwald concentration camp:

> A violin in a dark barrack where the dead were piled on top of the living? Who was this madman who played the violin here, at the edge of his own grave? Or was it a hallucination?
>
> It had to be Juliek.

He was playing a fragment of a Beethoven concerto. Never before had I heard such a beautiful sound. In such silence.

How had he succeeded in disengaging himself? To slip out from under my body without my feeling it?

The darkness enveloped us. All I could hear was the violin, and it was as if Juliek's soul had become his bow. He was playing his life. His whole being was gliding over the strings. His unfulfilled hopes. His charred past, his extinguished future. He played that which he would never play again.

I shall never forget Juliek. How could I forget this concert given before an audience of the dead and dying? Even today, when I hear that particular piece by Beethoven, my eyes close and out of the darkness emerges the pale and melancholy face of my Polish comrade bidding farewell to an audience of dying men.

I don't know how long he played. I was overcome by sleep. When I awoke at daybreak, I saw Juliek facing me, hunched over, dead. Next to him lay his violin, trampled, an eerily poignant little corpse.[1]

The experience conveyed by Wiesel here describes an "enveloping darkness," "unfulfilled hopes," and an "extinguished future." Such is the experience of suffering. It eclipses hope. The enveloping darkness must not be underestimated. It is part of the fabric of affliction, and any articulation of hope must be, by the very nature of this darkness, subdued and understated. There was a violin playing in the darkness, yes. This would indicate some persistence of hope. But the cost of this hope was unfathomable—Juliek was "playing his life"; "his soul had become his bow"; "his whole being was gliding over the strings."

It is inevitable for our musings about hope to draw us into an almost romantic notion that hope resides at the root of all imaginable anguish; yet, there are still inklings that such statements belie the elements of despair, hopelessness, and despondency that are commensurate with all true suffering. Disappointment is very much part of the reality of most situations of suffering. Inevitably, before things get better, they get worse. This downward spiral of suffering upon suffering, of disappointment added to an already anguished circumstance, is hard to bear.

Joni Eareckson Tada gives the account of a friend of hers, John McCallister, who is afflicted with a degenerative nerve disease. Struggling with the debilitating and dehumanizing aspects of his suffering is bad enough, but then one night, terrible shifts to unspeakable:

John's wheelchair sits unused in the corner. He's too weak to sit in it much. His bed stands in the center of the living room. John is in it. Nighttime is no longer friendly. Shadows cast jerking, jagging shapes across the room. Gravity is his enemy as the weight of the air settles on his chest. Breathing is heavy labor. Calling out is impossible.

He needs to call out tonight. In the darkness an ant finds him. The scout sends for others and they come. First hundreds, then thousands. A noiseless legion inches its way down the chimney, across the floor, secretly crawling up his urine tube, up, over and onto his bed. They fan out over the hills and valleys of John's blanket, tunneling under and onto his body. He is covered by a black, wriggling invasion.

I'm across the ocean in England when the fax arrives at my hotel, relaying the story. John's wife, along with a nurse, found him in the early morning with ants still in his hair, mouth, and eyes. His skin was badly bitten and burned. Pray for him, the fax conveys, we've never seen him so depressed.

We might ask how the subtle persistence of hope is evident in this situation. The dynamics of hope in the situation require our reflection. It must certainly be admitted that the distressing situation that occasioned this prayer request is riddled with hopelessness. Hope, if it is present here at all, is hidden in the prevailing despondency of this helpless human being. Before moving to a biblical understanding of hope, therefore, I want to explore in detail the eclipse of hope that blurs our vision and cuts us off from the consolations that may come from religious hope.

## Eclipse of Hope

Suffering eclipses hope. This is true in every dimension of suffering: physical pain, psychological anguish, social degradation, and most especially in spiritual desolation. Very seldom can we distinguish the root cause of such concealed hopelessness. It may be that all of these dimensions together erode confidence in the goodness of God, and one begins to experience one's own life as forsaken, tormented, and outcast.

The biblical view of hope takes into full account the reality of suffering. The biblical record in both the Old and New Testaments gives account of common experiences of the eclipse of hope. In this sense, hope is more invisible than visible. The biblical perspective is that hope is more "difficult and risky."[2]

Our starting point, therefore, in articulating the subtle persistence of hope is not to describe the notable features of hope in its color but rather to pick up the ambiguity of the biblical record and find hope at the root of the experiences that contradict it. In other words, hidden hope is revealed only when we are able to come to terms with the reality of suffering as we experience it in this broken world. While there are certainly many other categories of the experience of the eclipse of hope that could be described, I have chosen to focus on five types of encounters that carry the ambiguity of hope and suffering.

## Spiritual Desolation

Spiritual desolation, at its root, is the experience of losing one's sense of communion with God. It was on the cross that Christ cried out in agony, "'*Eloi, Eloi, lama sabachthani*'—which means, 'My God, my God, why have you forsaken me?'" (Matt 27:46).

What does it mean to experience oneself as abandoned by God? Certainly, viewed from the context of the spiritual life of a believer, this is cause for the eclipse of hope. The nearness of God is celebrated in the Bible as one of the trustworthy dimensions of God's fidelity to those who trust him, particularly for those who are experiencing affliction (e.g., Pss 34:18, 119:151, 145:18-19; Lam 3:55-57; Phil 4:5). The expectation that God will come near to those who call on him intensifies the experience of suffering. Not only is the individual caught in the downward spiral of affliction but, at the core, experiences himself or herself as abandoned by God. All severe suffering shuts us off from spiritual communion with God, causing us to feel forsaken by God.[3]

While it may be important to distinguish between the experience of being forsaken by God and the actuality of God's removal from our experience, the reality for the suffering person is that the calamity and anguish of suffering hinders intimacy with God and the sense of God's nearness. It is to this encounter with abandonment that we must attend if we are to discover the subtle persistence of hope at the root.

If we pay attention to the experience of spiritual desolation, particularly as it is expressed in the Passion Narratives of Jesus, we can identify some of the common elements of this profoundly human experience so universal in suffering. We see in Jesus' passion on the cross the sense of abandonment, the encounter with absence, the experience of rejection, a sharp crying out, a collapse of trust, and a final self-surrender. Hope is barely perceptible in this sequence, until, at the end, we see only a glimpse in the self-surrender of Jesus.

## Disillusionment

On the road to Emmaus we read of the *disillusionment* of the disciples, who had "hoped that he was the one who was going to redeem Israel" (Luke 23:21). Their utter disappointment at the events leading up to the crucifixion of Jesus is evident as they walk "with faces downcast" (Luke 23:17), and rehearse to their companion on the road the discouraging events that have led to their despondency.

Disillusionment is the experience of having our beliefs crushed in such a way that we no longer find them a compelling source of consolation in our grief. This is often difficult for the suffering person or community to articulate, as the very fabric of their faith orientation disintegrates in ways that are quite disorienting, perhaps beyond their ability to express. However, even here in disillusionment, the subtle persistence of hope may be recognized. The experience of not having our trust realized, while discouraging one's sense of hope, is still supported at the root with a "hoping against hope." Patience sustains our spiritual capacity to hope. The biblical tradition of genuine patience is imbued with the qualities of steadfast endurance. Patience is an ally of hope because it enables the suffering person to remain steadfast, even when one is very much in danger of giving up.[4]

While disillusionment has, at its core, the experience of broken confidence, it maintains a key element of hope that is nurtured by patience. While downcast in spirit, the travelers on the road to Emmaus wrestle to hold on to their hope, not fully convinced that the events leading up to the crucifixion of Jesus have trampled the foundation of their trust. They declare their bewilderment: "But we had hoped that he was the one who was going to redeem Israel. And what is more, it is the third day since all this took place" (Luke 24:21). The instinctive response of these disillusioned believers is to move toward the impulse of hope that is described by the story of the women who "amazed" them by telling them that "they had seen a vision of angels, who said that he was alive" (Luke 24:22-24). The disbelief that was causing their disillusionment was mitigated by the hope that stirred as they came to terms with the amazing possibility of resurrection.

Disillusionment may not be comprehensive, and, even in dire circumstances, the subtle persistence of hope may prevail. Hope is eclipsed but not completely snuffed out. The residual elements of hopefulness linger underneath—a dying ember waiting to be fanned into flame.

### Ridicule

The account of the sufferings of Job instructs us about hope from the sapiential literature of the Bible. Job experiences all of the dimensions of suffering: loss, grief, pain, and much personal anguish. But the writer of Job also conveys the deep loneliness and bitter alienation that arises from the experience of ridicule. Job is forced to defend his honor and his theological commitments in the face of criticism and spiritual ostracism.

The social dimension of suffering is often neglected, and yet the experience of alienation, marginalization, and oppression is deeply injurious.

It is also important for us to see how hope is operative in this situation of ridicule and social rejection. Common experiences of rejection, defamation, and social ostracism can diminish hope. The question of how hope is operative in this situation is important for our explorations on this theme. Perhaps, as in most dimensions of suffering, there is the hope that this social suffering will come to an end. The hope of relief from the ridicule allows one to move forward in self-protection. It is instructive here, as well, for us to acknowledge the corrective impulse to turn to God when our fellow humans let us down. Nowhere is the need for God so great as when all others have rejected and maligned to the point where self-esteem is destroyed. Social dimensions of suffering leave us feeling rejected and alienated by others.

## Exclusion

Joseph is alienated from his brothers in a violent act of exclusion. Motivated by their jealousy and envy, these siblings subject their brother Joseph to an extreme act of exclusion, selling him as a slave to Egyptian traders who are passing through. This action leaves Joseph desolate, betrayed, and rejected by his family and closest relatives. This experience is marked with a sense of the tragic, as is the case in many families today.

How does the experience of exclusion hinder one's own orientation in the world? The person who is rejected by near relatives feels oneself to be unworthy of love. This hinders all personal relationships, and one is always on one's guard in respect to the relationships that emerge from that time on. The biblical account of Joseph's rejection by his brothers contains very few hopeful turning points, until in the text we read of Joseph's long view of the situation, "You intended to harm me, but God intended it for good to accomplish what is now being done, the saving of many lives" (Gen 50:20).

## Punishment

One of the questions asked by those who suffer is the question of the punitive possibility—is God punishing me? As we saw in chapter 1, one of the common explanations of suffering is the retributive justice approach, which sees all suffering as deserved. In this view, suffering is associated with direct disobedience to God. We rejected, in that chapter, the idea that retributive justice can be considered as an explanation for all suffering, given that there are many innocents who suffer. However, the Bible does allow for a retributive interpretation of suffering in some cases. Any attempt to reconcile the biblical view of hope with the realities of experienced suffering must take this question on. In the story of Nathan's rebuke of David's sin in 2 Samuel 12, the severe punishment by God includes the death of David's son. "This is what the Lord says: 'Out of your own household I am going to bring calamity upon you.' . . . After Nathan had gone home, the Lord struck the child that Uriah's wife had borne to David, and he became ill. David pleaded with God for the child. He fasted and went into his house and spent the night lying on the ground. The elders of his household stood beside him to get him up from the ground, but he refused, and he would not eat any food with them. On the seventh day the child died" (2 Sam 12:11a, 15-18a).

Even though the text states elsewhere that David had been forgiven for his sin (2 Sam 12:13, *"The Lord has taken your sin away"*), the "Lord struck the child," and "on the seventh day the child died." Here is a complicated situation of retributive justice that directly implicates Yahweh. Even though David "pleaded with God for the child," the child dies. Three implications for our purposes here should be explored: Why did pardon of David's sin not include the relenting of the Lord's decision to strike "the child that Uriah's wife had borne to David"? (v. 15). Why did David's earnest pleading to God to spare the child's life fail? (vv. 16-17). And, perhaps most importantly for our concerns here, how can one hope at all when the hand of the Lord would strike a child with a fatal illness in punishing one's sin?

These are very difficult questions, but they must be asked if we are to discover the stillpoint of biblical hope. To be specific, the text does convey the message of God's forgiveness through David's repentance. To David's repentant statement, "I have sinned against the Lord" (v. 13a), Nathan offers the divine perspective of forgiveness and continuing consequences of sin. "Nathan replied, 'The Lord has taken away your sin. You are not going to die. But because by doing this you have made the enemies of the Lord show utter contempt, the son born to you will die'" (13b-14). However, for most of us there is little comfort that our own life would be spared in forgiveness while our child would die as a consequence of our sin.

Not wanting to resolve this ambiguity, I think this point illustrates well the anguish that comes with hoping in the context of retribution.

David still hopes, even through the turmoil of his son's illness, that the consequences of his sin will not result in the death of his son. "While the child was still alive, I fasted and wept. I thought, 'Who knows? The Lord may be gracious to me and let the child live'" (v. 22). David is not surprised, however, that his pleading is in vain. He accepts the death of his child as a consequence of his own disobedience. When the child dies, the text announces David's response: "David noticed that his servants were whispering among themselves and he realized the child was dead. 'Is the child dead?' he asked. 'Yes,' they replied, 'he is dead.' Then David got up from the ground. After he had washed, put on lotions and changed his clothes, he went into the house of the Lord and worshiped. Then he went to his own house, and at his request they served him food, and he ate" (vv. 19-20).

David's hope is twofold in spite of the tragic consequences of his son's death. His hope in the covenant established by Yahweh will restore him and allow him to fulfill his destiny as Israel's monarch despite the events surrounding his transgression. Further, he hopes to see his child again, indicating the innocence of the suffering child and the restored confidence that he will gain access to Yahweh in his death.

Yet, this hope is spoiled by the reality of God's action in punishing David by sending a fatal illness to his child. Here even the "subtle persistence of hope" would seem to be overshadowed by despair. Who can stand when the hand of the Lord is against you? Despite the overwhelming loss and grief associated with the illness of his son, David finds an inner strength in the possibility of seeing his child once again (after this life) and in the consolation that the Lord had spared him despite his deserving death. It is hard for us to imagine hope if it were our very own child who was not spared because of the offense to our sin taken by the Lord. However, here again, we can observe that hope (at least in some form) persists.

It is on this point that I would like, therefore, to turn to the notion of hope itself and the subtle persistence of hope as the qualifying activity of the human spirit even in the most anguished situations. We have seen that the experiences of forsakenness, disillusionment, ridicule, exclusion, and punishment erode hopefulness and, in some ways, eclipse hope altogether. And yet, the resilience of hope itself is able to "take on board," as it were, all of the darkness of these human experiences without completely being suffocated or snuffed out. It is to this resilience and tenacity of hope that I now want to turn.

## The Subtle Persistence of Hope

Winter is "the season bereft of hope."[5] The barren landscape defies any signs of life, vitality, or sustainability. Winter is a severe testing of hope's capacity to endure. There is little assurance that the plants will recover from the harsh northern winds, the crushing cold, and the freezing of all life. It is impossible to imagine that the seeds will ever find warmth again so as to germinate in what is now frozen earth and harsh, vacant tundra. The questions of winter, like the search for hope, leave us cold, exposed, and immobile. It is difficult to act without hope, because there, at the root of suffering, is the experience of forsakenness, loneliness, alienation, and the deep sense that the world cannot be trusted.

Hope enters this bleak and desolate landscape despite our loss of the capacity to see. The dark night is difficult to bear. So it is with suffering—a dark night of the soul, the bleakness of the spiritual winter erodes confidence in God's presence. Every indication is only of darkness and the stark panorama of nothingness. "How do men and women 'clap their hands and shout with a voice of joy to God' (Ps 47:1) in the midst of pain, suffering, heartache, and throbbing despair?"[6]

The question is an important one and one that has been asked by every seeking generation. Hope prevails despite the all-consuming winter of our lives. It springs up from nowhere. Hope catches our despair off guard and awakens us to God's abiding presence. Here is the spiritual meaning of hope: God comes near to us even though the evidence seems otherwise. God comes to sustain us despite the dark abode of suffering's night. God is awake to our sorrow and, somehow, participates in overcoming it. Everything in life protests suffering, but, where it most matters, it is God's own presence that brings comfort and joy even in the darkest circumstances of life. In the darkness and travails of life, God's silence is difficult to endure, yet even here there can be the most subtle and gentle awakening to hope.[7]

Hope's tenacity is dependent on something or someone to enter into the situation of the oppression with us. While we endure the winter of life's sorrows in infinite ways, the reality of something else breaking through is an important corollary to suffering. Hope is eroded by suffering but suffering is ameliorated by hope. This tension is part of the way things really are. Hope involves, at the core, taking our stand against despair."[8] At the root of hope is the experience of near despair; "hoping against hope," we find ourselves at the abyss created by fear of death and in desperate need of divine intervention. Those who have experienced such despair have also come to experience the elements of hope.

## Correspondences of Hope

Hope has to do with the future, with possibility, and with the resolution of suffering. In this dialectic, hope enters in, however meekly, and contradicts the experience of suffering itself, thus opening up the prospect of a better future. Hope vitiates suffering. As we have seen, hope is subtler than its usual portrayal in popular Christian belief as "triumph." It might rather be seen as dialectic with despair—hope teeters, as it were, between despair and confidence. It plays out in the balancing act of the assurance of a particular future versus resignation to an uncertain future.

Suffering creates anxiety about the certainty of an outcome in such a way that it calls out the correspondences of hope. In the next section we will explore some of the key insights of the theologians of suffering in regards to these particular correspondences and locate them in connection with the aspects of the eclipse of hope that we have already reflected on. Theologians who have particularly impacted my thinking are Dorothee Soelle, Jürgen Moltmann, and Gustavo Gutiérrez. I will take each of these in turn and locate their "dared suspicions" about suffering and hope—looking all the while for correspondences to the subtle persistence of hope. These three scholars all take a different approach to the theology of suffering; however, as I hope to demonstrate, there are certain corresponding ideas that are shared in these approaches and serve to clarify our understanding of hope in suffering.

### Dorothee Soelle
### Hope as Solidarity

Dorothee Soelle invests heavily in the social protestation of suffering. In her view, suffering should not be easily tolerated or accepted in a fatalistic way. Such easy acquiescence to suffering leads to what she thinks of as the premature acceptance of suffering. She insists that resistance to suffering is imperative in all circumstances, and she argues against any theological justification for pietistic acceptance of suffering as God's will. Soelle is careful to show that she is not attacking the ways that people use the Bible to support their hope, but she is critical of theological systems that pigeonhole and systematize suffering in inappropriate ways.[9]

This is an important corrective to suffering that is embraced in defeat, especially to those causes of suffering that underlie the social and preventable aspects of suffering to which the Christian faith is opposed. Hope is active, in this view, as an impetus to overcome the root causes of suffering. It compels us to action—to overcome the origins of that suffering. Soelle sees hope as the capacity to protest the unfair reality of suffering as it crushes our individual and collective spirit.

In Soelle's approach hope involves the expression of suffering in order to mobilize the caring community to confront and overcome the causes of suffering. This element emerges, in her view, through the expression of lament, which is the language of pain. The hopeful pro-testation of suffering, articulated in the prayer of lament, is called for as an act by which people dare to put their desires into words.[10] Hope-lessness is accentuated through the inability to express suffering or the reality of the suffering situation.[11] Hope catalyzes the suffering person to describe the situation of suffering rather than acquiesce to it in pre-mature acceptance.

This act of lament is also a call to the community to share in hope through the active participation in solidarity with the suffering situa-tion. This impulse to fight against suffering and to embrace the responsi-bility of overcoming its causes is founded on the "conviction that we live in a world that can be changed."[12] Hope and action are fundamentally entwined as we act on the responsibility to share in the suffering of oth-ers and organize for liberation of the oppressed.[13]

Soelle's movements of hope may be summarized in her paradigm: isolation—expression/communication—solidarity. In many ways this activity is the pattern of hoping in the situation of suffering. Rather than accept suffering as "willed by God" and thereby surrender to help-lessness, the suffering situation calls for lament, which is the begin-ning point for hope in Soelle's scheme. In describing the expression of suffering by a fifty-five-year-old foundry worker from a metal factory in Düsseldorf, Soelle identifies what, for her, is the locus of hope: "A phrase like 'Believe me, folks!' is a modern day psalm. The worker's objectives are not organized as yet; they still appear—as in prayer—as utopian wishes. What is depicted is really suffering, but it is no lon-ger at the stage of submissiveness. His language is 'psalmic language.' . . . The repeated phrase, 'Believe me, folks!' occupies exactly the same place occupied in the ancient psalms by, 'Hear me, O God; hear my supplication.'"[14]

Soelle's approach to the subtle persistence of hope therefore contests the common retributive approach that sees the root cause of suffering as a deserved punishment caused by offense to God. She prefers to start by assuming that the conditions of suffering have their root cause in unjust structures and the actions of oppressors. The corresponding elements of hope include the expression of the true situation of suffering itself and the organizing of the community in solidarity with those who suffer. Rather than *premature acceptance* of suffering, sufferers are invited to act on their hope through petition and expression, thereby overcoming the posture of acquiescence and inviting the participation of the community to overcome the causes of suffering itself.

The commendable framework for Dorothee Soelle's view of hope is its powerful insistence on human agency in overcoming suffering. Hope is enacted as the community works together for justice and for the elimination of suffering. Soelle develops her theological ideas of hope in the context of the most difficult questions of life in Germany in the time of writing. She faces up to the memory of the Holocaust, the war in Vietnam, and other tragedies of her day. The posture of resistance and determination are embedded in her view of hope. This too is rooted in a radical mysticism—or prayer. Her mysticism denotes "attention . . . from which creative ability springs, and at its highest level it is equivalent to prayer."[15] Soelle sees prayer as a subversive act, and in many ways she offers us a potent reminder of the focus of true prayer in the spiritual struggle against suffering.

There are important lessons in this approach to the theology of hope. The first is the call to anchor our theology of suffering in history and concrete reality. Many times we speak about suffering generally and fail to take seriously the rooted situation of suffering and the concrete situation that has given rise to that suffering. The insistence that we must truly see the concrete situation and the social conditions that underlie it is an important idea. Only then can suffering be expressed and overcome. This is an important corrective for much theologizing on the theme of suffering and is, in its own way, a support for a theology of hope.

Another element that is crucial is the insistence that the "lament" phase of suffering cannot be skipped. What gave Soelle this insight is not clear. However, here lies one of her most important contributions (in my view) to the theology of suffering—the almost innocuous principle "to at least say what the situation is."[16] In Soelle's terms, "The first step towards overcoming suffering is, then, to find a language that leads out of the uncomprehended suffering that makes one mute, a language of lament, of crying, of pain, a language that at least says what the situation is."[17]

This insight also leads to the expression of hope in language that is experience-near. Soelle issued a challenge not to give up theological language but rather to embark on the search for a new theological language.[18] It is her view that theology, in its essence, has the task of enlarging the borders of our language.[19] This has been an important test of the word-articulating efforts of the theology of suffering attempted in this volume. I am grateful to Soelle for her skillful challenge and the inspiration that it gave me to search for new language, even theopoetic language, to correspond with the reality of suffering and the subtle persistence of hope.

**Ich komme aus meinen Schwingen heim**

I come home from the soaring
in which I lost myself.
I was song, and the refrain which is God
is still roaring in my ears.

Now I am still
and plain:
no more words.

To the others I was like a wind:
I made them shake.
I'd gone very far, as far as the angels,
and high, where light thins into nothing.

But deep in the darkness is God.

—Rainer Maria Rilke, I, 50[20]

*Jürgen Moltmann*
## Resurrection as Protest

Jürgen Moltmann's contribution to the theology of suffering has been important and constructive. His theology of the cross was a serious attempt to locate the suffering of God within God the Trinity. But before I move to some of the seminal insights in his theological treatises, I want to show how his own prayerful and hopeful way of seeing life has impacted his voice as a theologian.

In *Experiences of God*, Moltmann describes what he calls "signposts and experiences" that led to his particular "theological perception."[21] Among the things he shares in this autobiographical piece is his experience as a prisoner of war from February 1945 to April 1948:

I was taken prisoner by the British, and for over three years I was moved about from camp to camp in Belgium, Scotland and England. . . . The break-up

of the German front, the collapse of law and humanity, the self-destruc-
tion of German civilization and culture, and finally the appalling end of
9 May 1945—all this was followed by the revelation of the crimes which had
been committed in Germany's name—Buchenwald, Auschwitz, Maidanek,
Bergen-Belsen and the rest. And with that came the necessity of standing up
to it all inwardly, shut up in camps as we were. I think my own little world
fell to pieces then too. The "iron rations" I had with me were quickly used
up, and what remained left a stale taste in the mouth. In that Belgian camp,
hungry as we were, I saw how other men collapsed inwardly, how they gave
up all hope, sickening for the lack of it, some of them dying. The same thing
almost happened to me. . . .

And yet the experience of misery and forsakenness and daily humiliation gradually built up into an experience of God. It was the experience of
God's presence in the dark night of the soul: "If I make my bed in hell, thou
art there." A well-meaning army chaplain had given me a New Testament. I
thought it was out of place. I would rather have had something to eat. But
then I became fascinated by the Psalms (which were printed in an appendix)
and especially by Psalm 39: "I was dumb with silence, I held my peace, even
from good; and my sorrow was stirred" (but the German is much stronger—
"I have to eat up my grief within myself"). . . . "Hold thou not thy peace at my
tears: for I am a stranger with thee, and a sojourner, as all my fathers were."
These psalms gave me the words for my own suffering. They opened my eyes
to the God who is with those "that are of a broken heart." He was present
even behind the barbed wire—no, most of all behind the barbed wire. But
whenever in my despair I wanted to lay firm hold on this experience, it eluded
me again, and there I was with empty hands once more. All that was left was
an inward drive, a longing which provided the impetus to hope.[22]

This self-disclosure is an important springboard for understanding the theology of Moltmann. The revelations of his experiences are
at the root of his theological approach, and he will go on to say things
like, "Christianity is completely and entirely and utterly hope—a looking forward and a forward direction; hope is not just an appendix. So
Christianity inevitably means a new setting forth and a transformation
of the present."[23]

Moltmann sees the divine protest at the root of hope. A crucial
insight into his theology of hope is set forth in *Experiences of God*,

For [the hoping person] the resurrection of Christ is not merely consolation
in suffering; it is also the sign of God's protest against suffering. That is why
whenever faith develops into hope it does not make people serene and placid;
it makes them restless. It does not make them patient; it makes them impatient. Instead of being reconciled to existing reality they begin to suffer from
it and to resist it.[24]

Moltmann sees implications for Christian discipleship in the embracing
of the cross of the risen Christ. Those who hope in Christ can no longer

put up with reality as it is, but begin to contradict it.[25] Moltmann follows this line of thinking through and expands in several key volumes the seminal insight contained in this vision. He is compelled, from his own experience of almost losing hope, to articulate a reason for Christian hope and the compelling idea of how hope functions. He maintains his deep commitment to discipleship and calls the church to live out this discipleship in concrete commitments of faith, hope, and love.

Moltmann's contribution to a theology of suffering is primarily the working out of the suffering and compassion of God in a Trinitarian theology. Here Moltmann attempts to say how it is that God suffers and offers the meaning of God's suffering for the sufferings of the world.

There are several elements of Moltmann's correspondences with hope that I want to acknowledge. First, Moltmann is careful to attend to the seriousness of suffering. He is intent to demonstrate that a theology of suffering will take into account the painful realities of all those who feel themselves cut off from God. The key concept of *godforsakenness* in the cross of Christ is at the center of this theological exposition of God's suffering.[26] Here Moltmann creatively combines a profound concern for the reality of affliction in the lives of those who trust in God with a theological understanding of what the "cross of the risen Christ" means for God. Moltmann's lively views have sparked heightened interest in the theology of the cross.

More than his theology of the cross, Moltmann's theology of hope became a crucible for the correspondences of hope. In particular Moltmann expresses a new "expectation-thinking" that corresponds to the Christian hope.[27]

A third important dimension of Moltmann's theology is his concept of God's solidarity with suffering. God's solidarity with those who suffer does not abolish suffering; it eliminates suffering in isolation.[28] In both his articulation of what suffering means for God and what suffering means for humanity, Moltmann pushes the limit of experience. He attempts to pursue the threads of suffering at its root. What does suffering mean for God in the cross of the risen Christ? And what does suffering mean for those who find themselves in the silence of God or in the experience of godforsakenness?

The subtle persistence of hope, for Moltmann, is not, as one would expect, the great horizons of eschatological fulfillment. While he attends to this horizon as the fundamental orientation of his theology, he is also very careful to express what this means for the present. The hope that we experience in the midst of godforsakenness is hope founded on the promises of God who is making the future.

Moltmann shares the commitment of those theologians who have a high view of human responsibility in the care of the creation. He does not explain away aspects of human sin and suffering that are the result of human error. In fact, he sees the responsibility of the church to live out its vocation as the community of hope and to work for the restoration of justice in the world.

This theocentric option gives light to the question of the subtle persistence of hope. True hope comes from God. God, who is for us, is the author of the promise of hope. God, who is for us, establishes intervention at the point of our greatest need. And God, our source and origin, is making all things new. There is a kind of mysticism in Moltmann's voice—he sees something that he is compelled to articulate. This invitation to see God as the one who suffers the "sufferings of Christ" probes the very mystery of our hope that is rooted in trust.

### Gustavo Gutiérrez
### The Hope of Spiritual Struggle in Job

Gustavo Gutiérrez approaches the question of hope by a careful exposition of the book of Job from the perspective of "the center of the world"— "so called because the crucified Jesus dwells there, and with him all who suffer unjustly, all the poor and despised of the earth."[29] His interest is to explore the kind of language or talk about God that would be appropriate from this center point and to find, in the theology of the book of Job, fresh insight into the suffering of the innocent.

In order to do this, Gutiérrez explains his method of spiritual reflection that precedes theologizing. For Gutiérrez the hope that God brings must first be contemplated and lived. In his words, "God is first contemplated when we do God's will and allow God to reign; only after that do we think about God."[30]

Gutiérrez reformulates authentic theology as "speech enriched by silence."[31] Gutiérrez then uses this method to explore the book of Job. Armed with the deep conviction that the Bible should be read from the perspective of our deepest need,[32] Gutiérrez explores the themes of the book of Job to test the authenticity of "disinterested faith"[33]—can Job believe for nothing? If so, Job becomes a paradigm of the suffering innocent who are always in the mind of Gutiérrez as he writes. In fact, he is conscious of the reality of *suffering of the innocent* as the backdrop for his entire interpretation of the book of Job.

He notes that, much like the suffering innocent of Latin America, Job expresses his hope by not giving into despair about the desperate suffering he is enduring. The book of Job, in Gutiérrez' reading, is a "gradual immersion in suffering."[34] While Job's "comforters" believe in their theology, Job resists the "convenient and soothing doctrine"[35] of retribution because it fails to account for Job's experience of suffering (Job 13:1-4).

Gutiérrez also declares his perspective that at the center of suffering is loneliness. Job is alienated first by the doctrine of retribution, which he does not accept as the cause of his suffering. Second, he is alienated by the friends whose "sorry comfort" deepens Job's loneliness. And finally, Job turns in on himself—the low point of loneliness and abandonment.

Yet, hope continues to spur Job on to "penetrate more deeply"[36] and refine his thinking about God. Job refuses to do the kind of theologizing that is not grounded in the reality of suffering. Here Gutiérrez makes one of his key points in the theology of suffering: "The language we use depends on the situation we are in. Job's words are a criticism of every theology that lacks human compassion and contact with reality; the one-directional movement from theological principles to life really goes nowhere."[37]

Gutiérrez sees a fivefold theological progression in the book of Job:[38]

1. widening the scope to the plight of the poor (a key interpretive move in Gutiérrez' approach to Job);
2. engagement in debate/dialogue through the speeches;
3. certain nuances come to the fore in this widening progression;
4. there is something "new to say"; and
5. the dialogue broadens to speak meaningfully about God in suffering.

This, in turn, in Gutiérrez' reading of Job, leads to a threefold spiritual struggle. Job's need of an arbiter (Job 9:33); Job's call for a witness to his innocent suffering (16:19); and finally, the hope of a *go'el*—a liberator or defender who will come to Job's rescue (19:25). The subtle persistence of hope is seen in Job's growing faith that God will be the *go'el*— and come to Job's defense. This growing conviction is the center of the spiritual struggle. Gutiérrez recognizes the growing flame of hope in the progression of Job's resistance. The book of Job demonstrates, according to Gutiérrez, a gradual increase in Job's faith and hope. From the small request for the presence of an arbiter, Job moves to the need for a witness and finally to a profound expression of confidence in a liberator who will come to rescue him. "The spiritual struggle with himself, with his friends, and, above all, with God brings him to a conviction that for the time being amounts to no more than a cry of hope: then he will see, and with his own eyes, his liberator, his *go'el*, and be able to look upon him as a friend."[39]

It is only here that Gutiérrez is able to bring his theology of suffering into full view. We see in the concluding dialogue between Job and God a correct way of speaking about God—mystical and prophetic language. "Mystical language expresses the gratuitousness of God's love; prophetic language expresses the demands this love makes."[40] God is not indifferent to suffering, but in God's freedom he has acted in love toward humanity. The cross is the fulcrum of God's love in the world.

Protest and lament in the Bible point to God's freedom and God's love most fully expressed in the suffering and abandonment of Christ. "To adopt a comparison that Bonhoeffer uses in another context, the cry of Jesus is the *cantus firmus*, the leading voice to which all the voices of those who suffer unjustly are joined."[41]

## Conclusion

In this chapter we have pursued the delicate relationship between suffering and hope as presented in the Bible and in the dared suspicions of theologians who have articulated their best understandings. The subtle persistence of hope is a veiled reality at the root of suffering. Many expressions of hope in Christian thought are much more triumphal than what we have presented in this chapter. However, there are several congruencies of thought between the various perspectives we have explored. All of the theologians, in their own words, have articulated some aspect of human responsibility to act in the interest of justice and to work for the alleviation of human suffering as part of the gospel ethic. The alleviation of suffering, in all three theologians that dare their suspicions, is a core dimension of authentic discipleship and a path to shared hope. There is further agreement that the loneliness and abandonment that are experienced by the most forgotten and forsaken of this world have been taken up in the suffering, passion, and cross of Christ. Each of the theologians we have studied offers a caution concerning words about God and suffering—true affliction is not easily articulated. We must find a new language—a language that is equal to the reality of suffering itself. Furthermore, this reality must be grounded in concrete situations of suffering that pay attention to the dynamics of suffering and hope. This requires a new way of doing theology—a contemplative and prophetic theology. In order to accomplish this, we need to practice absolute, unmixed attention—prayer. We must attend at once to the signs of suffering and the subtle persistence of hope in all of life.

# Ministry with the Afflicted

Ministers and caregivers have the sacred task of entering into the suffering of others. This work is very difficult and challenging. We have seen throughout this volume the complexities of the reality of suffering in the world. We have also attempted to articulate the presence and absence of God in the face of these realities. This moves us inextricably to the terrain of mystery—both the mystery of suffering and, even more, the mystery of God's love in the face of unspeakable affliction. Hints at the responses of ministering persons have been noted throughout the volume, but it behooves us to explore in greater detail those actions and practices that might enable a more hopeful participation in life for those who suffer in extremis.

The spiritual work of ministry with those who suffer begins with the recognition that at the root of a theological interpretation of suffering is the greater challenge of *helping people in very concrete and complex situations.* The exploration of the depths of these situations of suffering has always been at the heart of pastoral theology as a discipline. This volume, therefore, seeks to bring into focus both the framework for ministry with the afflicted and concrete proposals for the actions and practices that enable compassionate ministry. I begin this chapter by outlining four foundations for ministry with the afflicted: a willingness to embrace suffering, a life marked by prophetic engagement, the courage to risk compassionate involvement, and finally, communion with God who suffers with us.[1] In the second half of this chapter, I wish to move to specific actions and practices that would alleviate the suffering of the afflicted in the hope that these would enable the Christian community to respond with compassionate protest as the pilgrim community of God. The first foundation for our framework for ministry to the afflicted is a willingness to embrace suffering.

## A Willingness to Embrace Suffering

> *What is a poet? A poet is an unhappy being whose heart is torn by secret*
> *sufferings, but whose lips are so strangely formed that when the sighs and the*
> *cries escape them, they sound like beautiful music . . . and men crowd about the*
> *poet and say to him: "Sing for us soon again"; that is as much as to say,*
> *"May new sufferings torment your soul, but may your lips be formed as before;*
> *the cries would only frighten us, but the music is delicious."*[2]

Ministry involves embracing suffering and ministering out of the depths of our experiences in life. I have referred to this elsewhere as the work of "the attentive poet."[3] This metaphor of the ministering person captures both the "speaking" and the "silence" aspects of compassionate communication. Pastoral responses to the anguish of others require full attention or, as we have already seen, "absolutely unmixed attention."[4]

There are several features of this prayerful response of absolute, unmixed attention that I would like to suggest. First, the attentive poet gives heeds to the reality of brokenness in the world. She resists easy classification of persons, values, ideas, concepts, or experience. The attentive poet is immersed in "the depth dimension of reality,"[5] realizing that only by our own immersion in the suffering of the world are we able to begin to speak about the dimensions that are opened up by the words we use.[6] The core skill of the attentive poet is what Henri Nouwen terms "sensitive articulation."[7]

The sensitive articulation of the attentive poet requires that we speak in careful ways to those who are suffering, shifting our attention from theological reflection to spirituality and from prose to theopoetic speaking.[8] This must be more than merely calling up religious imagination for the purpose of making the faith more interesting. Rather, the call to the theopoetic must search out a language that can express the ineffable mysteries of suffering.[9] Theopoetic speaking, much like the laments of the Old Testament, is able to absorb the angst of life and communicate the hidden dimensions of suffering that lie buried in the experience of the afflicted.

Secondly, the attentive poet reads the wind (Heb. *ruach*) of God. She gives her absolute, unmixed attention to the wind of God, the brokenness in the world, and the suffering in our own hearts. To be God's people in a broken world requires spiritual lives that embrace suffering. Also, this is a call to live lives that are marked by attention to the contours of suffering and hope. Spiritual maturity is required if we are going to be able to take on board the complexities and ambiguities of the life situations of suffering. Such spiritual living involves a commitment to enter into the community of God as participants who are attentive, listening, and obedient. We hear the wind blow and we do not know where it is coming from or where it is going (cf. John 3:8).

Finally, the work of the attentive poet is an invitation to take heed to the contours of suffering and hope. The attentive poet is near to those who suffer, and by this sustaining presence, becomes a sign of hope. Donald Capps reminds us of the narrative in *Pilgrim's Progress* as the signature of pastoral engagement with those in need of hope.[10] Like Pilgrim's friend Hopeful, the attentive poet calls out to the one who is sinking in despair—"Do not be afraid, I have felt the bottom and know that it is good."

## Engagement with the Suffering World

The second foundation for ministry to the afflicted is engagement with the suffering world. This requires openness to the world and a capacity to move into the situations of despair, anguish, and hopelessness. In order to cultivate this spirit of openness, we must be prepared to give up on premature answers and probe more deeply into the complexities of life. The moral vision for deep engagement with suffering requires a new way of seeing and a new way of living. We must live with our hearts open to the brokenness of the world in all of its complexity and with all of its ambiguities.

The discipline of solidarity is more than simply acknowledging the suffering of others. It requires the capacity to be open to the risks of entering into the situations of suffering with compassion. Furthermore, this requires careful listening to the call of God the Spirit who invites us to participate in the ministry of reconciliation.[11]

The person who abides in God is engaged with culture not as a distant observer but as a participant who is grounded in eternal hopefulness. To be God's person is to remain postured toward God in a disposition of God who is "for us."

How is this enacted? First, it will call for the expression of the "lament" of the community. In recognizing the seriousness of suffering, we do not call out from a safe distance, but rather we enter into the ambiguity of the situation. Prophetic speaking requires participation in the human condition and an ongoing commitment to the life with and for others. As we live faithfully in a broken world, we form the lament of the community.

The action of true solidarity requires that we stay in the situation of the afflicted, the excluded, the forgotten, and the most vulnerable. This posture in the world provides a critical perspective and gives form to the lament of the community in search of God. This moral posture in the world is in radical opposition to the type of religious piety that claims moral supremacy while neglecting the root causes of injustice. To engage the brokenness of the world means recognizing the interconnectedness of all human situations and taking up a broader commitment to the well-being of others—a commitment that is fundamentally grounded in the intentions of God and God's infinite love expressed most fully in the cross.

## The Courage for Compassionate Ministry

Compassionate ministry requires a profound courage. This is the third foundation for ministry to the afflicted. This courageous risk of "suffering with" others is an essential element of pastoral ministry to the most afflicted. In order to move into the situations of the afflicted, we need to dare involvement. Moral vision is not enough. We must find the inner animation of God's Spirit that moves us into action. We must move toward suffering rather than withdraw from it. This countercultural pull to service requires a kind of spiritual daring.

In his description of courage, Edward Farley outlines three aspects of courage: relativizing, consent, and risk of being.[12] He distinguishes relativizing from relativism in that the former is an "existential attitude" that "restores to goods at hand their historical character, thus, their contextuality, their fragility to change and demise, and even corruptibility."[13] We therefore cannot succumb to idolatry as we come to terms with the biblical picture of reality as it really is. Consent is an aspect of courage that Farley (following Jonathan Edwards and Friedrich Schleiermacher) understands to be "more like the positivity of aesthetic experience than the negativity of resignation."[14] Consent allows for contingency, tragedy, and brokenness by affirming the reality of life as it is without attitudes of "discontent, anxiety, and the refusal of finitude that is part of the complex posture of courage."[15] Risk of being is the third attitude that "shapes the posture of courage."[16] This results in a posture of turning toward the world even in the face of "perilous situations of being," as the "self is founded by the presence of the sacred."[17]

Courage in the face of the complexities of life in a good but fallen world is at the heart of a pastoral theology of suffering. Ministry inherently moves into the complexity of suffering with awareness that only in the presence of God can we enter such an abyss. This, then, leads to the fourth foundation of our framework for ministry with the afflicted, communion with a suffering God.

## Communion with a Suffering God

We turn to the fourth and final element of a framework for ministry with the afflicted, communion with God. Communion with God is the foundation of our spiritual life together. At the root of this communion is the experience God's abiding love. Our first love is directed toward intimacy with God. However, at the core of this call to communion with God is the question of God's suffering love. The very question of God's presence or absence in times of distress and affliction is at the core of the themes addressed in this volume. If we take communion with God as a central motif of the Christian experience, then is it crucial that we explore God's suffering love. The person who suffers wonders if indeed God can be encountered in the very depths of his or her anguish. Restoring communion with God is no simple task for the person whose spiritual life has been disrupted by the reality of intense suffering. Yet this is the very aspect of ministry with the suffering that requires our noblest effort.

## Practices of Ministry to the Suffering

Affliction, we have seen, threatens all dimensions of life. Therefore our efforts to protect the spiritual vitality of those who are in affliction calls for our efforts to sustain them in all dimensions of their suffering: relieving physical pain, healing psychological anguish, restoring social dignity, and alleviating spiritual despondency. While not exhaustive, the following practices are intended to help those who care for the most afflicted to discern that work with care and precision of response to the needs of those who suffer in extremis.

*Enact the Paradigm*
## From Silence to Lament, from Indifference to Compassion, from Loneliness to Community

In this book I have been arguing for a paradigmatic approach to the theology of suffering. The paradigm proposed in this volume offers a framework from which to minister meaningfully and respectfully with those who suffer. This paradigm assists ministering persons who intuitively recognize the complexity of the task of caring for the afflicted. Moving into the multivalent situation of those who suffer requires more than pastoral sensitivity. It requires a mature understanding of the contours of suffering and hope so that the very realities of this situation can be navigated without minimizing the seriousness of the circumstances involved.

### From Silence to Lament

Our initial encounters with suffering persons call for a profound acknowledgment that their suffering is so severe that nothing can be said (mutism/silence). This is difficult for those who often feel obligated to speak for God in the situation. However, our first response as pastors and caregivers must be to share in the hushed silence of the most afflicted. Lament, the sensitive articulation of the situation, comes only after an appropriate period of silent grief. Enacting the paradigm begins with the willingness to live with the questions and to demonstrate our solidarity through tears more than words. In due course, lament emerges, but in the beginning we must be ever vigilant about the respect due to those who suffer in extremis.

### From Indifference to Compassion

The practice of entering into the suffering of others with active help (compassion) requires a deeper understanding of the dynamics of why we withdraw from the suffering of others in the first place. Compassion is not a practice that we can easily take up as though it were our natural response to suffering. It is a countercultural and spiritual skill of entering into to the anguishing situation of others. When we acknowledge our indifference, we break its power in our lives and are free to pursue compassion as our deepest vocation. We can test how often we in fact move away from situations of conflict, of pain, and of suffering. If we self-consciously would come to terms with the roots of apathy and indifference that still appear in our lives, we would begin to see how to shape our capacity to act in compassion where we are most needed.

From Loneliness to Community

Suffering cuts us off from others in such a way that the afflicted person [or family] feels that the help required is not forthcoming. Loneliness is *the suffering in suffering*. The inner experience of suffering in isolation increases the sense of desolation and abandonment that often comes with the experience of affliction. This calls for a reorientation of the faith community to a posture of support and presence. Telling people they are not alone in their suffering is not enough. We must demonstrate our care through the act of showing up in their lives. At its core, ministry to the suffering means coming near in their time of grave concern and anguish. The activity that we must generate as the compassionate community of God is the capacity to discern where the greatest needs are and to simply show up. In this way we dispel the dark cloud of abandonment and rejection, enabling suffering persons to experience themselves as loved and cared for by others.

We must remember that it is more natural to move away from suffering. The reality of anguish, affliction, and pain is very hard to bear. Knowing this is an important step to helping. Our tendency to withdraw requires that we heighten our awareness of our movement away from rather than toward those who are suffering. In our ministry, our movements must enter into the experience of the other in such a way as to relieve the person's sense of isolation, forsakenness, and abandonment. Our presence in the life situation of the suffering is a concrete measure of authentic compassion.

### Renew the Liturgical Practice of Lamentation

There are many calls for the renewal of the practice of lament in the church. Artful attention to Sergei Rachmaninoff's *All-Night Vigil* may be the beginning of a reorientation—the sounds of "deep calling to deep" (Ps 42:7). We have not only lost the capacity to lament because of theological triumphalism, we have also lost the language of lament and the mood of lamentation as core spiritual aspects of this spiritual practice. Part of the work required is a renewal of lament as a theological category, but the reforms must go further, effecting the transformation of our liturgical practices in the church. The practice of lament will begin with sighs and groans. The spiritual searching of the lament is not merely a mood that needs to be set in our ecclesial contexts, but rather an orientation to darkness, to night, to suffering, and to the abyss of the soul far from God.

## *Stay Near to the Fires of Affliction*

Fire might well be thought of as a significant biblical metaphor for affliction. "When you walk through the fire, you will not be burned; the flames will not set you ablaze" (Isa 43:2). The seriousness of suffering is like a situation where fire consumes and destroys. Nearness is an important pastoral response to the afflicted. A theology of nearness is required that allows us to confront the danger of entering into the terrain of affliction. The spiritual disciplines required to shape this moral engagement of suffering will be characterized by prayer, fasting, and contemplation. So much of Christian ministry is rooted in the practices of vital communion with God. Without these disciplines anchoring us in the situations of affliction, we ourselves are at risk. Spiritual ministry requires profound spiritual preparation.

## *Protect the Spiritual Vitality of Those Who Are Suffering*

The hope of those who are in affliction is already diminished by their situation. To come alongside those who are suffering requires attention to their vulnerable spiritual state. Pastors and caregivers should be awake to the fragility of the hope that resides in those whose life is torn apart by affliction. Protecting hope requires a vigilant accompanying of persons in need. Our very presence in the life situations of the afflicted is a sign of hope and an important counterweight to the oppressive anxiety and fear that come with suffering.

The presence of a consoling person in the darkness nurtures the anguished soul. The presence of a caring person or persons dispels the mounting angst that accompanies affliction. Here, in the very depths of the abyss of suffering, the very world of the afflicted is threatened. It is this spiritual dimension that is at the core of the pastoral task—to restore hope where hope has been all but destroyed by life. The work of ministering persons is to accompany those who are afflicted by life in the darkness of their spiritual night. Suffering persons need to know that they are not abandoned in their situation, and they need to experience the tangible care of the Christian community.

John Feinberg describes what he terms the "things that help"[18] as he recalls the painful journey of watching his beloved wife, Pat, die of Huntington's chorea. He writes,

> I have written about the need to care and show it, in the midst of a person's suffering, because I am so convinced of how crucial that is. By our words and deeds, we must show those who are hurting that we really care. And, by all

means, we must show it by not avoiding those who suffer for fear that we may say the wrong thing. Be there anyway, even if you say nothing. Your presence and willingness to listen is enough. When we keep our distance from those who suffer, we confirm their worst fears that no one cares and no one will help.[19]

## Cultivate Practices That Instill Hope

### Facilitate a Perception That What Is Wanted Will Happen

Hopeful presence means helping persons to gain conviction that those things which they hope for can happen. "Without the sense that what we want to happen will in fact happen, there is no hope. Without this sense of things, we are hopeless, bereft of hope."[20] Hoping is unexplainable in purely objective terms. There is "a subjective element in hoping."[21] It is because of this subjective element that hoping is often experienced as a "solitary act."[22] Wherever hoping occurs, we are likely to see deep disagreements among individuals as those who do not share the other's hope.

### Help Others to Name the Persisting Desire That Gives Rise to Their Hopes

Hope and desire are closely linked. The clarification of our desires can actually strengthen the spiritual staying power of those who are broken by life and diminished by the lack of clarity in their desires.[23] We have seen how suffering erodes our capacity to say what is really going on. The clarification of desires opens up the anticipation of a new future and begins the process of healing. Hope and desire are linked in this capacity to articulate what it is that we really want to see happen in a situation that otherwise seems hopeless.

### Help People to Restore What Has Been Lost

Hope and deprivation are inextricably linked: we hope for something we had but lost and deeply desire to retrieve or we hope for something that we have never had but that we strongly believe will make our life more meaningful and therefore hold it as a deep longing. "One reason our hopes are sometimes so difficult to identify or define is because the lack we feel is deeply personal, and these deep personal deprivations are hard to put into words."[24] Our unnamed losses have a profound effect on our capacity to remain hopeful. We have a deep-seated need to retrieve or restore something valuable. As Fredrick T. Melges states, "With hope, the personal future is not certain and fixed but is viewed as being open, unfrozen, and full of opportunities."[25]

*Nurture the Formation of the Congregation*
*as a Community of Care*

Church congregations are an odd mixture of doing and being. When ecclesial communities try to separate actions from their identity as a faith community, they are often reduced to mere pragmatism and perfunctory actions. Therefore, the call to the practices of care must be combined with the identity-forming vision of renewing the ecclesial communities in which we participate. The compassionate community of God involves the cultivation of caring clusters that inhabit the gospel.[26]

This doing/being community of care requires a formative vision. By articulating and living into a formative vision of the church as a caring community, Christian congregations define improved parameters of what it means to practice authentic ministry. This book has advocated for a vision of *the compassionate community of God* as the defining description of ecclesial communities whose desire is to care for the suffering. Living out this conception of the church necessitates a deeper acknowledgment of the full significance of such a vision.

Compassion must not be seen as an optional aspect of authentic Christian ministry, but a summative depiction of our core identity as a people who imitate God. If, as I have argued, compassion is a controlling metaphor of God's own character, then it is the theological nexus to take this metaphor as a central and abiding depiction of the church's mandate in the world. We witness to the mission of God and take up God's own compassionate action in the world as we live the true ecclesial vocation of the church as the compassionate community of God.

*Intercede for Those Who Suffer*

Prayer for those who suffer is a core action of alignment with the Spirit of God who "intercedes for us with groans that words cannot express" (Rom 8:26b). Entry into the depths of the situation of the afflicted is painful and difficult. The Christian community is called, in that darkest place, to intercede on behalf of those who suffer, even if "we do not know what we ought to pray for" (Rom 8:26a). There is a mystery to suffering. This mystery is rooted in the groaning of creation (Rom 8:22). The promptings of the Spirit to pray for those in affliction must be carefully heeded. This inner sensitivity to the Spirit's whisper moves us to the ministry of intercession. This deepens the recognition that all suffering requires God's intervention and comfort. Prayer is more than alignment with the purposes of God. It is also a full participation in the mind of the

Spirit and a reorientation to God's own reconciling action in the world. The situation of those who suffer involves intractable complexities that are rooted in a broken creation. Without God's help and intervention such realities are too much to bear.[27]

Ministry with those who suffer will call for a persistent action of prayer. While we fight against the root causes of suffering, the compassionate community of God must also lift up the anguish of those who suffer to the "Father of compassion and the God of all comfort, who comforts us in all our troubles" (2 Cor 1:3-4).

### Protest and Resist the Underlying Causes of Suffering

Ministry has a prophetic dimension that will not put up with the conditions that give rise to the suffering of others. So much suffering is caused by oppression, injustice, and blind acquiescence to conditions that ought to be protested, resisted, and overcome. The church must not prematurely accept suffering and thus reinforce apathy. We must recognize the suffering that we can curtail and the suffering that we can eliminate through efforts of compassionate engagement. Compassionate ministry has a profound un-ease with the conditions that give rise to the suffering of others and works tirelessly to overcome these conditions. As Henry David Thoreau stated, "For every thousand hacking at the leaves of evil, there is one striking at the root."[28]

### Cultivate the Wise Embodiment of a Theology of Suffering in the Community of Faith

One of the primary aims of this volume has been to expose premature and incomplete "answers" to what is often termed "the problem of suffering." By proposing a riddle approach to the theodicy question, we have often misplaced our thinking about God and the experience of suffering. This approach reduces the reality of suffering to a propositional exchange. Our posture of faith in responding to the reality of the afflicted requires a lived theology rather than a propositional approach to the questions of theodicy. Suffering, we have noted, is a reality to be confronted with God's help. The biblical affirmation of this reality needs to be our starting point for any thoughtful approach to the theology of suffering. The Christian community must live out its faith in a way that "takes on board" the complexity and ambiguity of a life in a broken world.

Taking up a biblical theology of suffering is no easy task. However, when approached from the perspective of lived wisdom, this task is grounded in the biblical vision of a reconciled creation. We cannot fully know what God is doing at any given time, but the orientation of faith in God grounds our very lives and communities in the narrative of God's reconciling action in the world. At the root, this lived wisdom confronts and replaces a propositional approach and enables a resilient fidelity despite the sorrows and hurts of life in a broken world.[29] The church must live out the compassion of God in the face of unspeakable suffering. While knowledge may be fragile and incomplete, it is nonetheless a matter of fidelity to God who is revealed in Scripture as "compassionate and gracious, slow to anger and abounding in love" (Ps 103:8).

## Conclusion

Entering into the complex situations of the most afflicted will require a more fully developed framework of pastoral theology and greater tenacity in employing those practices that will foster and sustain hope in the lives of the most afflicted. The call of this book has been to *absolute, unmixed attention* to the contours of suffering and the subtle persistence of hope. A theology of suffering will be more tears than words, as the words are symbols of a deeper experience that cannot be fully named. The experiences of suffering often leave the sufferer mute and alone in their experience of forsakenness. The "whole creation has been groaning," "we ourselves . . . groan," and the Holy Spirit of God "intercedes for us with groans that are too deep for words" (Rom 8:22-27). This is the mystery of the reality of suffering in our lives. We move into the sacred with prayerful attention—awake to the call of compassion—to *suffer with* those whose lives have been threatened in every dimension.

Persons who are in affliction and experiencing the multivalent realities of physical pain, psychological anguish, social degradation, and spiritual desolation are in desperate need of the consolation and love of the Christian community. Failure to fully understand the depths of the suffering situation eclipses hope and the capacity for compassion. The call to courageous engagement is an invitation to new risks of compassionate protest. The roots of suffering will seldom be open to us. However, the church must not easily acquiesce to the situation of suffering or succumb to the indifference that often accompanies overexposure to the suffering of others. The God of hope, whose own protest against suffering was most fully expressed on the cross of Christ, invites the Christian community to share in God's own divine protest through actions of solidarity and tenacious helping.

Afflicted persons need the responsive ministry of the authentic community of God. I close with a prayer of Henri Nouwen from an unpublished manuscript:

> Dear Lord, give me eyes to see and ears to hear. I know there is a light in the darkness that makes everything new. I know there is new life in suffering that opens a new earth to me. I know there is joy beyond sorrow that rejuvenates my heart. Yes, Lord. I know that you are, that you act, that you love, that you indeed are Light, Life, and Truth. People, work, plans, projects, ideas, meetings, buildings, paintings, music and literature all can only give me real joy and peace when I can see and hear them as reflections of your presence, your glory, your kingdom. Let me then see and hear. Let me be so taken by what you show me and by what you say to me that your vision and hearing become my guide in life and impart meaning to all my concerns. Let me see and hear what is really real, and let me have the courage to keep unmasking endless unrealities, which disturb my life every day. Now I see only in a mirror, but one day, O Lord, I hope to see you face to face—Amen.[30]

# Notes

*Introduction*

1 James W. Johnson and J. Rosamond Johnson, eds., *The Books of American Negro Spirituals* (New York: Viking, 1977), 1:145–47.

2 Dorothee Soelle, *Suffering*, trans. Everett R. Kalin (Philadelphia: Fortress, 1975), 70.

3 Edward Farley, "Interpreting Situations," in *The Blackwell Reader in Practical and Pastoral Theology*, ed. James Woodward and Stephen Pattison (Oxford: Blackwell, 2000), 119. "The believer's interpretive activity is not simply in one direction, for instance, toward Scripture. Faith itself is an existence in situations, and that existence involves interpretative acts of everything that structures faith's situation."

4 Farley, "Interpreting Situations," 120.

5 Farley, "Interpreting Situations," 121.

6 Farley, "Interpreting Situations," 122.

7 Harold S. Kushner, *When Bad Things Happen to Good People* (New York: Avon Books, 1983), 2–3.

8 Peter Kreeft, *Making Sense out of Suffering* (Ann Arbor, Mich.: Servant Books, 1986), 16. Kreeft states, "This book is for everyone who has ever wept and wondered. That includes everyone who has ever been born. For these are the two most distinctively human acts of all."

9 The New International Version has been used here and throughout the book for quotations of Scripture.

10 Dorothee Soelle follows Simone Weil in the description of affliction as having three dimensions: physical pain, psychological anguish, and social degradation. Soelle, *Suffering*, 13–15. Cf. Simone Weil, *Waiting for God*, trans. Emma Craufurd (New York: G. P. Putnam's Sons, 1951), 117. I expand this template to include a fourth dimension to affliction, *spiritual desolation*.

11 Gustavo Gutiérrez, *On Job: God-Talk and the Suffering of the Innocent*, trans. Matthew J. O'Connell (Maryknoll, N.Y.: Orbis Books, 1996), 12.

12 Gutiérrez, *On Job*, 12.

13    Rubem Alves, *The Poet, the Warrior, the Prophet* (London: SCM Press, 1990), 101.

14    Brennan Manning, *Ruthless Trust* (San Francisco: HarperSanFrancisco, 2000), 57. "All that is elusive, enigmatic, hard to grasp will eventually yield to our intellectual investigation, then to our conclusive categorization—or so we would like to think."

15    Manning, *Ruthless Trust*, 57. This term was coined by Henri J. M. Nouwen in *The Wounded Healer* (New York: Doubleday, 1990), 39. I am convinced that what Nouwen refers to here as the task of pastoral conversation and preaching is even more relevant to speaking to and with those who are afflicted about their experiences of God. In this sense every dialogue about God in suffering can also be said to be "a deep human encounter in which a man [sic] is willing to put his [sic] own faith and doubt, his [sic] own hope and despair, his [sic] own light and darkness at the disposal of others who want to find a way through their confusion and touch the solid core of life."

16    Soelle, *Suffering*, 68.

17    Dorothee Soelle states, "Theologians have an intolerable passion for explaining and speaking when silence would be appropriate." *Suffering*, 19. Peter Kreeft invites this further reflection, "I look for clues more than answers because I do more looking than calculating . . . most books, especially in philosophy and especially in modern times, are strong on figuring and weak on seeing." *Making Sense*, 22.

18    Thomas G. Weinandy argues, "Many if not most, theologians who argue for a suffering God (process theologians and Moltmann being the prime, but not exclusive examples) readily admit, and rightly so (and those who do not miss the logic of their stance), that their theodicy is panentheistic. Since panentheism holds that, while God's being is more than all else and is not exhausted by all else, his being includes all else, these theologians clearly perceive that if God is to suffer he must share in the same ontological order as everything else. However, to place God and all else in the same ontological order has disastrous philosophical and theological consequences." *Does God Suffer?* (Notre Dame, Ind.: University of Notre Dame Press, 2000), 154. I will attempt to demonstrate that the theology of a suffering God requires neither a panentheistic theology nor a formal theodicy.

19    Simone Weil, *Gravity and Grace*, trans. Arthur Wills (New York: G. P. Putnam's Sons, 1952), 170.

20    Soelle, *Suffering*, 77.

21    Soelle, *Suffering*, 78.

22    Soelle, *Suffering*, 78.

23    I am indebted here to Jürgen Moltmann, who understands this verse as an ontological reality of life in a broken world. I employ this idea here intentionally in the same way in order to draw together the phenomenology of the experience of suffering and the supernatural encounter with the life of the divine Trinity in active prayer.

24    Phil Zylla, "Contours of the Paradigmatic in Henri Nouwen's Pastoral Theology," in *Turning The Wheel: Henri Nouwen and Our Search for God* (Maryknoll, N.Y.: Orbis Books, 2007), 208–10.

25    Zylla, "Contours of the Paradigmatic," 208.

26    This dialectic between hope and suffering is expressed well by J. Christiaan Beker: "The possibility for authentic hope in the face of suffering is determined by the way we manage to relate suffering to hope. If we divorce hope from suffering, then we become victims of illusion and create images of false hope. If we divorce suffering

from hope, then we become victims of cynicism or despair and surrender hope alto-gether. All too often suffering is divorced from hope in our world because forging a meaningful bond between suffering and hope seems ever more difficult to achieve. However, the task of establishing a meaningful relation between hope and suffer-ing will decide whether our hope is authentic or inauthentic, and whether we are crushed by suffering or not—especially 'meaningless suffering.'" *Suffering and Hope: The Biblical Vision and the Human Predicament*, 2nd ed. (Grand Rapids: Eerdmans, 1994), 39.

27  Soelle, *Suffering*, 68.

28  This phrase was coined by Jürgen Moltmann in *The Crucified God*, 3rd ed. (Min-neapolis: Fortress, 1993), 46. "For *the suffering in suffering* is the lack of love, and the wounds in wounds are the abandonment, and the powerlessness in pain is unbelief. And therefore the suffering of abandonment is overcome by the suffering of love, which is not afraid of what is sick and ugly, but accepts it and takes it to itself in order to heal it" (emphasis added). It is an important insight that is also captured by others who have written on the theme of the theology of suffering. Gustavo Gutiér-rez notes that Job feels more and more isolated by the words of his "sorry comfort-ers." "He feels more alone than ever. The discussion begun with his friends has quickly turned into a dialogue of the deaf. . . . Those who experience at close range the sufferings of the poor, or of anyone who grieves and is abandoned, will know the importance of what Job is asking for. The poor and the marginalized have a deep-rooted conviction that no one is interested in their lives and misfortunes." *On Job*, 24.

29  Wayne Whitson Floyd Jr., "Compassion in Theology," in *Compassionate Ministry*, ed. Gary Sapp (Birmingham, Ala.: Religious Education Press, 1993), 42.

30  Donald P. McNeill, Douglas A. Morrison, and Henri J. M. Nouwen, *Compassion: A Reflection on the Christian Life* (New York: Doubleday, 1983), 4.

31  S. Dennis Ford, *Sins of Omission: A Primer on Moral Indifference* (Minneapolis: For-tress, 1990), 12.

32  Soelle, *Suffering*, 41.

33  Soelle, *Suffering*, 19.

34  Dietrich Bonhoeffer, *Letters and Papers from Prison* (New York: Macmillan, 1971), 360. "Here is the decisive difference between Christianity and all religions. Man's [sic] religiosity makes him [sic] look in his [sic] distress to the power of God in the world: God is the *deus ex machina*. The Bible directs man [sic] to God's powerlessness and suffering: *only the suffering God can help*."

35  "To say that God is passible is not to project on him our own powerlessness: it is to cross, in trembling, the threshold beyond which it is finally revealed, with a tre-mendous clarity, that vulnerability is part of his essence, although we cannot point to more than an imperceptible hint of its presence." Father Georges Morel, *Christus*, no. 83 (1974): 311–12.

## Chapter One

1  Peter Kreeft, *Making Sense out of Suffering* (Ann Arbor, Mich.: Servant Books, 1986), 16.

2  "A fleeting, incomplete glimpse of God's back—the obscure yet real, penetrating, and transforming experience of his incomparable glory—awakens a dormant trust.

Something is afoot in the universe, Someone filled with transcendent brightness, wisdom, ingenuity, and power and goodness is about. In the face of overwhelming evidence to the contrary, somewhere deep down a Voice whispers, 'All is well, and all will be well.'" Brennan Manning, *Ruthless Trust* (San Francisco: HarperSan-Francisco, 2000), 65.

3   "In this way one represses all other causes of suffering, particularly the social causes, and doesn't deal rationally with the actual causes." Dorothee Soelle, *Suffering*, trans. Everett R. Kalin (Philadelphia: Fortress, 1975), 18.

4   Andrew Lester, "Why Hast Thou Forsaken Me? Anger at God," *The Journal of Pentecostal Theology* 16, no. 2 (2006): 64.

5   Dorothee Soelle states, "Almost all Christian interpretations, however, ignore the distinction between suffering that we can and cannot end." *Suffering*, 19.

6   Lester, "Why Hast Thou Forsaken Me?," 55–56.

7   John Feinberg, "A Journey in Suffering," in *Suffering and the Goodness of God*, ed. Christopher W. Morgan and Robert A. Peterson (Wheaton, Ill.: Crossway Books, 2008), 221.

8   Yacob Tesfai, ed., *The Scandal of a Crucified World* (Maryknoll, N.Y.: Orbis Books, 1994), 2.

9   Paul E. Billheimer, *Don't Waste Your Sorrows* (Minneapolis: Bethany House, 1977), 83.

10   "It is not surprising that compassion, understood as suffering with, often evokes in us a deep resistance and even protest. We are inclined to say, 'This is self-flagellation, this is masochism, this is a morbid interest in pain, this is a sick desire.' It is important for us to acknowledge this resistance and to recognize that suffering is not something we desire or to which we are attracted. On the contrary, it is something we want to avoid at all cost." Donald P. McNeill, Douglas A. Morrison, and Henri J. M. Nouwen, *Compassion: A Reflection on the Christian Life* (New York: An Image Book by Doubleday, 1983), 4.

11   John Swinton picks up on Martin Buber's observation that "evil is the consequence of distractions and in particular of inattention. In order to achieve the good, one needs to consciously strive toward it. To move toward evil requires no formal work, only inattention to the good. One stumbles into evil by being distracted and inattentive." Swinton, *Raging with Compassion: Pastoral Responses to the Problem of Evil* (Grand Rapids: Eerdmans, 2007), 181.

12   "Compassion is neither our central concern nor our primary stance in life. . . . We do not aspire to suffer with others. On the contrary, we develop methods and techniques that allow us to stay away from pain. Hospitals and funeral homes often become places to hide the sick and the dead. Suffering is unattractive, if not repelling and disgusting. The less we are confronted with it, the better." McNeill, Morrison, and Nouwen, *Compassion*, 6–7.

13   C. S. Lewis, *The Problem of Pain* (New York: Macmillan, 1944), 93.

14   C. S. Lewis, *A Grief Observed* (London: Seabury, 1963), 4.

15   Lewis, *A Grief Observed*, 38.

16   Gustavo Gutiérrez, *On Job: God-Talk and the Suffering of the Innocent*, trans. Matthew J. O'Connell (Maryknoll, N.Y.: Orbis Books, 1996), 30.

17   Gutiérrez, *On Job*, 29. "It is a rejection of a way of theologizing that does not take account of concrete situations, of the sufferings and hopes of human beings."

18   "Philosophical theodicy tends to forget its roots in the lives of real people and to

carry out its reflective activities in abstraction from the lived experience of evil and suffering. Consequently, many apparently logical theodicies make little sense when they encounter the reality of evil and suffering as people experience them in 'real time.' When this happens, rather than solving the problem of evil, theodicy can easily become a source of evil in and of itself." Swinton, *Raging with Compassion*, 17.

19  Soelle, *Suffering*, 19.

20  One of the most important popular critiques of these truncated explanations of suffering is Harold S. Kushner's volume *When Bad Things Happen to Good People* (New York: Avon Books, 1981). My argument, while supplemented by others' writings, essentially follows the five common explanations originally proposed by Kushner.

21  E.g., Walter Kaiser, "Eight Kinds of Suffering in the Old Testament," in Morgan and Peterson, *Suffering and the Goodness of God*; and Kristine M. Rankka, *Women and the Value of Suffering: An Aw(e)ful Rowing toward God* (Collegeville, Minn.: Liturgical Press, 1998), 37–43. Rankka offers a typology of seven theodicies that give traditional answers to the problem of suffering. See also, Alister E. McGrath, *Suffering and God* (Grand Rapids: Zondervan, 1992). In each of these volumes, some summary of the common explanations of suffering is offered. While drawing on these sources significantly, I have elected to follow the more popular categories originally proposed by Harold S. Kushner.

22  Kaiser, "Eight Kinds," 22.

23  Kaiser, "Eight Kinds," 22.

24  Kaiser, "Eight Kinds," 22.

25  Kaiser, "Eight Kinds," 70.

26  Philip Yancey, *Where Is God When It Hurts?* (Grand Rapids: Zondervan, 1996), 5.

27  "The idea that God gives people what they deserve, that our misdeeds cause our misfortune, is a neat and attractive solution to the problem of evil at several levels, but it has a number of serious limitations. . . . It teaches people to blame themselves. It creates guilt even when there is no basis for guilt. It makes people hate God, even as it makes them hate themselves. And most disturbing of all, it does not even fit the facts." Kushner, *When Bad Things Happen*, 10.

28  Kaiser, "Eight Kinds," 70 (emphasis original).

29  Wendy Farley, *Tragic Vision and Divine Compassion* (Louisville, Ky.: Westminster John Knox, 1990), 21. Cf. Swinton, *Raging with Compassion*, 11.

30  Harold S. Kushner summarizes Thornton Wilder's depiction of this argument, "Looked at from underneath, from our vantage point in life, God's pattern of reward and punishment seems arbitrary and without design, like the underside of a tapestry. But looked at from outside this life, from God's vantage point, every twist and knot is seen to have its place in a great design that adds up to a work of art." Kushner, *When Bad Things Happen*, 18.

31  See McGrath, *Suffering and God*, 11–12. McGrath cites John Mackey's *Preface to Christian Theology* as the source of the balcony and the road analogy. The balcony perspective is the vista view from the Spanish patio that overlooks the valley and the road below; the perspective of the road is the difficult place where life is lived.

32  Alister McGrath makes such an argument when he states, "Those on the Balcony could be of help to those on the Road—above all, if they were fellow travelers engaged on the same journey. For at its best, the Balcony perspective can be profoundly helpful. Those on the Balcony can see further on account of their elevated position. Where those on the Road see only to the next bend, those on the Balcony

can see where the Road is going and what it avoids. The Balcony provides perspective to make sense of the Road." *Suffering and God*, 12–13.

33    John Swinton states this emphatically, "To tell a mother whose baby is dying of starvation that it is really for the good and that she will learn valuable lessons through the experience is to develop a theodicy that may be theoretically interesting, but that in practice is evil. What kind of God are we left with if we manage, through clever intellectual moves, to fit such obscene forms of cruelty and evil into a framework that somehow justifies it and draws it within the boundaries of the love and righteousness of God?" *Raging with Compassion*, 13.

34    Kristine M. Rankka describes this approach when she writes, "In this model a test [is] imposed by God for the refinement or strengthening of an individual or humanity as a whole. In this model, that which seems harsh, difficult, even unendurable is actually beneficial when seen in the proper light. Suffering can lead one back to righteousness, a stronger faith, a closer relationship with God, and according to John Hick, one of its proponents, is constitutive of a 'soul-making' process. It acts as a stimulus to growth, offers the opportunity to learn humility, and reveals a greater depth of human experience and a richer understanding of the meaning of being human." *Women and the Value of Suffering*, 41.

35    Nicholas Wolterstorff, *Lament for a Son* (Grand Rapids: Eerdmans, 1987), 66–68 (emphasis original).

36    Harold Kushner cites this teaching from the Talmud, "If you go to the marketplace, you will see the potter hitting his clay pots with a stick to show how strong and solid they are. But the wise potter hits only the strongest pots, never the flawed ones. So too, God *sends such tests and afflictions only to people He knows are capable of handling them*, so that they and others can learn the extent of their spiritual strength." *When Bad Things Happen*, 25 (emphasis added).

37    In popular Christian literature the idea is often suggested that tragedy can even be preferred to a normal life situation because of the formative power of suffering. Joni Eareckson Tada writes, "Without suffering, she could be like an unbridled horse who lacks the restraints that guide and direct. The bit, martingale, tie down, spur, and crop school the horse without the aid of his master, to train himself up in the way he should go. It's the same for humans. Hardship is our bit and bridle." Joni Eareckson Tada and Steven Estes, *When God Weeps* (Grand Rapids: Zondervan, 1997), 183.

38    As a heartless expression of this explanation of suffering, Harold Kushner quotes from the eulogy of a clergyman at the death of a five-year-old boy struck down by a car, "This is not a time for sadness or tears. This is a time for rejoicing, because Michael has been taken out of this world of sin and pain with his innocent soul unstained by sin. He is in a happier land now where there is no pain and no grief; let us thank God for that." *When Bad Things Happen*, 27.

39    Dorothee Soelle makes the very important and lasting distinction that "almost all Christian interpretations [of suffering] . . . ignore the distinction between suffering that we can and cannot end." *Suffering*, 19.

*Chapter Two*

1    Walter Kasper, *The God of Jesus Christ*, trans. V. Green (New York: Crossroad, 1984), 160.

2    Gustavo Gutiérrez, *On Job: God-Talk and the Suffering of the Innocent*, trans. Matthew J. O'Connell (Maryknoll, N.Y.: Orbis Books, 1996), xiv. "God is first contemplated when we do God's will and allow God to reign; only after that do we think about God. To use familiar categories: contemplation and practice together make up a first act; theologizing is a second act. We must first establish ourselves on the terrain of spirituality and practice; only subsequently is it possible to formulate discourse on God in an authentic and respectful way."

3    "Go, said the bird, for the leaves were full of children, / Hidden excitedly, containing laughter. / Go, go, go, said the bird: human kind / Cannot bear very much reality." T. S. Eliot, "Quartet No. 1: Burnt Norton," *Four Quartets* (London: Faber & Faber, 1974), 14.

4    Dietrich Bonhoeffer, *Letters and Papers from Prison* (New York: Collier Books, 1972), 17.

5    James Gustafson, *Christ and the Moral Life* (Chicago: University of Chicago Press, 1968), 242.

6    Gustafson, *Moral Life*, 242.

7    Gustafson, *Moral Life*, 249.

8    Gustafson, *Moral Life*, 249, 253, 255.

9    "The hoping person can never come to terms with the laws or necessities of this world . . . or with the evil that continually breeds evil. For him [*sic*] the resurrection of Christ is not merely consolation in suffering; it is also the sign of God's protest against suffering. That is why whenever faith develops into hope it does not make people serene and placid; it makes them restless. It does not make them patient; it makes them impatient. Instead of being reconciled to existing reality they begin to suffer from it and to resist it." Jürgen Moltmann, *Experiences of God*, trans. Margaret Kohl (Philadelphia: Fortress, 1980), 12.

10   John Claypool, *Tracks of a Fellow Struggler*, 2nd ed. (New Orleans: Insight, 1995), 71.

11   Elie Wiesel, *Night*, trans. Stella Rodway (New York: Bantam Books, 1986; copyright, MacGibbon and Kee, 1960), 268–73.

12   Dietrich Bonhoeffer, *Ethics*, trans. Neville Horton Smith (New York: Macmillan, 1955), 270 (emphasis added).

13   Rubem Alves articulates this sensitive expression of the deep concerns of human life when he writes, "There are words which grow out of ten thousand things and words which grow out of other words: endless. . . . But there is a Word which emerges out of silence, the Word which is the beginning of the world. This Word cannot be produced. It is neither a child of our hands or of our thoughts. We have to wait in silence, till it makes itself heard: Advent . . . Grace." *The Poet, the Warrior, the Prophet* (London: SCM Press, 1990), 4.

14   Simone Weil, *Gravity and Grace*, trans. Emma Crawford and Mario von der Ruhr (London: Routledge, 1952, repr. 2007), 3.

15   Paul Tillich, *Theology of Culture* (New York: Oxford University Press, 1959), 54.

16   Paul Tillich, *Theology of Culture*, 56.

17   Paul Tillich, *Theology of Culture*, 57.

18   Paul Tillich, *Theology of Culture*, 59.

19   Dorothee Soelle, *Suffering*, trans. Everett R. Kalin (Philadelphia: Fortress, 1975), 69.

20   Paul Tillich explains, "Some of the greatest of those who have searched for ultimate reality spoke in a way that is very similar to the way in which the Bible speaks.

The term 'blindness' for the ordinary state of mind is used in all periods of philosophical thought. The experience of being awakened out of the sleep of the natural worldview, the sudden awareness of the light of the ontological question, the breaking through the surface on which one lived and moved before—these events are described like a religious conversion. . . . Ontology presupposes a conversion, an opening of the eyes, a revelatory experience. It is not a matter of detached observation, analysis, and hypothesis." *Biblical Religion and the Search for Ultimate Reality* (Chicago: University of Chicago Press, 1955), 65.

21    Tillich, *Biblical Religion*, 65.

22    This phrase was coined by Henri J. M. Nouwen in his volume *The Wounded Healer* (New York: Doubleday, 1979), 39. It is a crucial concept in pastoral theology. Sensitive articulation of the suffering of others requires both an attentiveness to the situation of suffering itself and then, the carefully constructed words that describe and give recognition to that suffering in ways that the one suffering finds meaningful.

23    Soelle, *Suffering*, 70 (emphasis added).

24    Soelle, *Suffering*, 16.

25    Alves, *Poet*, 8.

26    Jürgen Moltmann, *The Crucified God*, 3rd ed. (Minneapolis: Fortress, 1993), 46.

27    "In the midst of his [Job's] sufferings he has no other way of expressing himself, and therefore he pleads to be heard and given an answer. He feels more alone than ever. The discussion begun with his friends has quickly turned into a dialogue of the deaf. The doctrine these theologians profess does not allow them to hear what others are saying; the echo of their own words stops up their ears." Gutiérrez, *On Job*, 23.

28    Peter Kreeft, *Making Sense out of Suffering* (Ann Arbor, Mich.: Servant Books, 1986), 17.

29    Gustavo Gutiérrez remarks, "It is important to keep in mind from the very outset that theological thought about God is thought about a mystery. I mention this here because it influences an attitude to be adopted in the effort to talk about God. I mean an attitude of respect that is incompatible with the kind of God-talk that is sure, at times arrogantly sure, that it knows everything there is to know about God." Gutiérrez, *On Job*, xi.

30    This is an expansion of Dorothee Soelle's original three categories. Cf. Soelle, *Suffering*, chap. 3.

31    Donald McNeill, Douglas Morrison, and Henri Nouwen, "Compassion is neither our central concern nor our primary stance in life. . . . We do not aspire to suffer with others. On the contrary, we develop methods and techniques that allow us to stay away from pain. Hospitals and funeral homes often become places to hide the sick and the dead. Suffering is unattractive, if not repelling and disgusting. The less we are confronted with it, the better." *Compassion: A Reflection on the Christian Life* (New York: Doubleday, 1983), 6–7.

32    Dorothee Soelle explains, "Apatheia is a Greek word that literally means nonsuffering, freedom from suffering, a creature's inability to suffer. . . . We are using the term here in a broader sense. Apathy is a form of the inability to suffer. It is understood as a social condition in which people are so dominated by the goal of avoiding suffering that it becomes a goal to avoid human relationships and contacts altogether. In so far as the experiences of suffering, the *pathai* (Greek for the things that happen to a person, misfortunes) of life are repressed, there is a corresponding

disappearance of passion for life and of the strength and intensity of its joys." *Suffering*, 36.

33   Robert Lifton and Richard Falk, *Indefensible Weapons: The Political and Psychological Case against Nuclearism* (Toronto: CBC Publications, 1984), 103.

34   Douglas John Hall comments on the development of psychic numbing in our society when he states, "We probably have more data about human suffering than any generation before us. Every news broadcast deluges us with more information . . . than we can absorb, even at the intellectual level. . . . But just as at the personal level people in our society find it taxing to visit their own sick and dying relatives in hospitals and nursing homes, so they appear incapable of absorbing at the level of feeling, compassion, or (in its deepest sense) sympathy the plight of the world's hungry, politically oppressed, or war-ravaged—including the degradation and dehumanization of minorities within our own midst." *God and Human Suffering* (Minneapolis: Augsburg, 1986), 45.

35   Paul Fiddes states correctly, "If God's suffering is to be of healing effect for a suffering world, then it must be recognizably God's, and not merely our human suffering projected onto God. We cannot simply analyze what suffering means in human experience and transfer the results to God without recollecting the uniqueness of his Being." *The Creative Suffering of God* (Oxford: Clarendon, 1988), 110.

36   As Jürgen Moltmann states in *Crucified God*, "The theological traditions have always considered the cross and the resurrection of Jesus within the horizon of soteriology. . . . This is by no means false, but it is not radical enough. We must go on to ask: 'What does the cross of Jesus mean for God himself?'" *Crucified God*, 201.

37   Thomas G. Weinandy argues, "The contemporary experience of human suffering, which seemed to demand a passible God, found a ready ally and firm warrant, it appeared, in the biblical revelation of God. Thus contemporary theologians, in turning to the Bible, saw the God portrayed within it as not only sanctioning their felt need for a God who suffered, but one that actually advocated what they had perceived. . . . But what is it that contemporary theologians found in the Bible that supported and nurtured their conviction that God is passible?" *Does God Suffer?* (Notre Dame, Ind.: University of Notre Dame Press, 2000), 6. Cf. James F. Keating and Thomas Joseph White, eds. *Divine Impassibility and the Mystery of Human Suffering* (Grand Rapids: Eerdmans, 2009).

38   Anthony Clarke, *A Cry in the Darkness: The Forsakenness of Jesus in Scripture, Theology and Experience* (Macon, Ga.: Smyth & Helwys, 2002), 217.

39   Gutiérrez, *On Job*, xiii.

40   Simone Weil, *Gravity and Grace* (New York: G. P. Putnam's Sons, 1952), 171.

41   Brazilian theologian Rubem Alves offers this lyrical description of the phenomenon I am attempting here to convey, "But there are occasions when the safe, familiar world, comes to its end. Suddenly, the flat land of the ex-plained is interrupted by cliffs and canyons, and it is no longer possible to proceed. . . . Or the smooth surface of the ex-plicated begins to crack and one realizes that what was believed to be a solid foundation was nothing more than frozen water, ice which begins to melt, as one's body sinks" *Poet*, 17.

42   Rubem Alves, *Theology of Human Hope* (St. Meinrad, Ind.: Abbey Press, 1972), 3.

43   Soelle states correctly, "The recognition of the three dimensions of suffering—physical, psychological, and social—is fundamental for probing the problem more deeply." *Suffering*, 13–14, 65–66. This insight has moved the discussion in theology

from a general "suffering" to specific dimensions of suffering. In much theological literature on the topic of suffering these distinctions have not been made and I think it has helped our understanding immensely to break down these dimensions of suffering and to have a view of the composite of affliction.

44    Soelle, *Suffering*, 13.

45    For a fuller critique of the theodicy approach see Terrence W. Tilley, *The Evils of Theodicy* (Washington, D.C.: Georgetown University Press, 1991) and Sarah K. Pinnock, *Beyond Theodicy* (Albany, N.Y.: State University of New York Press, 2002).

46    Jennifer L. Geddes offers this supporting statement: "Viewing suffering as embedded in events, situations, and relations resists a static view of suffering that can lead to inaction and hopelessness and pushes for an exploration of its causes and consequences." *Evil after Postmodernism* (London: Routledge, 2001), 5.

47    Claus Westermann summarizes the discussion of the centrality of this text in the book of Lamentations this way: "For Haller the religious significance of Lamentations lies particularly in chapter three. That this chapter forms the center—the core or the pivot—of the Book of Lamentations is also the opinion of Rudolph, Notscher, Weiser, Kraus, Hillers, Ploger, Gottwald, Childs, Boecker, and Johnson. Boecker calls it '. . . the central song of Lamentations.' . . . Such wide agreement regarding the central, indispensable significance of chapter three is little short of amazing. In fact I have yet to come across a clearly contrasting opinion." *Lamentations*, trans. Charles Meunchow (Edinburgh: T&T Clark, 1994), 67.

48    F. W. Dobbs-Allsopp states, "The voice is distinctly male. Here NBSV's translation of the poem's opening line, 'I am the one who has seen affliction,' though well intentioned in its attempt to utilize inclusive language, obscures the important fact that the speaker is specifically a 'man' (*geber* in Hebrew). By the end of the poem the man's voice will become more inclusive, but not initially. One of Lamentations' key accomplishments is to fashion and inclusive and communal voice and response that can only be accessed through human individuality and which is, therefore, necessarily gendered." *Lamentations* (Louisville: John Knox Press, 2002), 106–7.

49    Emily Dickinson, "The Mystery of Pain," in *Women's History: Poems by Women*, ed. Jone Johnson Lewis, accessed March 4, 2010, http://womenshistory.about.com/library/etext/poem1/blp_dickinson_mystery_pain.htm.

50    Penny Giesbrecht, *Where Is God When a Child Suffers?* (Hannibal, Mo.: Hannibal Books, 1988).

51    Giesbrecht, *Where Is God?*, 77–85.

52    See Sarah Coakley and Kay Kaufman Shelemay, eds., *Pain and Its Transformations* (Cambridge, Mass.: Harvard University Press, 2007).

53    "I am convinced that pain gets bad press. Perhaps we should see poems, statues, and hymns to pain. Why has my attitude changed? Because, up close, under a microscope, the pain network is seen in an entirely different light. . . . Why do I need pain? When I hurt, what is my body telling me? . . . The pain network deserves far more than token acknowledgment. It bears the mark of creative genius." Philip Yancey, *Where Is God when It Hurts?* (New York: Harper Paperbacks, 1990), 13.

54    Not her real name; the story is used with the permission of the young woman.

55    Søren Kierkegaard states, "This is the way a person always gains courage; when he [sic] fears a greater danger, he always has the courage to face a lesser one; when he is exceedingly afraid of one danger, it is as if the others did not exist at all. But the most appalling dangers that the Christian has learned to know is 'the sickness

unto death.'" *The Sickness unto Death: A Christian Psychological Exposition for Upbuilding and Awakening*, ed. and trans., Howard Hong and Edna Hong (Princeton: Princeton University Press, 1980), 9.

56   Nicholas Wolterstorff, *Lament for a Son* (Grand Rapids: Eerdmans, 1987), 24, 25.

57   Soelle, *Suffering*, 66.

58   Soelle, *Suffering*, 18–19.

59   Dorothee Soelle cites Simone Weil on this important observation: "The lack of solidarity with the afflicted is therefore the most natural thing in the world. . . . It is natural for us more or less to despise the afflicted, 'although practically no one is conscious of it,'" *Suffering*, 14–15.

60   Simone Weil, *Waiting for God*, trans. Emma Craufurd (New York: G. P. Putnam's Sons, 1951), 117. Cf. Soelle, *Suffering*, 13–16.

61   Dorothee Soelle does not explicitly use this fourth dimension in her description of affliction; however, upon closer reading of her work, she does explore this idea of spiritual desolation in the lament psalms and in Jesus' own passion narrative. Her view of suffering goes on to include abandonment, betrayal, isolation, ostracism, loneliness, and, even more, God's silence and forsakenness. *Suffering*, 16, 72, 78–79, 81.

62   Martin Buber, *Eclipse of God* (New York: Harper & Row, 1952), 127.

63   Iain Provan states, "This is perhaps the lowest point of the whole poem. The catalogue of suffering which the narrator has endured has so taken its toll that even the hope which might make it tolerable seems to have deserted him. He is a man in the deepest despair." *Lamentations: The New Century Bible Commentary* (Grand Rapids: Eerdmans, 1991), 90.

64   James Loney, "When God Dies," in *The Bruised Reed: A Christian Reflection on Suffering and Hope*, Canadian Council of Churches' Commission on Faith and Witness, accessed October 22, 2010, http://ecumenism.net/archive/2009/10/the_bruised _reed_a_christian_reflection_on_suffering_and_hope.htm.

65   Brennan Manning writes, "When tragedy makes its unwelcome appearance and we are deaf to everything but the shriek of our own agony, when courage flies out the window and the world seems to be a hostile, menacing place, it is the hour of our own Gethsemane. No word, however sincere, offers any comfort or consolation. The night is bad. Our minds are numb, our hearts vacant, our nerves shattered. How will we make it through the night? The God of our lonely journey is silent." *Abba's Child* (Colorado Springs, Colo.: NavPress, 1994), 105–6.

66   "How do men and women 'clap their hands and shout with a voice of joy to God'? (Ps 47:2) in the midst of pain, suffering, heartache, and throbbing despair? Is it possible to endure and eventually move beyond the bleak and melancholy landscape of evil and destruction?" Brennan Manning, *Ruthless Trust* (San Francisco: HarperSanFrancisco, 2000), 47–48.

67   Moltmann, *Crucified God*, 241.

68   Carlo Carretto articulates the spiritual desolation of the forsaken when he writes, "But it is precisely when thinking about him that no answer comes. I might even say that he himself is the difficulty. If he is so good, why does he make me suffer? If he can do all things, why does he leave me in my distress? What do you want from me, God? . . . It looks like you are indifferent to my pain, my anguish, since you, yes, you are the one who sends me these trials. Why Lord?" *Why, O Lord?*, trans. Robert R. Barr (Maryknoll, N.Y.: Orbis Books, 1986), 24.

69   "I am not after conclusions. Conclusions are meant to shut (from the Latin *con* plus *claudere*, to shut). . . . Every conclusion brings the thought process to a halt." Alves, *Poet*, 8.

## Chapter Three

1   Kathleen D. Billman and Daniel L. Migliore, *Rachel's Cry: Prayer of Lament and Rebirth of Hope* (Cleveland, Ohio: United Church Press, 1999), 105.

2   See chapter 2 for a detailed account of these elements.

3   Dorothee Soelle, *Suffering*, trans. Everett R. Kalin (Philadelphia: Fortress, 1975), 70.

4   "Acute suffering attacks a person's self-respect." Billman and Migliore, *Rachel's Cry*, 106.

5   See chapter 1.

6   Howard W. Stone and James O. Duke articulate the concept of "embedded theology" as the learned understandings that we accumulate through our religious encounters, our educational experiences, and our reading. See Stone and Duke, *How to Think Theologically* (Philadelphia: Fortress, 1996), 13–15.

7   Or as Gustavo Gutiérrez puts it, "The language we use depend on the situation we are in." *On Job: God-Talk and the Suffering of the Innocent*, trans. Matthew J. O'Connell (Maryknoll, N.Y.: Orbis Books, 1996), 30.

8   Billman and Migliore, *Rachel's Cry*, 105.

9   "Physical pain has the power to destroy language. When the body is tormented with pain, a person may lose the capacity to concentrate her attention and coordinate her breathing and voice-producing organs in ways necessary to speak clearly and coherently. She may be able only to sigh and groan. In her study of the experience of pain, Elaine Scarry writes that 'physical pain does not simply resist language but actively destroys it, bringing about an immediate reversion to a state anterior to language, to the sounds and cries a human being makes before language is learned.'" Billman and Migliore, *Rachel's Cry*, 105.

10   Old Testament scholar Patrick Miller states, "The frequent designation of the psalmic prayers for help as 'lament' or 'complaint' tends to create a sense that the primary function of the prayer is to complain or lament . . . however the fundamental aim is to seek help from God. So the petition or plea is where one discerns the basic intention of the prayer for help. All of the language of complaint or lament serves to ground the petition and, like the more explicit motivation sentences, . . . to encourage and justify, from the angle of one praying, the intervention of God as a necessary and appropriate step to overcome suffering and distress." *They Cried to the Lord: The Form and Theology of Biblical Prayer* (Minneapolis: Fortress, 1994), 86–87.

11   Miller, *They Cried*, 86. Also on page 55 he states, "All of these need to be considered in thinking about the character and circumstances of human pleas to the Lord."

12   Patrick Miller explains, "The call of God to 'hear,' to 'give ear,' or to 'attend=heed' is sounded often in the Psalms, as well as, but less frequently, the plea to 'see' or to 'consider.' . . . But this call for a hearing is fundamental especially in those frequent situations when the psalmist feels that God is hidden or silent, when God has forgotten or forsaken the one in trouble. Getting God's attention is the crucial turning point." *They Cried*, 97.

13    Dorothee Soelle's insight is very key to my interpretation of this movement from silence to lament. In her schema, the articulation of the situation of the suffering person is a first step and an important breakthrough to the ability to articulate one's suffering. She states, "The first step towards overcoming suffering is, then, to find a language that leads out of the uncomprehended suffering that makes one mute, a language of lament, of crying, or pain, a language that *at least says what the situation is.*" *Suffering*, 70 (emphasis added).

14    Patrick Miller conveys the occasion of the lament psalms as rooted in the crises of life. He states, "It is . . . unusual to find prayers for help that do not represent situations of distress of some sort. They are virtually nonexistent in the Psalms. In narrative texts, there are some prayers for God's help or direction that do not appear to belong to a setting of crisis or trouble. Most of these, however, in fact, do reflect a situation of stress of some sort." *They Cried*, 56.

15    John Swinton calls lament "a crisis of understanding" and offers this perspective: "Lamentation is first and foremost a mode of communication with God; it is a form of prayer. It is not 'mere rage' or 'therapeutic catharsis.' Lament has a purpose and an endpoint beyond the simple expression of pain: reconciliation with and deeper love of God. As a form of prayer, lament is both transformative and subversive." *Raging with Compassion: Pastoral Responses to the Problem of Evil* (Grand Rapids: Eerdmans, 2007), 111.

16    Nicholas Wolterstorff, *Lament for a Son* (Grand Rapids: Eerdmans, 1987), 70–71.

17    Ann Weems describes her modern book of lamentations as a book "for those whose souls struggle with the dailyness of faithkeeping in the midst of life's assaults and obscenities . . . for those who are living with scalding tears running down their cheeks." *Psalms of Lament* (Louisville, Ky.: Westminster John Knox, 1995), xv.

18    Weems, *Psalms*, 40–41.

19    Wolterstorff, *Lament*, 71.

20    As Billman and Migliore state, "The prayer of lament is the language of the painful incongruity between lived experience and the promises of God." *Rachel's Cry*, 107.

21    Billman and Migliore offer this important insight into the relationship of faith and lament when they state, "We are convinced that faith does endure for those who cry out to God in the outrage and sorrow, but it may be thoroughly reshaped and reformed in the crucible of suffering." *Rachel's Cry*, 104.

22    On God as "hidden or absent" in the theology of the complaint psalms, see Ingvar Floysvik, *When God Becomes My Enemy* (St. Louis, Mo.: Concordia Academic, 1997), 146–49.

23    Patrick Miller states it this way, "The narrative prayer, therefore, suggests that the prayer for help may begin with the plea that God will turn toward the petitioner, will pay attention to the plight and the plea. There is an implicit assumption that God's attention means God's help. To catch God's ear and eye—to use one of the Bible's anthropomorphic phrases—is to be able to expect God's help." *They Cried*, 87.

24    Ekman Tam articulates this concept when he writes, "Spiritual wounding . . . occurs when one perceives no reason or purpose whatever for one's suffering. Job is a good case of this condition. In addition to his physical pain, Job experienced more anguish in his ability to find a meaning or purpose for his suffering. . . . He could not find a reason for his suffering. Job was in a total void. He simply suffered

for suffering's sake. This made his suffering extremely unbearable." "Wounding, Doubting, and Trusting in Suffering," *Journal of Pastoral Care* 55, no. 2 (2001): 161.

25    J. Richard Middleton comments, "The Hebrew attitude toward the apparent existence of evil in the world has generally been to adopt the principle that the individual should not deny his [sic] own experience." "Why the 'Greater Good' Isn't a Defense," *Koinonia* IX/1&2 (1997): 93.

26    John Swinton clarifies this when he writes, "Jesus' cry of lament from the cross reveals something significant about his experience. Jesus' movement from silence into speech startles us not just with its bold and unrelenting challenge to God, but also with the particular form of language he uses to address God." *Raging with Compassion*, 98.

27    Jürgen Moltmann, *The Crucified God*, 3rd ed. (Minneapolis: Fortress, 1993), 204.

28    Moltmann states, "What happened on the cross of Christ between Christ and the God whom he called his Father and proclaimed as 'having come near' to abandoned men [sic]? According to Paul and Mark, Jesus himself was abandoned by this very God, his Father, and died with a cry of *godforsakenness*." *Crucified God*, 241 (emphasis added).

29    Moltmann, *Crucified God*, 244, 255.

30    Anthony Clarke writes, "Jesus' cry for forsakenness moves the theodicy discussion forward from its theoretical impasse, and finds instead God sharing in the suffering of creation. In the godforsakenness of Jesus, God shows himself to be with and for the godless and godforsaken." *A Cry in the Darkness: The Forsakenness of Jesus in Scripture, Theology and Experience* (Macon, Ga.: Smyth & Helwys, 2002), 238.

31    John Swinton uses the famous painting *The Scream* by Edvard Munch as the framework for mutism, stating, "The silent scream reflects the voicelessness imposed by suffering, a silent, disorienting entrapment that defies language but remains, nonetheless, meaningful." *Raging with Compassion*, 95.

32    Melissa Johnston-Barrett offers this understanding of the lament word-form as it comes to fruition: "It is only at the threshold of speech that the sufferer can begin to regain a sense of agency and identification with oneself and others. These small steps begin to reconnect the sufferer to others. If she has true listeners, those who are willing to give extra attention to her words, her speech will be particularly fruitful." "Making Space: Silence, Voice and Suffering," *Word and World* 25, no. 3 (2005): 333.

33    Soelle, *Suffering*, 71–72.

34    David Morris states, "Suffering is voiceless in the metaphorical sense that silence becomes a sign of something ultimately unknowable. . . . In this sense, suffering encompasses an irreducible nonverbal dimension that we cannot know—not at least in any normal mode of knowing—because it happens in a realm beyond language. The quality of such suffering remains as blank to thought as the void opened up by a scream." "Voice, Genre, and Moral Community" in *Social Suffering*, ed. Arthur Kleinman, Veena Das, and Margaret Lock (Berkeley: University of California Press, 1997), 27.

35    Terence E. Fretheim describes the significance of this when he writes, "The verbs with God as subject are striking: God 'heard'; God 'remembered'; God 'saw'; God 'knew.' . . . God has not only heard their cries of suffering, but God has also seen the people. . . . In some real sense, God is depicted here as one who is intimately

involved in the suffering of the people, having entered into their sufferings in such a way as to have experienced what they are having to endure, too." *The Suffering of God* (Philadelphia: Fortress, 1994), 128.

## Chapter Four

1   Dorothee Soelle, *Suffering*, trans. Everett R. Kalin (Philadelphia: Fortress, 1975), 70.
2   S. Dennis Ford, *Sins of Omission: A Primer on Moral Indifference* (Minneapolis: Fortress, 1990), 12.
3   Soelle, *Suffering*, 36.
4   Dorothee Soelle describes apathy as a lack of "awareness of their own suffering and sensitivity to the suffering of others. They experience suffering, but they 'put up with it,' it doesn't move them. They have no language or gestures with which to battle suffering." *Suffering*, 37.
5   "It is important for us to acknowledge this resistance and to recognize that suffering is not something we desire or to which we are attracted. On the contrary, it is something we want to avoid at all cost. Therefore, compassion is not among our most natural responses. We are pain-avoiders and we consider anyone who feels attracted to suffering as abnormal, or at least very unusual." Donald P. McNeill, Douglas A. Morrison, and Henri J. M. Nouwen, *Compassion: A Reflection on the Christian Life* (New York: Doubleday, 1983), 4.
6   We must acknowledge Simone Weil's observation that "it is natural for us more or less to despise the afflicted, although practically no one is conscious of it." Soelle, *Waiting for God*, trans. Emma Craufurd (New York: G. P. Putnam's Sons, 1951), 122.
7   Ford clarifies, "The academic study of mythology and, more recently, of ethics demonstrates the power of stories to inform the way we see and structure experience, including our moral experience. . . . If indifference, as well as commitment, can be attributed to the artful models and symbols expressed by and contained within stories, then freedom to act on behalf of others requires first freeing ourselves from the narratives that reinforce our deep-seated propensity for moral indifference." *Sins of Omission*, 53; 54.
8   Ford explains, "Persons do not individually decide to remain indifferent; they are indifferent because they have—as participants in their culture and local communities—inherited ideas, rituals, mythologies, stories, and methods that foster or legitimize indifference rather than commitment. We acquire indifference in the same way we acquire language: unself-consciously, without deliberation or malice, almost innocently." *Sins of Omission*, 13.
9   Diane Bergant states, "A careful reading of the Bible will show that underlying each and every divine activity, whether creation, liberation, or judgment, is a God revealed as 'compassionate and gracious, slow to anger, rich in steadfast love and faithfulness.' It is this fundamental character that informs all divine activity and, therefore, can be considered a controlling metaphor." She further expresses that this is a recent turn in Old Testament theology when she writes, "Only recently have scholars turned with renewed interest to the characterization of God as compassionate." "Compassion in the Bible," in *Compassionate Ministry*, ed. Gary L. Sapp (Birmingham, Ala.: Religious Education Press, 1993), 12; 13.

10    Bergant comments, "The ultimate goal of God's compassion—restoration. This restoration would include: reestablishment of covenant union; commitment to God and to all others in covenant with God; and a life of fullness that comes from restored harmony." "Compassion in the Bible," 24.

11    Hence Bergant comments, "The compassion of God is more than comforting, it is creative. As the womb brings to birth life with all of its possibilities, so divine compassion brings to rebirth life that was threatened or perhaps lost." "Compassion in the Bible," 25.

12    "Compassion is not a bending toward the underprivileged from a privileged position; it is not a reaching out from on high to those who are less fortunate below; it is not a gesture of sympathy or pity for those who fail to make it in the upward pull. . . . Compassion means going directly to those people and places where suffering is most acute and building a home there." McNeill, Morrison, and Nouwen, Compassion, 27.

13    McNeill, Morrison, and Nouwen, Compassion, 27.

14    Wayne Whitson Floyd Jr., "Compassion in Theology," in Sapp, Compassionate Ministry, 48.

15    Floyd, "Compassion in Theology," 48.

16    Floyd, "Compassion in Theology," 49.

17    Floyd, "Compassion in Theology," 51.

18    Floyd, "Compassion in Theology," 48.

19    Jürgen Moltmann, The Crucified God, 3rd ed. (Minneapolis: Fortress, 1993), 39.

20    This imitation of God requires a more profound understanding of God's compassion. Wayne Whitson Floyd Jr. expresses this well when he states, "God's solidarity with creation extends to God's radical involvement with that creation's very brokenness itself, a voluntary displacement of the divine self onto the cross, that the world might be redeemed from its own brokenness for its vocation as God's creature." "Compassion in Theology," 55.

21    "Jesus Christ is the displaced Lord in whom God's compassion becomes flesh. In him, we see a life of displacement lived to the fullest. It is in following our displaced Lord that the Christian community is focused." McNeill, Morrison, and Nouwen, Compassion, 65–66.

22    "We must never forget that this world has played a very active role in forming us into the people we have become. . . . We are not separate from the world. In many ways, we are the world. The reign of God challenges our preconceived judgments, our unexamined values, and our uncritical perception of reality. . . . The implications of the reign of God are quite radical when we look at this alternative way of living from the perspective of compassion." Bergant, "Compassion in the Bible," 32.

23    Diane Bergant explains, "Of special interest [in 34:18-23] is the fact that the revelation of God accorded to Moses here is a manifestation of divine attributes rather than a kind of physical appearance. Along with this display of divine goodness is the proclamation of God's name, 'Lord.' Here God's name, which is a revelation of God's essential being, is explicitly identified with God's graciousness and compassion. This identification would suggest that compassion is constitutive of the very nature of God." "Compassion in the Bible," 17.

24    "Those who offer us comfort and consolation by being and staying with us in moments of illness, mental anguish, or spiritual darkness often grow as close to us as those with whom we have biological ties. They show their solidarity with us by

willingly entering the dark, uncharted spaces of our lives. For this reason, they are the ones who bring new hope and help us discover new directions." McNeill, Morrison, and Nouwen, *Compassion*, 14.

25    "If God's compassion reveals itself in the downward path of Jesus Christ, then our compassion toward each other will involve following in his path and participating in this self-emptying, humiliating movement." McNeill, Morrison, and Nouwen, *Compassion*, 28.

26    In this sense I agree with Anthony Headley, Joe Abbot, and Gary Sapp, who suggest that "human compassion is derived and is indeed an *'imitatio dei.'* Such imitation of God must demonstrate itself in efforts of active compassion that seeks to alleviate the suffering of others," "Compassion in Religious Counseling," in Sapp, *Compassionate Ministry*, 127.

27    "Granting that human empathy can be efficacious, is there any way of conceiving the efficacy of divine empathy? On the basis of this theory of entities, I can say generally that God functions to draw self-oriented entities out of fear and solipsism into union and cooperation with others. If entities (and therefore a world) are to form at all, they must be attracted out of their self-orientation not just toward the beauty of the other but to an empathetic concern for the larger environment of others, to others-together-in-peril. Only in this more comprehensive transcending is the entity attracted to acts of mutual enhancement." Edward Farley, *Divine Empathy: A Theology of God* (Minneapolis: Augsburg Fortress, 1996), 304.

28    John Thiel writes, "In Jesus' innocent suffering, God identifies with humanity at the heart of evil's most powerful and scandalous presence to the human condition. God enters into solidarity with the innocent suffering that all human beings endure, and by doing so joins the community of moral witness that judges innocent suffering to be a terrible diminishment of life as it was originally created." *God, Evil, and Innocent Suffering: A Theological Reflection* (New York: Crossroad, 2002), 160.

29    Jürgen Moltmann, *Experiences of God*, trans. Margaret Kohl (Philadelphia: Fortress, 1980), 12.

30    Moltmann, *Experiences of God*, 12.

31    Moltmann, *Experiences of God*, 12 (emphasis added).

*Chapter Five*

1    This seminal insight is stated by Moltmann in *The Crucified God*, where he writes, "This mysticism of the passion has discovered a truth about Christ which ought not to be suppressed by being understood in a superficial way. It can be summed up by saying that suffering is overcome by suffering, and wounds are healed by wounds. For *the suffering in suffering* is the lack of love, and the wounds in wounds are the abandonment, and the powerlessness in pain is unbelief. And therefore, the suffering of abandonment is overcome by the suffering of love, which is not afraid of what is sick and ugly, but accepts it and takes it to itself in order to heal it. Through his own abandonment by God, the crucified Christ brings God to those who are abandoned by God." *The Crucified God*, 3rd ed. (Minneapolis: Fortress, 1993), 46 (emphasis added).

2    Carlo Carretto captures this emotional anguish in his descriptive writing, "When you are suffering, in flesh or in spirit, the natural response is to weep. And what a lot of weeping there is! . . . Why, Lord, all this weeping? The answer does not come

easily. And again we begin to weep and our thoughts become all tangled and even more sorrowful, and we stumble about like wounded birds. Then we start again asking: why? Why? Under the heavy hand of suffering we can fail to grasp the reason for life, and curse life as a hopeless misfortune. That is the pit of the abyss and total darkness where the gleam of faith has gone out altogether. But the matter is much more complex. Even if I am screaming I realize that my words are sense-less. A way of releasing pressure. Not meant to produce an answer. Then again the weeping begins, and swells the level of the great sea of suffering" *Why, O Lord?*, trans. Robert R. Barr (Maryknoll, N.Y.: Orbis Books, 1986), 19.

3    "Loneliness is one of the most universal human experiences, but our contempo-rary Western society has heightened the awareness of our loneliness to an unusual degree. . . . The contemporary society in which we find ourselves makes us acutely aware of our loneliness. We become increasingly aware that we are living in a world where even the most intimate relationships have become part of the competition and rivalry. . . . Loneliness is one of the most universal sources of human suffer-ing today. . . . Children, adolescents, adults and old people are in growing degree exposed to the contagious disease of loneliness in a world in which a competitive individualism tries to reconcile itself with a culture that speaks about togetherness, unity and community as the ideals to strive for." Henri J. M. Nouwen, *Reaching Out: The Three Movements of the Spiritual Life* (New York: Doubleday, 1975), 24–25.

4    Roger Helland, *The Journey: Walking with God* (Kent, U.K.: Sovereign World, 2000), 94–96.

5    Brennan Manning's insight is apropos here, "The bromides, platitudes, and exhor-tations to trust God from nominal believers who have never visited the valley of desolation are not only useless, they are textbook illustrations of unmitigated gall. Only someone who has been there, who has drunk the dregs of the cup of pain, who has experienced the existential loneliness and alienation of the human condition, dares whisper the name of the Holy to our unspeakable distress." *Ruthless Trust* (San Francisco: HarperSanFrancisco, 2000), 44–45.

6    Ann Weems, "Lament Psalm Thirty-eight," *Psalms of Lament* (Louisville, Ky.: West-minster John Knox Press, 1995), 76–77.

7    Dorothee Soelle expounds Jesus' experience of abandonment at Gethsemane and its implication for the theology of suffering when she writes, "The Gethsemane story tells of Jesus' pain. Its duration is depicted through the threefold trip back and forth between the sleeping disciples and the place where he prayed. One can think of the repeated praying as the 'scream,' the absolute high point, and the return of the disciples as the increasingly unbearable waiting for the scream. . . . All extreme suffering evokes the experience of being forsaken by God. In the depth of suffering people see themselves as abandoned and forsaken by everyone." *Suffering*, trans. Everett R. Kalin (Philadelphia: Fortress, 1975), 84–85.

8    Miroslav Volf offers this further perspective on abandonment, "Jesus' greatest agony was not that he suffered. Suffering can be endured, even embraced, if it brings desired fruit. . . . What turned the pain of suffering into agony was the aban-donment; Jesus was abandoned by the people who trusted in him and by the God in whom he trusted. 'My God, my God, why have you forsaken me?' (Mark 15:34)" *Exclusion and Embrace* (Nashville: Abingdon, 1996), 26.

9    Nicholas Wolterstorff captures the uniqueness of every grief and the solitude

of suffering. "Each death is as unique as each life. Each has its own stamp. Inscape. . . . The son of a friend—same age as Eric—died a few weeks before Eric. The friend's son committed suicide. The pain of his life was so intense that he took the life that gave the pain. I thought for a time that such a death must be easier to bear than the death of one with zest for life. He wanted to die. When I talked to the father I saw that I was wrong. Death is the great leveler, so our writers have always told us. Of course they are right. But they have neglected to mention the uniqueness of each death—and the solitude of suffering which accompanies that uniqueness. We say, 'I know how you are feeling.' But we don't." *Lament for a Son* (Grand Rapids: Eerdmans, 1987), 24–25.

10   Roy F. Baumeister and Mark R. Leary, "The Need to Belong: Desire for Interpersonal Attachments as a Fundamental Human Motivation," *Psychological Bulletin* 117, no. 3 (1995): 497–529.

11   Baumeister and Leary, "Need to Belong," 522.

12   "The wise pastor or companion is ready to hear without prejudice or reaction the cries of dereliction, of godforsakenness, the accusations and complaints against God, the pleading and bargaining with God that are necessary aspects of human grieving. By so doing, the one who extends care to another in times of grief acts as priest in the name of Christ the high priest on behalf of God and the community of faith, hearing the outpouring of human lament, reminding the sufferer—often simply through the ministry of presence and the willingness to hear—that the God who allows us to be broken will heal us, and that the community which seems so far away, in fact surrounds the sufferer and is ready to respond in lovingkindness and hospitality. Only to unfold in its own time can we at last come to that 'new orientation' which Brueggemann believes is the ultimate goal of the psalms of lament." Michael Jinkins, *In the House of the Lord: Inhabiting the Psalms of Lament* (Collegeville, Minn.: Liturgical Press, 1998), 119. Cf. Walter Brueggemann, *The Message of the Psalms: A Theological Commentary* (Minneapolis: Augsburg, 1984), 51; and Phil C. Zylla, "What Language Can I Borrow?: Theopoetic Renewal of Pastoral Theology," *McMaster Journal of Theology and Ministry* 9 (2007–2008): 129–43.

13   Consider, e.g., John Ackerman's compelling idea that "the Trinity is the mysterious community of God; God invites the church to be transformed into such a community." *Spiritual Awakening: A Guide to Spiritual Life in Congregations* (Herndon, Va.: Alban Institute, 1994), 81.

14   Stanley J. Grenz, *Theology for the Community of God* (Nashville: Broadman & Holman, 1994), 30.

15   Stanley Grenz outlines the relationship of the kingdom of God to the concept of community when he writes, "The kingdom dimension reminds us of the biblical assumption that history is meaningful. History is directed toward a goal—the kingdom of God or the presence of the will of God throughout the earth (Matt 6:10). The concept of community fills the idea of the kingdom of God with its proper content. When God's rule is present—when God's will is done—community emerges." *Theology for the Community*, 30–31.

16   "The fellowship that God intends for his creation begins in the present. But it is ultimately an eschatological reality, an enjoyment that will be ours in its fullness only at the consummation of history." Grenz, *Theology for the Community*, 66.

17   Grenz, *Theology for the Community*, 99.

18    Grenz states, "Participation through Christ in the divine life . . . is, of course, ulti-
      mately an eschatological event." *The Social God and the Relational Self* (Louisville, Ky.:
      Westminster John Knox, 2001), 323.
19    Stanley J. Grenz offers this compelling picture of the shaping of the community
      of God's people: "The indwelling Spirit shapes the fellowship of Christ's followers
      after the pattern of the love that preexists in the triune life. In this manner, the
      Spirit-fostered mutuality of unifying love—the perichoretic life—within the eccle-
      sial community marks a visual, human coming-to-representation of the mutual
      indwelling of the persons of the Trinity. As this occurs, the Spirit forms the com-
      munity of Christ, comprising it truly as the 'church of God,' to cite Paul's illuminat-
      ing descriptor. By means of this formative work, the Spirit constitutes the church
      ontologically to be the prolepsis of the imago dei and hence the sign not only of
      God's way of being in creation but of the dynamic of the eternal, triune God. In
      short, the indwelling Spirit leads and empowers the church to fulfill its divinely
      mandated calling to be a sacrament of trinitarian communion, a temporal, visible
      sign of the eternal, dynamic life of the triune God." *Social God*, 336.
20    Roland Chia summarizes four key ideas in Colin Gunton's ecclesiology that are
      relevant to our theme here. Chia, "Trinity and Ontology: Colin Gunton's Ecclesiol-
      ogy," *International Journal of Systematic Theology* 9, no. 4 (2007): 452–68.
21    Chia, "Trinity and Ontology," 458.
22    Colin Gunton states, "Relationality is thus the transcendental which allows us to
      learn something of what it is to say that all created people and things are marked
      by their coming from and returning to God who is himself, in his essential and
      inmost being, a being in relation." *The One, The Three and the Many: God, Creation and
      the Culture of Modernity* (Cambridge: Cambridge University Press, 1992), 229.
23    *Koinonia* "transcends mere reciprocity and takes the form of creative subordination
      in conformity to Christ." Chia, "Trinity and Ontology," 460.
24    "When used to describe the church," says Chia, "koinonia designates both commu-
      nion between God and humankind and within humankind. . . . Humankind has its
      true being in communion." "Trinity and Ontology," 460.
25    "The concrete nature of the church means that it becomes an echo of the life of the
      Godhead—the church points to the creative and recreative presence of God to the
      world." Chia, "Trinity and Ontology," 461.
26    Chia, "Trinity and Ontology," 461.
27    Colin Gunton, "The Church on the Earth: The Roots of Community," in *On Being
      the Church*, ed. Colin Gunton and Daniel Hardy (Edinburgh: T&T Clark, 1989), 79.
28    Chia, "Trinity and Ontology," 461.
29    Moltmann argues in *The Crucified God* for "a theology of the cross which under-
      stands God as the suffering God in the suffering of Christ and which cries out with
      the godforsaken God, 'My God, why have you forsaken me?' For this theology,
      God and suffering are no longer contradictions . . . but God's being is in suffering
      and the suffering is in God's being itself, because God is love" (227).
30    Moltmann, *Crucified God*, 244.
31    Moltmann, *Crucified God*, 245.
32    Jürgen Moltmann, *The Way of Jesus Christ* (Minneapolis: Fortress, 1993), 174.
33    Moltmann, *Way of Jesus Christ*, 180–81.
34    "'The sufferings of Christ' are God's sufferings because through them God shows

his solidarity with human beings and his whole creation everywhere: God is with us. 'The sufferings of Christ' are God's sufferings because through them God intervenes vicariously on our behalf, saving us at the point where we are unable to stand but are forced to sink into nothingness: God is for us. 'The sufferings of Christ' are God's sufferings, finally, because out of them the new creation of all things is born: we come from God. Solidarity, vicarious power and rebirth are the divine dimensions in the sufferings of Christ. Christ is with us, Christ is for us, and in Christ we are a new creation." Moltmann, *Way of Jesus Christ*, 181 (emphasis original).

35  Moltmann states, "The person in whose heart God has put peace can no longer come to terms with the discord in the world, but will resist it and hope for 'peace on earth.' Injustice and suffering acquire a meaning only to the degree in which we refuse to accept them. Faith and hope for the righteousness and justice of God are the spur to keep us from surrendering to them, and to make us fight injustice and suffering wherever and however we can." *Way of Jesus Christ*, 187.

36  Henri J. M. Nouwen states, "Loneliness is one of the most universal sources of human suffering today. . . . Children, adolescents, adults and old people are in growing degree exposed to the contagious disease of loneliness in a world in which a competitive individualism tries to reconcile itself with a culture that speaks about togetherness, unity and community as the ideals to strive for." *Reaching Out*, 25.

37  Rainer Maria Rilke, *Letters to a Young Poet* (New York: Norton, 1954), 19.

38  Nouwen, *Reaching Out*, 40.

39  Henri J. M. Nouwen states, "It is through this movement that we reach out to God, our God, the one who is eternally real and from whom all reality comes forth." *Reaching Out*, 114.

40  Simone Weil, *First and Last Notebooks* (New York: Oxford University Press, 1970), 99.

41  Simone Weil describes God's movement toward us and the implications of this for prayer. "In prayer we must not have in view any particular thing, unless by supernatural inspiration, for God is the universal being. To be sure, he descends into the realm of particular things. He has descended, he descends in the act of creation; as also in the Incarnation, the Eucharist, Inspiration, etc. But the movement comes from above, never from below; it is a movement on God's part, not on ours. We cannot bring about such intercommunication except when God decrees it. Our role is to be ever turned towards the universal." *Gravity and Grace* (London: Routledge, 1952; repr. 2007), 47.

42  Nouwen, *Reaching Out*, 128.

43  Nouwen, *Reaching Out*, 154.

44  "The word 'community' usually refers to a way of being together that gives us a sense of belonging. . . . It is important to remember that the Christian community is a waiting community, that is, a community which not only creates a sense of belonging but also a sense of estrangement. In the Christian community we say to each other, 'We are together, but we cannot fulfill each other . . . we help each other, but we also have to remind each other that our destiny is beyond our togetherness.' The basis of the Christian community is not the family tie, or social or economic equality, or shared oppression or complaint, or mutual attraction . . . but the divine call." Nouwen, *Reaching Out*, 152–53 (emphasis added).

45  Nouwen, *Reaching Out*, 154.

46    "In prayer," states Nouwen, "the nature of the community becomes visible because in prayer we direct ourselves to the one who forms the community. We do not pray to each other, but together we pray to God, who calls us and makes us into a new people. Prayer is not one of the many things the community does. Rather, it is its very being." *Reaching Out*, 156.

47    Grenz, *Social God*, 336.

*Chapter Six*

1    "Similar lists are well known elsewhere, particularly in Stoic literature; *peristasen-katalog* = catalogue of difficult circumstances (Gk. *peristaseis*). . . . The list here contains several elements in common with 2 Cor 11 and 2 Cor 12. Like the 2 Cor 11 list, it focuses exclusively on outward tribulation, without evincing the consciousness of an inner dimension which elsewhere is so typical of Paul's sense of eschatological tension. To that extent the list here is nearer to the Stoic parallels in its immediate form; but, of course, the thought of Christian suffering continues to be controlled by v. 17, echoed in v. 35a. The parallel with 2 Cor 11:23-27 also makes clear that such a list is not a mere literary form but is a firsthand expression of Paul's own experience. Since he regarded his own experience as the outworking of the eschatological tension between the ages (of Adam and of Christ), he naturally saw his experience as typical for all his fellow believers." James D. G. Dunn, *Romans 1–8*, WBC 38a (Dallas: Word, 1988), 505.

2    "In our literature διωγμός *always means persecution for religious reasons.*" Dunn, *Romans 1–8*, 505.

3    Sword is "an obvious metonomy for violent death or war." Dunn, *Romans 1–8*, 505.

4    "Paul uses the simple verb 'groan' in 8:23, and in 2 Cor 5:2 and 4 to depict the 'groans of eschatological anticipation.'" Douglas Moo, *The Epistle to the Romans* NICNT (Grand Rapids: Eerdmans, 1996), 518.

5    Robert Jewett comments, "There is an unparalleled coherence in this expression that combines the suffering of creation from the time of Adam with a metaphor of hope—travail, the agony that leads to new birth." *Romans* (Minneapolis: Fortress, 2001), 517.

6    Paul is describing "the slow animal-like writhing of creation's discomfort at the present alienation from and distortion of what might have been and will yet become. This is how the course of creation's history can be characterized 'up to the present.'" Dunn, *Romans 1–8*, 489.

7    Paul is contrasting "the present suffering and the future glory." Charles H. Talbert, "Tracing Paul's Train of Thought in Romans 6–8," *Review and Expositor* 100 (2003): 60.

8    "In such groaning and travail Paul sees the eschatological expectation of material creation, awaiting the glory of Christian humanity." Joseph A. Fitzmyer, *Romans* (New York: Doubleday, 1992), 509.

9    C. E. B. Cranfield emphasizes that this verse restates two thoughts that have already been stated in v. 19 with heightened clarity: "on the one hand, the thought of creation's present painful condition, and on the other hand, the thought that the painful condition is not to no purpose but will have a worthwhile issue (expressed by the image of travail)." *The Epistle to the Romans*, vol. 1, ICC (Edinburgh: T&T Clark, 1975), 417.

10  C. K. Barrett, *The Epistle to the Romans* (New York: Harper & Row, 1957), 167.

11  Karl Barth, *The Epistle to the Romans*, trans. Edwyn C. Hoskyns (London: Oxford University Press, 1933), 311.

12  "The term 'eschatological imagination' . . . refers to a way of perceiving the world that is not bounded by assumptions about the way that things seem to be according to our present understanding. Eschatological imagination is inspired and sustained by God's promises in scripture of how things will be." John Swinton, *Raging with Compassion: Pastoral Responses to the Problem of Evil* (Grand Rapids: Eerdmans, 2007), 55.

13  Celia Deane-Drummond argues for the renewal of the virtue of temperance in its original meaning as "the ability to distinguish basic needs and wants." Such renewal, she suggests, will heighten our understanding of just ecological decisions that occur through the selfless awareness of the intricate connection between all living things. See "Environmental Justice and the Economy: A Christian Theologian's View," *Ecotheology* 11, no. 3 (2006): 294–310; 299.

14  "The transition from creation to Christian is made via the idea of 'groaning'; not only is the creation 'groaning together' but 'we ourselves, having the first fruits of the Spirit, groan in ourselves, awaiting adoption, the redemption of our bodies.'" Moo, *Romans*, 519.

15  Karl Barth eloquently argues, "We too are subjected to vanity, to the contrasts of life and death, light and darkness, beauty and ugliness. We groan, as the creation does; we travail in pain together with it. We too bear within us the eternal Future, which we know can never be realized in time. We too are God's prisoners, and therefore we too—hope. . . . My final possibility is to groan—and to await the promise." Barth, *Romans*, 313.

16  Fitzmyer comments that "the 'groaning' expresses the association of them with the groaning of physical creation; it is, in reality, but another way of expressing the 'sufferings' of 8:18." *Romans*, 510.

17  Dunn states, "The implication that this travail of creation is of a piece with the eschatological tension experienced by believers is already clear. The suffering of the saints is part of the cosmic drama into which all creation, inanimate as well as animate, is drawn. But lest the point be insufficiently clear Paul spells it out. We ourselves are caught up in the same cosmic unease too deep for words." *Romans 1–8*, 489.

18  Craig Dykstra and Dorothy C. Bass state, "Insofar as a Christian practice is truly attuned to the human condition in a given time and place and to the intentions of God, participating in it increases one's knowledge of humanity and all creation. . . . The content of each practice challenges, lures, and sometimes drags its practitioners into new ways of being and knowing that are commensurate with that practice—and thus, if it is rightly attuned, commensurate with the well-being of creation. Living within such a practice gives men and women certain capacities that enable them to read the world differently—even, we would argue, more truly." "A Theological Understanding of Christian Practices," in *Practicing Theology: Beliefs and Practices in Christian Life*, ed. Miroslav Volf and Dorothy C. Bass (Grand Rapids: Eerdmans, 2002), 25.

19  Rubem Alves, *The Poet, the Warrior, the Prophet* (London: SCM Press, 1990), 29.

20  Rubem Alves cites the poem of Carlos Drummond de Andrade: "the words . . . Still wet and sleepy, they roll in a difficult river." *Poet*, 30.

21   Alves, *Poet*, 33–34.

22   Joseph Fitzmyer states, "Paul mentioned earlier that Christians 'groan' together with the groaning material creation (8:23); now he affirms that the Spirit too groans with Christians who have hope and long for the glory of the risen life. [The Spirit] enables Christians by its assistance to formulate the proper prayer of hope." *Romans*, 517.

23   Old Testament scholar Terence E. Fretheim states, "The very act of creation thus might be called the beginning of the passion of God. God has so entered into the world that God cannot but be affected by its life, including its sinful life. Because this condescending God fully relates to sinful creatures with integrity, and with the deepest possible love, God cannot but suffer, and in manifold ways." *The Suffering of God: An Old Testament Perspective* (Philadelphia: Fortress, 1984), 58.

24   Theologian Clark H. Pinnock comes closest to this interpretation of the groaning of the Spirit when he writes, "The Spirit grieves and suffers with creation, not only with those sufferings involved in natural processes but also in the new ways brought about by sin. Because of it creation groans in travail, but Spirit keeps hope alive in humanity even in the midst of suffering. Such sufferings are the birth pangs of a new creation, when we along with creation are united with the life of God. Despite everything, Spirit persists toward the goal of freeing us along with the universe (Rom 8:23)." *Flame of Love: A Theology of the Holy Spirit* (Downers Grove, Ill.: InterVarsity, 1996), 76.

25   Matthew Black comments, "Prayer here is conceived as the working of the Spirit within us; our inarticulate groans and sighing mingle with the sighs and groans that cannot be uttered in the Spirit's joint intercession with us." *Romans*, NCBC (Grand Rapids: Eerdmans, 1973), 123.

26   Jürgen Moltmann's Trinitarian theology of hope completes this understanding of divine protest when he states that "hope finds in Christ not only a consolation *in* suffering, but also the protest of the divine promise *against* suffering." Moltmann, *Theology of Hope* (New York: HarperCollins, 1991 ed.; London: SCM Press, 1967), 21 (emphasis original).

27   Kevin Hughes states eloquently, "The language of our hopes thus breaks open, leaving us with a hope that is deeper than language or concept or symbol. In the end, the infinite God is our hope, and life in the unknowable God will shatter even our most profound eschatologies. . . . Hope is the infinity of love. Hope, then, is the longing that remains when we have crossed our hopes, where we are vulnerable at the foot of the cross in unknowing longing for the resurrection union with the Bridegroom. . . . Hope is the longing itself for the deeper reality of a love that is beyond all loves, for the beauty that lies beneath, before, behind, above, and within those symbolic, evocative visions, for the time when 'God will be all in all.'" "The Crossing of Hope, or Apophatic Eschatology," in *The Future of Hope*, ed. Miroslav Volf and William Katerberg (Grand Rapids: Eerdmans, 2004), 124.

28   Kristine M. Rankka speaks of "radical suffering" when she writes, "In radical suffering, as exemplified in Job's experience, nothing is ultimately explained or settled once-for-all but new insights (revelations) can be gained in the midst of suffering, which can change one's entire point of reference." *Women and the Value of Suffering: An Aw(e)ful Rowing Toward God* (Collegeville, Minn.: Liturgical Press, 1998), 188–89.

29 Stanley J. Grenz states, "Eschatological hope does not allow us simply to sit back and wait for God's future. In fact, the apostles spoke out against this type of quietism (2 Thess 3:6-13). We wait for the Lord's return, of course, but ours is an active waiting. Because we are certain that God will bring his plan to completion, we become actively involved in that program. In this way, hopeful living means living hopefully. Motivated by hope of the final consummation, we seek to fulfill our divinely given mandate in the world, proclaiming in word and action by the power of the Holy Spirit the good news about God's activity in the world." *Theology for the Community of God* (Nashville: Broadman & Holman, 1994), 855.

30 Nicholas Wolterstorff invites us to return to a fundamental posture of hope. He writes, "It's time that we returned to hope. The Christian hopes for two things: she hopes for consummation, and she hopes for redemption; she hopes for a transformed mode of existence that goes beyond God's work as creator and sustainer—a new creation, a new age, not in any way brought about by 'flesh and blood,' that is, by the dynamics of creation; and she hopes for deliverance from injustice. Two distinct hopes, neither to be assimilated to the other: hope for a new creation, and hope for the just reign of God within this present creation." "Seeing Justice in Hope," in Volf and Katerberg, *The Future of Hope*, 87.

31 "Unwavering trust is a rare and precious thing because it often demands a degree of courage that borders on the heroic. When the shadow of Jesus' cross falls across our lives in the form of failure, rejection, abandonment, betrayal, unemployment, loneliness, depression, the loss of a loved one; when we are deaf to everything by the shriek of our own pain, when the world around us suddenly seems a hostile, menacing place—at those times we may cry out in anguish, 'How could a loving God permit this to happen?' At such moments the seeds of distrust are sown. It requires heroic courage to trust in the love of God no matter what happens to us." Brennan Manning, *Ruthless Trust* (San Francisco: HarperSanFrancisco, 2000), 3–4.

## Chapter Seven

1 Elie Wiesel, *Night*, trans. Marion Wiesel (New York: Hill & Wang), 94–95.

2 J. Christiaan Beker in his book *Suffering and Hope* offers a perspective on this hiddenness of hope when he writes, "Hope in biblical terms is a difficult and risky commodity. When Paul writes, 'Now hope that is seen is not hope. For who hopes for what he sees? But if we hope for what we do not see, we wait for it with patience' (Rom 8:24-25), he seems to mislead us. Doesn't hope need some visible signs, some empirical warrant? How can we match 'invisible' hope with the so 'visible' reality of suffering? How can we trust in the forthcoming power of what in our present experience is such a powerless God? It seems to me, however, that Paul's counsel that 'we wait for it with patience' (Rom 8:25) will constitute the measure of belief and unbelief for the Christian of our time." *Suffering and Hope: The Biblical Vision and the Human Predicament*, 2nd ed. (Grand Rapids: Eerdmans, 1994), xi.

3 Dorothee Soelle comments that "all extreme suffering evokes the experience of being forsaken by God." *Suffering*, trans. Everett R. Kalin (Philadelphia: Fortress, 1975), 85.

4 This experience of hidden hope requires the ally of patience as described by pastoral theologian Donald Capps: "Patience is what we develop by engaging in difficult

tasks without giving up. This inner capacity or virtue—call it steadiness, endur-ance, perseverance—keeps hopes alive. . . . The traditional Christian view, articu-lated by the author of the book of James, is that patience is what sustains us as we wait for our hopes to be realized. As the farmer waits for the precious fruit of the earth, being patient over it until it receives the early and the late rain, so 'you also must be patient. Strengthen your hearts, for the coming of the Lord is near' (5:7-8). Then, in what appears to be a misunderstanding of the book of Job, the author notes, 'You have heard of the endurance of Job, and you have seen the purpose of the Lord, how the Lord is compassionate and merciful' (5:11). The fact that Job was a very angry individual has led some to challenge the idea of 'the patience of Job,' claiming that he was anything but patient. Yet, perhaps it is fortunate that the tradition has ascribed patience to him, as this means that patience has nothing to do with serenity, self-composure, or equanimity. Patience is steadfastness, the abil-ity to continue to hope even as we are sorely tempted to give it up." *Agents of Hope* (Minneapolis: Fortress, 1995), 150.

5   Parker Palmer, *Let Your Life Speak* (San Francisco: Jossey-Bass, 2000), 102.

6   Brennan Manning, *Ruthless Trust* (San Francisco: HarperSanFrancisco, 2000), 59.

7   Manning states, "Needless to say, all questions, pertinent and impertinent, find no responding voice. The scandal of God's silence in the most heartbreaking hours of our journey is perceived in retrospect as veiled, tender Presence and a passage into pure trust that is not at the mercy of the response it receives." *Ruthless Trust*, 60.

8   Moltmann states, "We come to know its [hope's] truth if we are forced to stand our ground against despair." *Experiences of God*, trans. Margaret Kohl (Philadelphia: Fortress, 1980), 19.

9   Soelle states, "The difficulty here lies less in the existential interpretation that peo-ple give to their pain than in the later theological systematization, which has no use for suffering that hasn't been named and pigeonholed." *Suffering*, 20.

10   Soelle, *Suffering*, 78.

11   Soelle, *Suffering*, 70.

12   Soelle, *Suffering*, 70.

13   "Active behavior replaces purely reactive behavior. The conquest of powerless-ness—and this may at first consist only in coming to know that the suffering that society produces can be battled—leads to changing even the structures." Soelle, *Suffering*, 72–73.

14   Soelle, *Suffering*, 71–72 (emphasis added).

15   Soelle, *Suffering*, 77.

16   Soelle, *Suffering*, 70.

17   Soelle, *Suffering*, 70.

18   Soelle, *Suffering*, 7.

19   "A theology that could wrest land away from the sea of speechless death would be a theology worthy of that name." Soelle, *Suffering*, 7.

20   Rainer Maria Rilke, *Rilke's Book of Hours*, trans. Anita Barrows and Joanna Macy (New York: Riverhead Books, 1997), 83.

21   Moltmann, *Experiences of God*, 6.

22   Moltmann, *Experiences of God*, 7–8.

23   Moltmann, *Experiences of God*, 11.

24   Moltmann, *Experiences of God*, 12.

25  "Peace with God means conflict with the world, for the goad of the promised future stabs inexorably into the flesh of every unfulfilled present." Jürgen Moltmann, *Theology of Hope*, trans. James W. Leitch, 5th ed. (New York: HarperCollins, 1975), 21.

26  Moltmann outlines four elements of godforsakenness: (1) Christ was dehumanized on the cross, outcast, cursed, crucified; (2) Christ died with the cry of forsakenness, (3) the event of the cross was an event 'in God'; and (4) the history of God contained within itself the whole history of godforsakenness. In this scheme those who are forsaken "are already taken up by Christ's forsakenness into Divine history." *The Crucified God*, 3rd ed. (Minneapolis: Fortress, 1993), 241, 243, 244, 255.

27  Moltmann, *Theology of Hope*, 35.

28  Lucien Richard, *What Are They Saying about the Theology of Suffering?* (Mahwah, N.J.: Paulist, 1992), 49.

29  Gustavo Gutiérrez, *On Job: God-Talk and the Suffering of the Innocent* (Maryknoll, N.Y.: Orbis Books, 1996), xvii.

30  Gutiérrez continues, "To use familiar categories: contemplation and practice together make up a first act; theologizing a second act. We must first establish ourselves on the terrain of spirituality and practice; only subsequently is it possible to formulate discourse on God in an authentic and respectful way." *On Job*, xiii.

31  Gutiérrez, *On Job*, xiv.

32  Gutiérrez, *On Job*, xvii.

33  Gutiérrez, *On Job*, 1; 5.

34  Gutiérrez, *On Job*, 7.

35  Gutiérrez, *On Job*, 22.

36  Gutiérrez, *On Job*, 31.

37  Gutiérrez, *On Job*, 30.

38  Gutiérrez, *On Job*, 39.

39  Gutiérrez, *On Job*, 66

40  Gutiérrez, *On Job*, 95.

41  Gutiérrez, *On Job*, 99–101.

## Conclusion

1  These are adapted and changed from a proposal first put forward by John Westerhoff in *Spiritual Life: The Foundation for Preaching and Teaching* (Louisville, Ky.: Westminster John Knox, 1994), 30.

2  Søren Kierkegaard, *Either/Or*, vol. 1, trans. David F. Swenson and Lillian Swenson (New York: Anchor Books, 1959), 19.

3  Phil C. Zylla, *Virtue as Consent to Being: A Pastoral-Theological Perspective on Jonathan Edwards's Construct of Virtue* (Eugene, Ore.: Wipf & Stock, 2011), 113.

4  Simone Weil, *Gravity and Grace*, trans. Emma Crawford and Mario von der Ruhr (New York: Routledge, 1952; repr. 2007), 117.

5  Paul Tillich, *Theology of Culture* (New York: Oxford University Press, 1959), 59.

6  "What is a poet? An unhappy man [sic] who in his heart harbors deep anguish." Kierkegaard, *Either/Or*, 19.

7  "You say what I suspected. You express what I vaguely felt, you bring to the fore what I fearfully kept in the back of my mind. Yes, yes—you say who we are—you

recognize our condition." Henri J. M. Nouwen, *The Wounded Healer* (New York: Doubleday, 1990), 39.

8   John Westerhoff states, "We need to shift our attention from theological reflection to spirituality, from discursive prose to poetry, from reason to the imagination, from instruction to formation, from the sciences to the arts." *Spiritual Life*, 21.

9   Amos N. Wilder stated some years ago, "A vital theopoetic can renew the biblical faith for a living encounter with the deeper currents of the age. But at the same time our age must purge itself of its own complacencies." *Theopoetic: Theology and the Religious Imagination* (Philadelphia: Fortress, 1976), 23.

10   Donald Capps, *Agents of Hope* (Minneapolis: Fortress, 1995), 3.

11   "We need to take the time to reflect on our lives and listen to where God's Spirit is calling us. We then need to permit God to engage us, anticipating that God will empower us to follow that calling." Westerhoff, *Spiritual Life*, 36.

12   Edward Farley, *Good and Evil: Interpreting a Human Condition* (Minneapolis: Fortress, 1990), 146–50.

13   Farley, *Good and Evil*, 147.

14   Farley, *Good and Evil*, 148. For a deeper analysis of this concept, see Zylla, *Virtue*, 67–69.

15   Farley, *Good and Evil*, 148.

16   Farley, *Good and Evil*, 150.

17   Farley, *Good and Evil*, 150.

18   John Feinberg, "A Journey in Suffering," in *Suffering and the Goodness of God*, ed. Christopher W. Morgan and Robert A. Peterson (Wheaton, Ill.: Crossway Books, 2008), 225.

19   Feinberg, "Journey in Suffering," 227.

20   Capps, *Agents of Hope*, 53.

21   Capps, *Agents of Hope*, 55.

22   Capps, *Agents of Hope*, 56.

23   Pastoral theologian Donald Capps states, "I suggest, therefore, that hoping occurs as the identity of that which is desired becomes known to us. In this sense, hope does not exist until desire has been able to 'name' its object, to say, this is what I long and yearn for. Thus, hoping reflects the clarification of our desires, enabling us to 'know' where our desires lead and are leading us. Hoping entails the capacity to identify the object of our desire." *Agents of Hope*, 59.

24   Capps, *Agents of Hope*, 61.

25   Frederick Townes Melges, *Time and Inner Future* (New York: Wiley, 1982), 17.

26   "Congregations are repositories of wisdom about how suffering can be overcome. They are bearers of wisdom from sacred texts, founding forbears, and living saints who not only speak words of wisdom but also embody them in their lives. Somewhat transcending these saints and texts is the dynamic organism of the congregation, whose interconnections and habits and truths form a living entity itself." Susan J. Dunlap, *Caring Cultures: How Congregations Respond to the Sick* (Waco, Tex.: Baylor University Press, 2009), 56.

27   Jacques Ellul states this emphatically when he writes, "Prayer is the referral to God's decision, on which we are counting. Without that referral there can be no hope, because we would have nothing to hope for. Prayer is the assurance of the

possibility of God's intervention, without which there is no hope." *Hope in Time of Abandonment*, trans. C. Edward Hopkin (New York: Seabury, 1972), 272–73.

28    Henry David Thoreau, *Walden* (Princeton: Princeton University Press, 1971), 54.

29    "For the Christian, what the world is, its reality, is inseparable from the story of the God who created and redeemed the world by the power of the Word become flesh in the first-century Jew called Jesus. Moreover, this (true) world is opened to us not just as we add in certain supernatural facts about it to what facts we already naturally know, but as we are transformed in our passions and actions by charity, faith, and hope to see it as it is." Charles R. Pinches, *Theology and Action: After Theory in Christian Ethics* (Grand Rapids: Eerdmans, 2002), 198.

30    Henri J. M. Nouwen, unpublished prayer from an unpublished manuscript. Copyright © The Henri Nouwen Legacy Trust. All Rights Reserved. Used by permission.

# Index of Names

# Subject Index